Law and Society
Recent Scholarship

Edited by Eric Rise

A Series from LFB Scholarly

Liberty and Authority in Free Expression Law
The United States and Canada

Karla K. Gower

LFB Scholarly Publishing LLC
New York 2002

Copyright © 2002 by LFB Scholarly Publishing LLC

All rights reserved.

Library of Congress Cataloging-in-Publication Data

Gower, Karla K.
  Liberty and authority in free expression law : the United States and Canada / Karla K. Gower.
     p. cm.
Includes bibliographical references and index.
  ISBN 1-931202-34-6 (alk. paper)
  1. Freedom of speech--United States--History. 2. Freedom of speech--Canada--History. I. Title.
  KF4770 .G69 2002
  342.73'0853--dc21

2002007183

ISBN 1-931202-34-6

Printed on acid-free 250-year-life paper.

Manufactured in the United States of America.

Table of Contents

Preface and Acknowledgements · vii

Chapter 1 Introduction · 1
Review of the Literature · 5
   Organizing Principles · 6
   Protection of Individual Rights · 11
   The Canadian Charter of Rights and Freedoms
      and the Politicization of Rights · 14
   Comparisons of Freedom of Expression Law · 21
   Theories of Freedom of Expression in a Democracy · 23

Chapter 2 The Progressive Era: 1900–1920 · 27
The Last Half of the Nineteenth Century · 28
The Progressive Era · 34
Political Speech Cases · 46
Summary of Findings and Conclusion · 56

Chapter 3 Disillusionment with Democracy: 1921–1945 · 59
Political Thought from 1921 to the Great Depression · 60
Political Thought from the Great Depression to 1945 · 70
Political Speech Cases · 77
   American Political Speech Cases · 79
   Canadian Political Speech Cases · 85
Summary of Findings and Conclusion · 87

Chapter 4 The Consensus Years: 1946–1962	91
Political Thought from 1946 to 1962	91
Political Speech Cases	105
American Political Speech Cases	106
Canadian Political Speech Cases	120
Summary of Findings and Conclusion	129
Chapter 5 Change versus Continuity: 1963–1974	133
Political Thought from 1963–1974	133
Political Speech Cases	142
American Political Speech Cases	143
Canadian Political Speech Cases	154
Summary of Findings and Conclusion	157
Chapter 6 How do we want to live?: 1975–1999	161
Political Thought from 1975–1999	162
Political Speech Cases	178
American Political Speech Cases	178
Canadian Political Speech Cases	191
Summary of Findings and Conclusion	207
Chapter 7 Conclusion	209
Major Trends in Political Thought in the United States and Canada	209
The Correlation Between Political Thought and Freedom of Expression Law	213
The Resolution of the Tension Between Liberty and Authority	221
Endnotes	223
Bibliography	275
Index	287

Preface and Acknowledgements

The seeds of this study were planted on my arrival in the United States in 1992 as a master's student in mass communication. Being from Canada, I had been raised, essentially, on American culture. I thought moving to the United States would involve no more than would moving to another city in Canada. Therefore, I found myself surprised at how different culturally I was from my American colleagues. Perhaps it was because I was suddenly surrounded by journalists who were trained to be distrustful of authority, but I was most struck by our differing attitudes toward government and by their strong devotion to individual rights, especially in the area of freedom of expression.

The more I thought about the differences the more I came to wonder whether they stemmed in part from the difference in the way Americans and Canadians conceptualize the individual, the state, and their relationship. It was this difference in conceptualization that I set out to explore by comparing the political thought of each country and freedom of expression case law.

As with all writers, I need to thank many people for their support and encouragement in the course of my research. In particular, I want to thank Cathy L. Packer, associate professor of the University of North Carolina at Chapel Hill, for her guidance, sense of humor, and most of all friendship throughout the researching and writing of this book. Ruth Walden, Margaret Blanchard, Stephen Leonard, and Kevin McGuire also are to be thanked for their assistance and advice.

The editors at LFB Scholarly Publishing deserve a thank you for their patience and understanding. I especially thank Leo Balk. Without him, this book might never have seen the light of day.

And finally, I want to thank my family and friends who mean so much to me and who have always been there for me.

CHAPTER 1
Introduction

Freedom of expression is a hallmark of democracy. It is difficult to conceive of a working democracy that does not permit its citizens some right of free expression. In fact, as Robert Bork noted, "representative democracy would be meaningless without the freedom to discuss government and its policies."[1] Indeed, the history of the modern notion of freedom of expression is interwoven with the historical struggle for democracy and the rule of law.[2] Freedom of expression is, according to Thomas Emerson, "essentially a product of the development of the liberal constitutional state" that began with the Enlightenment.[3]

Prior to the Enlightenment, the attitude of the state toward expression was authoritarian. Freedom of expression was seen as both an instrument of and a threat to the state. Power was located in the state, and "command, obedience, and order [were] higher values than freedom, consent, and involvement."[4] Individuals were expected to obey the public law,[5] which was used by the state as an instrument to control expression and maintain order. With the Enlightenment came the rise of liberalism and liberal justifications for freedom of expression. Liberalism changed both the locus of power and the authoritarian instrumental notion of law. Since power was now located in individuals, free expression was seen as essential for the development of rational individuals and for the proper functioning of the democratic process. The legitimacy of state action or public law now depended upon the "rule of law." Instead of arbitrary and discretionary, the law had to be specific in its terms and universal in its application.

Despite these changes, the authoritarian tendencies of the state did not disappear completely but continue to linger. In a modern liberal democracy, they take their form in government restrictions on expression. Because freedom of expression is not absolute, the state is permitted to restrict expression in limited circumstances, such as when expression threatens public safety and welfare. This ability on the part of the state to restrict expression results in a tension between the liberal commitment to free expression on the one hand and the authoritarian tendencies of the state to curb expression in the name of public safety and welfare on the other. The tension is between liberty—the desire of individuals to freely express themselves without fear of government interference—and authority—the desire of the state to restrict expression to protect public safety and welfare. Implicit in the term liberty is a belief in the rationality of individuals and their ability to govern themselves. Correspondingly, implicit in the term authority is a belief in the need for individuals to be protected from themselves and each other.

Legal scholar Pnina Lahav has described "this dialectic between universal values under a liberal/constitutional order on the one hand, and the state with its instrumental conception of public law and speech on the other hand," as the key to understanding the law of freedom of expression in democratic societies.[6] Focusing on freedom of the press, Lahav has theorized that "the press law of a particular country is not so much determined by the existence of a particular type of constitutional commitment, or by the presence of a special press statute, as by the particular political philosophy which animates it."[7] In other words, how the tension between liberty and authority is resolved in a democracy depends on how the political thought of the country conceptualizes the individual, the state, and their relationship.

This study explores the tension existing in democracies between liberty and authority and how that tension affects the law of freedom of expression. This is accomplished through a comparative analysis of the political thought and the law of freedom of expression in the United States and Canada. Specifically, it examines how the political and legal theorists and philosophers in the two countries have conceptualized the individual, the state, and their relationship over the course of the twentieth century. After determining the major trends in the political thought of both countries, freedom of expression cases are examined for evidence of reflection of those trends in the decisions. At the same time, the cases are examined to see whether the views of the judges concerning the nature of the individual, the state, and their relationship are reflected in the political thought. Such an examination allows for patterns and connections to emerge that help shed light on the tension between liberty and authority in democracies and how that determines the level of protection for freedom of expression.

The United States and Canada are appropriate countries to comparatively analyze the tension between liberty and authority because they are so similar, and as one researcher noted, "the more similar the units being compared, the more possible it should be to isolate the factors responsible for differences between them."[8] The two countries share a language, legal heritage, mass culture, integrated economy, and lifestyle.[9] They are both liberal democracies based on the rule of law with federal forms of government, although the structure of those governments is different, and are committed to the protection of freedom of expression. Despite these similarities, there are differences in the extent of protection given to freedom of expression[10] and in the relationship between the individual and the state in the two countries. The United States is traditionally associated with individualism and a lack of respect for authority, while Canada is traditionally considered more communitarian and more deferential to authority. These differences in political thought and the law of freedom of expression in light of the extensive similarities between the two countries suggest a need to explore the relationship between these two factors. For these reasons, the United States and Canada are appropriate choices for an exploration of the tension between liberty and authority through a comparative study of freedom of expression law and political thought.

The cases analyzed are in the area of political speech. Political speech is defined here as criticism of public officials and policies, including speech advocating forcible overthrow of the government or incitement to violate democratically enacted laws.[11] The issue in political speech is at what point the state's duty to protect public safety and welfare takes precedence over the individual's right to criticize the government. Such speech brings into question the relationship of the individual to the state and directly involves the notion of self-governance, one of the primary liberal justifications for freedom of expression.[12] Therefore, it is an important type of expression in which to explore the tension between liberty and authority. At the same time, political speech allows for cases from many areas of the law to be examined, providing a better insight into the tension and its effect on freedom of expression.

Decisions of the supreme courts of both countries are examined because these courts set out the legal meaning of freedom of expression in any given period. In Canada, the Canadian Supreme Court was not the highest court of the land until 1949. Prior to that year, cases could be, and regularly were, appealed to the Judicial Committee of the Privy Council in Great Britain. However, it is the relationship between Canadian political thought and freedom of expression with which this work is concerned. Presumably, the Privy Council did not take Canadian political thought into consideration in making its decisions, nor would its members have been influenced by such thought. In addition, it appears there were no cases concerning freedom of expression heard by the Privy Council in the period.[13]

Although history cannot be divided into neat packages with definitive starting and ending points, for purposes of organization, this book divided the twentieth century into five periods based on either major events affecting both countries, such as world wars, or on major shifts in the political thought. Each of the chapters analyzes the literature by the major twentieth century legal and political theorists and philosophers of the United States and Canada published during the particular period. The major theorists and philosophers were determined through an examination of studies on twentieth century political thought in the two countries. Specifically, the literature was examined

Introduction 5

for trends in the conceptions of the individual, the state, and their relationship. The trends in both countries were examined for similarities and differences and cross-border influence. The chapters then analyze American political speech cases for explicit and implicit reflection of the American political thought, followed by an analysis of the Canadian political speech cases for reflection of Canadian political thought. Only those writers who published during the period and those cases decided by the courts in the specific years were examined together.

In today's increasingly international age, a greater understanding and appreciation for the dynamics at work in the law of freedom of expression in different democracies are needed. This study contributes to that understanding. The interdisciplinary nature of this study also strengthens the traditional legal research on freedom of expression and fits the law on freedom of expression into a larger context. The historical approach of the study adds to that process by examining the tension between liberty and authority across time.

REVIEW OF THE LITERATURE

Given the proximity of the two countries and their similar British roots, it is not surprising that scholars have spent considerable effort analyzing what accounts for the differences between the two. This section considers those studies as an introduction to the way scholars in the two countries view the individual, the state, and their relationship. Drawing on constitutional law, political science, and sociology, five topics are addressed: (1) the organizing principles of the two countries, (2) the protection of individual rights,[14] (3) Canada's Charter of Rights and Freedoms and the politicization of rights in both countries, (4) comparisons of freedom of expression law, and (5) theories of freedom of expression in a democracy.

Organizing Principles

American sociologist Seymour Martin Lipset, who has made a career out of comparing the United States and Canada, has argued that the differences between the two countries reflect differences in what he calls their basic organizing principles.[15] Those principles have affected how Americans and Canadians view sources of authority, their values, and their understanding of their societies.[16] The United States was founded on the principle of liberalism, which emphasized distrust of the state, egalitarianism, and populism.[17] Canada, on the other hand, was conservative in the British or European sense, accepting the need for a strong state, respect for authority, and deference. Although both countries have modified these principles over the years, they continue to be influenced by them.[18] It is these organizing principles that scholars have looked to for explanations of the differences in institutions and values.

These organizing principles determined in part how the two countries were founded and their notions of federalism. How the two countries were founded is important for an understanding of the development of their political thought because it established a difference from the beginning in the way these countries think about the individual and the state. Similarly, their notions of federalism are important to the later development of freedom of expression law because, as Ellis Katz and G. Alan Tarr stated, "federalism countenances particularism and encourages diversity, while the protection of rights seems to require universal standards and uniform treatments."[19] Those scholars advocating the "universality of rights" position argue that nationalization gives the greatest protection to individual rights, while regionalism promotes group rights at the expense of individual rights. Knowing whether the federalism of a country is oriented around the central government or regional governments is potentially important for understanding the law of freedom of expression and the tension between liberty and authority.

In explaining the political and cultural differences between the United States and Canada, most scholars emphasize that the United States was born of revolution, while Canada was created by evolution. Douglas Alderson, for example, noted that Canada has had forty-seven different constitutional acts from the first document in 1763 that created British North America until its most recent in 1982.[20] He described this process as a long evolution in which constitutional documents were changed to meet changing social, legal, and economic times without the need for revolution.[21] Alderson saw Canada's constitutional evolution as indicative of a particular historical and social understanding of the proper role and limits of government and a particular locus of sovereignty. In Canada, sovereignty resides in the Crown, while in the United States, it is with the people.[22]

Other scholars stress the importance of the American Revolution for the development of Canada's institutions and values. They claim that the Revolution in fact produced two nations. Richard Preston, for example, argued that although Canada gained its independence from England through the process of evolution, Canada's distinctive identity has been achieved, at least in part, by rejecting revolution rather than by experiencing it.[23] According to Lipset, Canadians had to justify their refusal to join the American Revolution, and the result was the nations' differing self-images in the nineteenth century. The Americans gloried in their tradition of revolution, while the Canadians defended a tradition of counterrevolution, embodied in the continued link with the mother country and elitist values, and cultivated the belief that the decision to refuse was morally superior to what the Americans had done.[24]

Lipset argued that it was not just English-speaking Canadians who were counterrevolutionary. French-speaking Canadians also sought to preserve their values and cultures by reacting against a liberal revolution. While British and American Tories fought against the American Revolution and for the protection of the rule of law and traditional values, French-speaking Canadians sought to isolate themselves from the anti-clerical, democratic values of the French

Revolution. The elites of both groups consciously attempted to create a conservative, monarchical, and ecclesiastical society in Canada.[25]

Lipset concluded that the revolutionary and counterrevolutionary themes were echoed in the constitutional documents of the two countries. The revolutionary theme, celebrating individualism, was subsumed in the American objectives of "life, liberty, and the pursuit of happiness." The counterrevolutionary theme was reflected in the Canadian objectives of "peace, order, and good government," contained within the 1867 British North America Act (BNA Act), the document that united Canada as a country.[26]

Jennifer Reid, a Canadian political scientist, described the Americans of the Revolution as forwarding-looking. They had overthrown the old society and were constructing a new one in the New World. The Canadians of the same period were intent instead on preserving the traditional society.[27] These conflicting visions of society were codified, Reid argued, in two eighteenth century documents—the American Constitution and the Quebec Act.[28] The Quebec Act was an attempt on the part of English-speaking Canadians to avoid Americanization and to codify the notion that Canada was simply England transplanted to the New World.[29] The American Constitution, on the other hand, signaled a disruption with the past and, because it provided for amendment, posited a unity with the future, according to Reid.[30]

Scholars agree that the American Constitution and Bill of Rights are an embodiment of the American distrust of governments and authority. Guaranteeing individual rights and limiting the authority of the state were very much the goals of the Constitution and Bill of Rights.[31] Scholars also agree that in 1867 when Canada became a country, the American experience with federalism was very much on the colonials' minds.[32] Canadian political scientist Jennifer Smith noted that for the colonists in British North America, as Canada was known until Confederation, federalism meant American federalism, and it was not a popular identification. She and others have argued that many Canadians drew a connection between federalism and the Civil War.

Federalism was seen as an arrangement that encouraged dissension rather than unity.[33] Smith argued, for example, that for John A. Macdonald, one of the Fathers of Confederation and Canada's first prime minister, state sovereignty was the weak link in the American Constitution.[34]

Scholars have explained the British North Americans' movement toward Confederation as a pragmatic response to political, economic, military, and diplomatic conditions and considerations.[35] Lipset, for example, noted that Confederation reflected in part the fear of Canadians that they would be easy targets for takeover or absorption by the United States in the aftermath of the Civil War. Furthermore, Britain had sought for some decades to give up much of its responsibility for the territories and wanted colonists to take political responsibility for domestic governments.[36] According to other scholars, Confederation was a pragmatic accommodation of English and French desires. The English monarchists, such as Macdonald, favored a single government system, like that of Great Britain, rather than a federal system, while the French political elite in Lower Canada sought greater provincial autonomy. For Calvin Massey, the BNA Act reflected "both Macdonald's centralizing bias and the demands of French Canadians that security be provided for the autonomous development of a separate cultural and linguistic identity within a confederated union."[37] Faced with a choice between the Westminster political tradition based on parliamentary supremacy and American federalism, the Fathers of Confederation opted for a new system they called "parliamentary federalism."[38]

Essentially, the Canadians took the British unitary system of parliament and grafted it onto American federalism, or a dual system of government. The British system is based on the doctrine of parliamentary supremacy, which means that parliament's power is unlimited. American federalism, on the other hand, contains two levels of government, each sovereign in its own right with separate jurisdiction and each limited by constitutions. The BNA Act provides for both a national and a provincial level of government and distributes powers between the two, reserving general residual power to the central government. Scholars agree that the BNA Act is a document by a government, for a government. It contains no bill of rights nor does it specifically guarantee individual rights. The Canadian goal of creating a strong central government was frustrated by outside factors. The BNA Act made no provision for a national court, although the federal legislature did establish the Supreme Court of Canada in 1875.[39] Until 1949, appeals from Canadian courts, including the Supreme Court, were to the Judicial Committee of the Privy Council in England. The committee, established in 1833, was part of the legislative branch, not the judicial; yet its decisions had long-lasting ramifications for Canada's constitutionalism.[40] William Eaton noted that the first three Canadian cases that came before the Privy Council were used by the Council to restrict the broad general powers of the federal government. It was established at once that the BNA Act was to be considered not as a constitutional document, but as a general statute of the British Parliament, which it essentially was.[41] Despite the plain wording and the intent of the BNA Act that residual power be left in the hands of the federal government, the Privy Council interpreted the Act narrowly and used it to restrict federal powers.[42] The Council decided that the federal government could only legislate to preserve "peace, order, and good government" in times of emergency so as not to infringe on provincial autonomy, although there is no mention of provincial autonomy in the BNA Act.[43] The result of the decisions of the Privy Council was a shift in power from the federal government to provincial governments.

Kenneth Holland argued that the process begun by the Privy Council was substantially reversed by the Supreme Court of Canada after 1949 when appeals to the Privy Council were abolished. The Court moved both to restrict the provincial power and to expand federal jurisdiction. Holland has detailed the shifts in the concept of federalism on the part of the courts in both countries from its beginnings to the present.[44] The swings from protecting the central governments to strengthening state or provincial governments and back are responses to particular historical periods and exist, Massey argued, without reference to the constitutional texts themselves.[45]

Despite the swings, the result overall is that federalism in the two countries has evolved in roughly opposite directions from that intended by their founders.[46] As Holland has observed, over the years, the U.S. federal government has gained greater policy and fiscal dominance over the states, and the Canadian federal government has conceded ever more powers to the provinces.[47] The judiciaries in both countries have played a leading role in that process.

It would appear, then, that the American Revolution produced two nations with different political structures and self-images. The American Constitution and Bill of Rights are reflections of a distrust of government and authority. The BNA Act, on the other hand, reflects an absence of such a distrust and promotes a link with the past. Changes wrought by the courts have frustrated the original intentions of the framers of these documents, leading to an emphasis on nationalism in the United States and regionalism in Canada.

Protection of Individual Rights

American and Canadian scholars agree on the importance of protecting individual rights in a democracy, but they disagree on the best means to protect them. The disagreement reveals the differing heritages of the scholars themselves and reflects the different way rights are discussed and protected in the United States and Canada.

As stated earlier, scholars see the American Bill of Rights as a natural outgrowth of a suspicion of authority.[48] The American colonials saw themselves as oppressed by an autocratic tyranny imposed from without that repressed all freedom of thought and discussion, enforced oppressive laws with unfair and arbitrary procedures, and sustained the whole effort by military force.[49] The new Americans produced a constitution and a bill of rights that expressed a strong commitment to freedom and the limited state.[50] At the same time, distrust and hostility toward government were institutionalized in a system of checks and balances and a separation of powers.[51]

Scholars see the BNA Act, which makes no mention of individual rights, as a reflection of trust of government. Lewis Katz and Alan Westin both noted that because Canada had no violent break with Great Britain, there was no need to incorporate a bill of rights.[52] The Canadians' apparent trust of government is illustrated by their adoption of the British parliamentary structure, in which the legislature has the responsibility in law and in politics of balancing liberty and order, as opposed to the courts being responsible for the balancing as in the United States.[53] This difference in attitude toward government has led to a difference in the discourse concerning individual rights and in the institutions expected to protect those rights.

Massey, for example, argued that the formation of the United States occurred in an intellectual climate that accepted the legitimacy of natural rights as paramount to the authority of government.[54] For other scholars, the most important accomplishment of the Bill of Rights was psychological: It gave credence to the Jeffersonian view that individuals had "inalienable rights" that could not be taken away by any government.[55]

Some Canadian scholars, on the other hand, have rejected the notion of natural rights. Leonard Leigh, writing in 1958 in the wake of decisions of the Supreme Court of Canada suggesting the possibility of an implicit bill of rights in the BNA Act, argued there could be no implicit bill of rights because of the doctrine of parliamentary supremacy. The only limitations on Parliament were based on practical politics and recognized conventions.[56] The question for Leigh was not whether a legislature could legislate in the area of individual rights but which could legislate, the federal legislature or the provincial legislature.[57]

Lipset argued that nineteenth-century Canadians believed the monarchy to be a superior guarantor of liberty and freedom.[58] These Canadians, he stated, were not impressed by American advantages gained from democracy as distinct from the monarchy. Essentially they

Introduction 13

believed that "freedom wears a crown."[59] Lipset said the Canadian attitudes toward liberty and order reflect the historical emphasis on the rights and obligations of the community over those of the individual.[60] This difference in the early discourse on rights led Lipset to describe the two countries as operating under differing models of law and order. America is based on a due-process model, which involves various legal inhibitions on the power of the police and prosecutors. The crime-control model evident in Canada, on the other hand, emphasizes maintenance of law and order and is less protective of the rights of defendants and individuals generally.[61] Lipset went on to say that in the United States the common law and the courts have been perceived and used as a check on the power of the state. In Canada, the courts have been much more closely identified with the state and perceived as an arm of the state.[62]

Douglas Schmeiser argued, however, that in the 1950s, the Supreme Court of Canada was probably the most progressive court in the English-speaking world.[63] Armed only with the responsibility for dividing legislative power between Parliament and the provinces and with developing common law principles, it took individual rights to an unprecedented level in Canadian jurisprudence.[64] He concluded, however, that the Canadian Supreme Court no longer attaches primary importance to the role of the individual in conflict with the state.[65] In the 1970s, there was a sharp reversal of this trend begun in the 1950s.[66] Today, the Court is more concerned with the collective good of society, whether expressed in terms of needs of the state, administrative efficiency, or law and order. In cases of doubt, the common good usually wins out over the individual good. Thus, the main thrust for the protection of individual rights in Canada recently has come from the legislatures, which generally have been more liberal than the courts. According to Schmeiser, this recent trend is in accord with traditional Canadian legal theory that has looked to Parliament as the champion of individual liberty and as the final court of the land.[67] In the United States, on the other hand, it is the Supreme Court that is looked to for protection of individual rights.

Thus, there appears to have been a difference from the outset in the way rights were discussed in Canada and the United States and in what was seen as the best way to protect them. The questions raised but remaining unanswered by the comparative literature are how the political thought on rights has changed in the two countries, if at all, and to what extent that thought is reflected in judicial opinions in freedom of expression cases.

The Canadian Charter of Rights and Freedoms and the Politicization of Rights

In the 1950s, the Canadian Supreme Court found an implicit bill of rights within the BNA Act. Shortly thereafter the federal government enacted the Canadian Bill of Rights.[68] Despite its earlier protection of individual rights, the Supreme Court refused to grant the statute more than perfunctory powers. The debate on rights continued in Canada until passage of the Charter of Rights and Freedoms (the Charter) in 1982, which for the first time constitutionally entrenched individual rights.[69] The Charter has generated interest among Canadian and American commentators who have questioned the potential impact of U.S. civil rights jurisprudence on Charter adjudication.[70] As Christopher Manfredi noted, the attitude of Canadian commentators toward the U.S. experience has ranged from enthusiastic praise for judicial enforcement of constitutional rights in the United States to cautious warnings about misusing and misunderstanding American constitutional theories and experience.[71]

William McKercher, writing just after passage of the Charter, stated that the wording of the Charter reflects the clear influence of the American experience.[72] McKercher is repeatedly cited by scholars as support for their contention that the Charter is simply a modern version of the Bill of Rights; yet McKercher proceeded in his article to outline the extensive differences between the two documents. The Charter, he noted, contains no due process clause, no explicit protection of property, and no right to bear arms. But it does contain, unlike the Bill of Rights, an affirmative action clause, a standard for judging the limits of rights, language and educational rights, mobility rights, aboriginal rights, and denominational school rights.[73] McKercher saw these differences as evidence of how the Charter embodies specific Canadian value choices.

Robert Sedler pointed out that the Charter and the Bill of Rights "are different documents in part because the Charter is a contemporary document written when Canada was at an advanced stage of its legal and political development."[74] The Bill of Rights, on the other hand, was promulgated when America was a new nation. There was no American experience on which to frame limitations; therefore, the limitations on government in the Bill of Rights were broad-based and open-ended.[75] In contrast, the drafters of the Charter could build on the Canadian experience. At the same time, they had the American experience with individual rights to guide them.[76] The result, argued Sedler, is that the Charter's clear language resolves some of the issues that required extensive interpretation by the U.S. Supreme Court or that have yet to be resolved by it.

The most notable difference between the Charter and the Bill of Rights is the inclusion in the Charter of sections 1 and 33. Section 1 provides that the rights and freedoms contained within the Charter are "subject only to such reasonable limits prescribed by law as can be demonstrably justified in a free and democratic society." In essence, section 1 prescribes the mode of analysis the Canadian courts are to use in evaluating governmental restrictions on rights.

According to Manfredi, the absence of such a "reasonable limits" clause in the Bill of Rights forces American courts to build limits into the substantive definition of rights. Section 1 of the Charter allows Canadian courts to balance the rights and freedoms guaranteed by the Charter against other considerations without necessarily restricting the substantive scope of the Charter's provisions.[77] Manfredi used the issue of secondary picketing to illustrate his point.[78] The Supreme Court of Canada held in *RWDSU, Local 580 v. Dolphin Delivery Ltd.*, [1986] 2 S.C.R. 573, that picketing is a form of expression but that the injunction against secondary picketing in the case before it constituted a reasonable limit under section 1. The Court was able to make the ruling without restricting the substantive definition of expression. The U.S. Supreme Court has been able to uphold similar state picketing regulations only by distinguishing between speech and conduct.[79]

But the most significant difference between the Charter and the Bill of Rights is section 33 of the Charter.[80] Section 33 provides that the legislatures of either the federal or provincial governments can declare that an act "shall operate notwithstanding a provision" of the Charter. The section permits the government to validly pass acts that would otherwise be unconstitutional under the Charter. American scholars see section 33 as evidence of Canada's reluctance to let go of tradition and the doctrine of parliamentary supremacy. As Steven Simpson asked, "how can a constitution describe and provide freedoms as 'fundamental' when they are subject to a simple legislative override?"[81] Canadian scholars are split on its significance. Some agree with the American view, arguing the naiveté of the clause's defenders.

McKercher, for example, criticized those who argue that it will be used only sparingly because no legislature would want to have to justify its use to the electorate. Such an argument is based on faith that certain events will not occur.[82] Such an assumption, agreed Clare Beckton, only works in peacetime, not in times of crisis.[83] Because of the inclusion of the "notwithstanding clause," Massey saw the Charter as a distinctly Canadian creation, combining the American model of judicial review and the British model of parliamentary supremacy.[84] The result has been not the nationalization of individual rights as was expected by many Canadians, but rather the regionalization of rights because provincial governments may override or legislate "notwithstanding" the fundamental rights constitutionally protected by the Charter.[85]

Others see the section as protecting Canadian democracy. Manfredi argued that section 33 is an attempt to refute "the paradox at the heart of liberal constitutionalism" that if the only limit on the courts' power is a constitution whose meaning courts alone define, then constitutional

Introduction 17

supremacy ultimately becomes judicial supremacy.[86] "What is undesirable about this consequence and what provides the principal justification for the legislative override of section 33, is that judicial supremacy of the type reflected in American jurisprudence used by the post-Charter [Canadian] Court potentially denies Canadians their most basic freedom and right of self-governance," he wrote.[87] Canadian views on section 33 are symptomatic of a deeper division existing among Canadian scholars with respect to the whole notion of an entrenched bill of rights and the role of the courts in protecting rights.

Scholars on both sides of the border agree that the role of the Supreme Court of Canada changed with the passage of the Charter. Those who wrote immediately after the Charter came into effect in 1982 predicted either that the Court would turn increasingly toward American jurisprudence for guidance and Canada would become an increasingly rights-based society or that the Court would act conservatively, cautiously feeling its way. The change in the role of the Court is important because it suggests a change in political thought and a change in freedom of expression law that needs to be examined.

In 1983, Beckton, for example, argued that the Charter was a clear direction to courts to depart from their past history of treating infringements of rights, such as freedom of expression, as simply requiring a division of powers analysis and to focus on the right itself.[88] Similarly, McKercher, writing in the same year, argued that the Canadian courts would be forced to limit government under the Charter and would become the "ultimate guardians of the rights of the people."[89] The Charter put the whole of the judiciary and the legal profession into a position very much closer to that of their American counterparts and, most importantly for McKercher, forced the Supreme Court into the center of Canadian political life, which previously had been dominated almost exclusively by the executive branch of government.[90] He predicted that Canada would reject its traditional political model of "elite accommodation," which is characterized by compromise reached between the executives of the two levels of government, in favor of a more active citizen participation model on rights issues.[91]

Sedler, however, argued the opposite. Because the Charter defines the nature and extent of the protection afforded individual rights more specifically than does the U.S. Constitution and because the Charter's text and structure prescribe the mode of analysis for the Canadian Court to use, he saw the role of the Canadian courts in the development of constitutional protection for individual rights as comparatively less significant than the role played by the U.S. courts.[92] For example, Sedler argued, the U.S. Supreme Court had to be activist to an extent to perform its constitutional function of defining the meaning of the Constitution because of the way the Constitution was written.[93] This is not the case for the Canadian Supreme Court under the Charter.

Scholars who have examined the post-Charter decisions of the Canadian Supreme Court for use of U.S. citations and for the level of activism have found mixed results. In examining the use of U.S. cases by the Canadian Court, Manfredi found that after increasing steadily between 1984 and 1987, the number of U.S. citations dropped in 1988. He concluded that American jurisprudence enjoyed its greatest influence in early Charter cases when the Canadian Supreme Court was grappling for the first time with general questions of constitutional interpretation and specific questions of application. As the Court has decided an increasing number of Charter cases, it has built a foundation of domestic constitutional doctrine and precedents on which it can build.[94] This kind of cross-border influence in cases and in political thought was looked for in this study.

Holland examined the results of Charter cases and argued that since the Charter, the Supreme Court has exerted strong integrative and centralizing influences on the provinces in the area of individual rights. No longer in the position of being umpire between the two levels of government, it can now place constitutional constraints on both. The first fifteen Charter cases went against the government, whether federal or provincial. By the end of 1986, the Court had shifted toward more frequent support of the governments. And by 1990, it was hearing approximately twenty-five Charter cases per year, about one-quarter of its total load. Charter claimants won approximately a third of the time.⁹⁵ Overall, Holland's research reveals that the Supreme Court is more likely to favor Charter claimants than the provincial courts of appeal.⁹⁶ Holland concluded that the Supreme Court of Canada is seeking to enhance national integration by shifting the balance of power toward the federal government and by developing a uniform national law on civil rights and liberties.

Scholars agree that the Charter has given the Court the potential to lead Canada in the direction of a more rights-based, citizen-participatory society. In Canada, that process has been described as the "judicialization of politics" because the Charter is seen as increasing judicial influence over public policy and it is expected that the courts will attract the attention of interest groups.⁹⁷ In the United States, the phrase "politics of rights" has been used to describe the same phenomenon. What the scholars do not agree on is whether this politicization of rights is a good thing and whether it is in fact happening.

Canadian constitutional historian F.L. Morton argued that a "politics of rights" was not possible in Canada prior to the passage of the Charter and that most attempts in Canadian history to use the judicial process to achieve political purposes have failed.⁹⁸ Roger Gibbons, however, claimed that rights have been becoming increasingly politicized in Canada since the end of World War II. Canada's political life after the War was marked by a much sharper regional and intergovernmental conflict than American political life.⁹⁹ The civil rights movement in the United States was centralist in character and an assault on the federal underpinnings of the American political system, but the Quebec nationalism movement that challenged Canada's constitutional order in the same time period was decentralized and federal in outlook.¹⁰⁰ The result of the Canadian conflict was a prolonged constitutional debate that began in the 1960s and has continued to the present.¹⁰¹

As Gibbons stressed, until 1982 the constitution was seen by Canadians as a document by and for governments. It had little relevance for the rights and responsibilities of citizens.¹⁰² Passage of the

Canadian Bill of Rights in 1960, which reflected the rights-based political culture of the United States, had little effect because the Canadian political culture was still predominantly parliamentary and governmental in character.[103] But the Charter infused "rights" directly into the Canadian constitutional political discourse. It has shifted Canadian constitutional culture toward an acceptance of popular sovereignty as citizens have come to see the constitution as theirs rather than as the property of governments.[104] For Manfredi, the entrenchment of rights also promotes unity by shifting political discussion away from regional conflicts toward universal questions about rights and by enhancing the power of a national institution — the Supreme Court.[105]

For Morton, the politicization of rights is undemocratic because it allows unelected and unaccountable judges to overrule decisions of democratically-elected legislators. Defenders of the Charter, Morton argued, frequently respond to such allegations by drawing sharp distinctions between law and politics and between questions of rights and questions of policy.[106] But Canadians should have been more skeptical of what he called the myth of distinction between rights and policy because Canada had no written constitution for the majority of its existence as a country and yet its civil rights record is better than that of the United States. This shows, he argued, that just as a society can protect its individual rights without a Charter, so the existence of constitutional rights cannot guarantee protection in the face of hostile public opinion.[107]

American scholars, then, praise the Charter for what they consider as bringing about long-overdue changes in Canadian law. Their only concern is with section 33, the notwithstanding clause, which permits a legislative override of Charter rights. Canadian scholars either agree with the American response and applaud what they see as the positive shift toward a rights-based, citizen-participatory society, or they lament the passage of the Charter and decry what they perceive as a negative shift toward an anti-democratic state because of the increased reliance on the judiciary instead of the legislative branch. What all scholars agree on is that the Canadian constitutional landscape has changed and with it

Canadian society. To what degree and with what effect society will change remains to be seen. What is interesting about the Canadian intellectuals who view the change as negative is that they see the change as producing a less democratic society. Their vision of democracy and of the relationship of the individual to the state are clearly different from their American counterparts.

Comparisons of Freedom of Expression Law

For the most part, scholars see the Charter as an opportunity for the Canadian Supreme Court to follow the American Supreme Court's example and give strong constitutional protection to freedom of expression.[108] Scholars advocated the wholesale adoption of American principles and doctrines by the Canadian courts, especially in the areas of civil libel and access to the courts. Most favored increased protection in Canada for press rights. For example, scholars suggested that the Court ought to adopt the *New York Times v. Sullivan* actual malice standard in civil libel cases to give greater protection to the media.[109]

Other scholars attempted to explain differences in the law between the two countries by looking at judicial attitudes and the historical context of the cases.[110] For example, until recently Canadian courts had followed common law doctrines respecting an individual's right to a fair trial and preferred that right to the public's right of access to courts.[111] The reason given by the scholars for the Canadian courts' favoring of the right of a defendant to a fair trial over the right of a free press was that the Canadian legal culture gave greater deference to precedent and tradition than did the American legal culture. The Canadian judiciary was seen as timid and overly deferential to the legislature.[112] It would appear, however, that the Canadian situation is more complex than these articles suggest.

Interestingly, very few studies compare the treatment of political speech in Canada with that of the United States. Writing in 1959, for example, W.F. Bowker discussed the development of freedom of expression law in the two countries in the sedition cases of the World

War I period. Bowker noted that a provincial court of appeal decision in 1916, in a case involving charges of sedition against German sympathizers, anticipated to some degree the American "clear and present danger" test of 1919.[113]

After World War I, both countries clamped down on Socialists and Communists. While Communists were being rounded up in the Palmer raids in the United States, Socialists who had led a general strike in Winnipeg, Manitoba, were being convicted of uttering seditious words in Canada.[114] The Winnipeg general strike prompted Parliament to amend the Criminal Code to make illegal any association whose purpose was to bring about governmental, institutional, or economic change by force. Bowker noted that during the Depression a few convictions were made under the section but a strong opposition to it developed and Parliament repealed it in 1936.[115] Four years later, Congress passed a similar statute in the United States, according to Bowker, which is still in effect.[116]

The first time the Supreme Court of Canada dealt with the issue of seditious speech was in the case of *R. v. Boucher* in 1951. For Bowker, this decision, in which Mr. Justice Rand declared that there could be no sedition without an incitement to violence, deserves to be ranked with the great opinions of Justices Oliver Wendell Holmes, Jr., and Louis Brandeis.[117] Kent Greenawalt, on the other hand, treats the case matter-of-factly. He wrote, "The case is often cited as an application of free speech principles operating prior to the Charter. That decision supports narrow construction of provisions regulating dangerous speech, but sheds little light on the bounds of section 2," the Charter's freedom of expression section.[118] This is the only mention of seditious speech in Greenawalt's comparison of Canadian and American speech cases. What is missing from the work of both scholars is an analysis of the Canadian Court's reasoning in the case and its conception of the individual, the state, and their relationship.

The majority of the comparisons of freedom of expression are largely descriptive studies. Although some of the scholars attempted to explain their findings as the result of historical differences or judicial attitudes, none provided a theoretical framework for their conclusions.

Theories of Freedom of Expression in a Democracy

Because this study explores the law of freedom of expression as it has developed in two different democracies, the abundant studies on First Amendment theory have not been discussed. Instead, theories that attempted to explain freedom of expression cross-nationally were sought out. Unfortunately, there is a shortage of studies in this area. Several scholars have listed the kinds of factors that should be examined when looking at individual rights in different countries, but these factors are not theories in themselves.

Alan Westin, for example, argued that the treatment of rights and freedoms in any democratic society is best understood as part of its politics.[119] According to Westin, liberal societies start with ideals embodied in a bill of rights. Then historians and political scientists look at the process by which each liberal society tries to apply its ideal goals to the realities of governance in a complex society.[120] He identified six factors that are primary in shaping the civil liberties politics of any democracy:[121]

- the act of founding
- the ideology or political culture of the society
- the structures of government that were created by the written constitution
- the political processes
- sociological make-up of the population
- the legal culture

These factors are not unlike those set out by Lawrence Beer in his comparative study of freedom of expression in Japan.[122] Beer's six factors were part of what Beer called a "transcultural approach" to comparative study. Such factors should be taken into account when making comparisons, but they do not in themselves constitute a theory of freedom of expression. In his article, Westin did set out his own theory of American civil liberties politics. He saw the history of rights in America as a Hegelian dialectical process between the desire of public officials to maintain the status quo in terms of rights on the one hand and the creation of interest groups who push for new rights on the other.[123] According to Westin, the history of the expansion of rights and liberties in the United States is a history of demanding change from those who are reluctant to change.[124] Westin did not apply his theory of American rights development to Canada, but he did acknowledge that there is a sense in Canada that liberty versus authority issues should be settled by the legislatures and not by the courts. Thus, the parliamentary structure has produced a different relationship between liberal issues and the political process in Canada than in the United States.[125]

Sedler, after finding considerable similarity between freedom of expression cases in Canada and the United States, theorized that any free and democratic societies sharing the same legal tradition are likely to be in substantial agreement with respect to constitutional limits on freedom of expression. He concluded, "To this extent, the constitutional protection of individual rights will be 'universal' in free and democratic societies."[126] He hypothesized that if England, Australia, and New Zealand were to adopt constitutional protections for individual rights the results would be substantially the same.

But Lahav has noted that constitutional commitments are not determinative of the level of protection for freedom of expression. Rather, the key to understanding the law of freedom of expression is the political thought of a country. Lahav argued that prior to the Enlightenment, the state considered the press both as a tool to advance the public good and as a threat to public order. At the same time, public law was conceived of as an instrument of the state to be used at the discretion of the ruler. The result was what Lahav referred to as an authoritarian/instrumental conception of press law.[127] With the Enlightenment came the development of liberal justifications for free expression and a different conception of public law. Under the new "rule of law," the legitimacy of governmental action depended on the uniformity of the law's application and a lack of the arbitrariness associated with the instrumental conception of public law.[128] Despite the shift to this liberal/constitutional conception of press law, as Lahav called it, states continue to hold onto the authoritarian/instrumental concept.[129] An example is when the state seeks to restrict the press on the grounds of protecting national security.[130] The result is a tension in modern democracies between the liberal commitment to free expression and the authoritarian tendencies of the state to curb expression in the name of national or collective interests.[131] She concluded that:

> It is the form this tension takes in the various societies that distinguishes them. Each has its own unique combination, peculiar to its history, philosophy, and political culture. The manifestations of the particular combination, the causes which contributed to its formation, and the results, in terms of the degree of freedom enjoyed by the particular national press, have not yet been adequately explored, and herein lies the challenge to scholars of comparative press laws.[132]

Lahav's work is clearly the most theoretical of the studies discussed here, but not the most original. Other scholars have mentioned this tension between liberalism and order or between liberty and authority. Alderson, for example, talked about the tensions that exist in a liberal democracy between public and private and the individual and the state.[133] James Buchanan, a political economist, described the same phenomenon as society's need to find a workable solution between anarchy and the leviathan.[134] What sets Lahav apart is her attempt to conceptualize the tension into a framework within which to compare different countries. In the following chapters, this study explores Lahav's notion that the political philosophy of a democratic country is the key to understanding the level of tolerance granted freedom of expression by examining the twentieth century political thought and political speech cases of the United States and Canada.

CHAPTER 2
The Progressive Era: 1900–1920

> The nineteenth century seems to have brought us to the edge of a precipice, and to have left us there gazing wistfully into outer space. That rather smug era led us to believe that we stood on *terra firma* whence . . . we might bridge any chasm that presented. It was a scientific century, and—so it seems to us now—rather a myopic one . . . given a collection of atoms and a law of evolution. . . . But things have changed. . . . [This is] an age that feels that the nineteenth century solution of the world problem was inadequate, . . . ; an age which sees that it must find a solution for itself, but has no data for the task, and as yet can do little more than stand shivering timorously at the brink.[1]

In the above passage from 1904, Canadian intellectual Arnold Haultain accurately described the reaction of both Canadian and American intellectuals to the turn of the century. They felt as though they were standing on the brink of a precipice, while society was changing all around them, challenging their understanding of the relationship of the individual to the state.

THE LAST HALF OF THE NINETEENTH CENTURY

In the United States, the major trend in political thought in the last half of the nineteenth century was individualism based on social Darwinism.[2] Individuals were seen as discrete, rational beings, locked in an evolutionary struggle to survive. Because nature rewarded only the fittest, individuals openly competed for survival. Based on this view of individuals, society was seen in mechanistic or instrumental terms. It was composed of autonomous individuals who had contracted together for their own protection. The role of the state was restricted to the protection of individuals from the actions of others that would threaten each individual's right to struggle to survive and the maintenance of order. The doctrine of laissez-faire, then, was a natural extension of such individualism. Government intervention was seen as tampering with the natural evolution of individuals and society.[3]

In Canada, on the other hand, although the government's role was the same—the protection of individuals from the interference of others and the maintenance of order—the focus was on the state, rather than the individual. The dominant political thought was idealism, which viewed society as an organic whole. Individuals were part of that whole but had no identity separate from their existence in society. It was through their self-identification with society that individuals could realize themselves and achieve a higher moral life. Individuals were autonomous to the extent that they had a duty to themselves and society to seek the higher moral life. The doctrine of laissez-faire in Canada, then, was based on the premise that government intervention in society would weaken the moral fiber of that society.[4] The difference in the Canadian and American approaches to these concepts can be explained in part by the economic situations of the two countries.[5]

The last half of the nineteenth century was a conservative time in America. People yearned for a period of stability to recover from the unrest of the Civil War years and to take advantage of the country's economic growth. In this atmosphere of conservatism, the social philosophy of England's Herbert Spencer struck a responsive chord.[6]

Spencer attempted to devise a universal system of philosophy, which he called systematic philosophy. Essentially, he argued that the entire universe, including individuals and societies, followed the same pattern of evolution, which was a process of simultaneous integration and differentiation.[7] When applied to societies, this meant that they evolved by integrating with one another. A strong tribe, for example, would conquer a weaker tribe. As the tribe or society grew larger, the individuals within the society became more differentiated. A clear ruler developed; a division of labor occurred. As in the case of nature, it was the strong who survived in Spencer's world. Weak tribes were integrated into stronger ones; the strongest man emerged the ruler; the most skilled basket maker became the basket maker for the tribe.[8]

Evolution, then, was a struggle with nature for existence. To survive, individuals had the right to do as they wished as long as they did not violate the equal right of others to struggle to survive. The state's role was limited to protecting the individual in the quest for survival by removing artificial impediments imposed by society on the natural law of the survival of the fittest.[9] Any positive action on the part of the state, such as providing care for the weak and the infirm, would upset the natural order of things, he argued.[10] Spencer's extreme individualism fit well with the long-standing American tradition of individualism and the mood of the country in the latter part of the nineteenth century. Given his individualism, it is perhaps not surprising that Spencer was even more influential in the United States than he was in his native England.

One of those American intellectuals who were influenced by Spencer's philosophy was William Graham Sumner. Sumner was arguably the most influential American writer of the time, perhaps because he sought to justify laissez-faire economics at a time when capitalists were beginning to feel pressure from reformers.[11] By the 1880s, it was becoming clear to many Americans that industrialization was producing an ever-widening gap between the haves and the have-nots. A vocal reform movement was beginning to push for legislative reform to curb capitalistic excesses.

In his *What Social Classes Owe Each Other*, Sumner took Spencer's social philosophy and applied it to the United States in an attempt to justify capitalism and the growth of wealth.[12] Sumner had to make capitalism a part of natural law to refute the suggestion that the wealthy owed something to the poor. He made it clear that individuals had to fight against nature to survive and that nature rewarded only the fittest. Therefore, individuals were in open competition with each other in the struggle for existence.[13] In detailing the role of the state in this struggle, Sumner distinguished between what he called the ills of nature and man-made ills.[14] Among Sumner's natural ills was poverty due to one's own laziness and inefficiency. Some men, he argued, were simply more intelligent and more adept at business than others were. This was a natural phenomenon and should not be tampered with by the state.[15] For example, if a legislative scheme improved the condition of the working classes, it would interfere with the natural competition among workers. In doing so, society would be lessening natural inequalities and destroying liberty by protecting the weaker members of society.[16]

After establishing that poverty and wealth were natural phenomena, dependent on the natural abilities of individuals, Sumner went on to refute the argument of reformers that the wealthy had a duty to help the poor. Such a "sentimental" notion might well exist in a society based on status, Sumner argued, but that was not the case in the United States. American society was based on contract, not status. When Americans entered this contract, they severed all ties with a status-based society and became equal to one another. In becoming equal, they threw off the duty to help others and relinquished the right to have others assist them. Thus, "in a free state every man is held and expected to take care of himself and his family, to make no trouble for his neighbors, and to contribute his full share to public interests and common necessities."[17] Taking care of one's own self and one's family was one's sole social duty. The doctrine that individuals should be left free to make the most of themselves, Sumner argued, was essentially the notion of civil liberty inherited by Americans from Great Britain.[18]

In plain English, it meant "mind your own business."[19] Government's role was to protect "the property of men, and the honor of women. These it has to defend against crime."[20]

Canadian intellectual Andrew Macphail, in the late 1800s, would have found much in Sumner with which he could agree. Like Sumner, Macphail had no faith in the ability of legislative enactments to reform society. Society was the product of a slow evolution and could not be improved upon by the acts of government.[21] Government's role was to maintain a state of affairs in which individuals were free to manage their own affairs in their own way, he argued.[22] Despite the similarities, there are significant differences between the philosophies of Sumner and Macphail, which reflect the differences in the dominant political thought in the United States and Canada at the turn of the century.

As indicated earlier, American intellectuals adopted Spencer's social Darwinism and its justifications for individualism and the doctrine of laissez-faire. Spencer, however, did not generate the same interest in Canada. The mood of intellectuals in Canada in the late 1800s was certainly as conservative as that in the United States, but the economic situation in Canada was different. Canada was still largely agrarian. It was beginning to industrialize, but the vast split between the haves and the have-nots produced by industrialization in the United States had not yet occurred. There was as yet no need to justify the doctrine of laissez-faire or capitalism.

More suited, then, to Canada's economic situation was the idealism of Hegel as filtered through English writers such as Carlyle.[23] Idealists saw society as a product of evolution, but it was an evolution that had been synthesized with Christianity. Evolution followed a natural law or a natural order that was preordained by God. It was, in other words, an ongoing act of creation, and the process of natural selection was seen as survival of the morally fit.[24] Improvement of society would arise through reform of the inner spirit of individuals, and correspondingly it was only through society that individuals could find satisfaction. Idealists, then, tended to stress individuals' roles in society and their obligations to that society.[25] At the same time, however, the British constitutional, liberal tradition, which emphasized the individual over society, remained strong in Canada, tempering the idealism. As Canadian historian Doug Owram described it, "the mixture of idealism and individualism meant a world in which the free will of man was untrammeled by institutions and where his moral sense and social leanings would, if properly directed, make that individual work toward the benefit of society."[26]

The preeminent Canadian philosopher at the turn of the century was John Watson. Watson followed a philosophic creed he called "intellectual idealism," which he described as "the doctrine that we are capable of knowing Reality as it actually is, and that Reality when so known is absolutely rational."[27] Watson argued against Spencer's individualistic point of view, which saw the objective world as made up of a number of individual things in space and time, each with their own peculiar properties. The idealist view, on the other hand, was that there is only one objective world, and what are distinguished as individual objects are merely particular aspects from which the objective world may be viewed.[28] Individuals, then, are bound up with the nature of existence as a whole and can only realize themselves as part of the whole,[29] in the same way that the hand cannot exist separate from the human body.[30] It follows that individuals are by their very nature social and form part of an organism in which the good of each is bound up with the good of all.[31]

For Watson, moral thought, which distinguishes between what is and what ought to be, implied two ideas—the idea of duty and the idea of freedom. The idea of duty implied the identification of the individual with the common weal. It was only through self-identification with the good of all that individuals could realize their true self.[32] Every duty was at once a duty to one's self and a duty to others. For example, the duty of furthering one's own physical and mental well-being was at the same time a duty to society because it was only through doing so that one could become a fit member of the social organism.[33] The idea of freedom was not the freedom of the mere individual, but the freedom that rested upon self-identification with the common good.[34]

Individuals were to view themselves as members of a community in which the rights of all were bound up with the rights of each. Community was therefore not formed by a contract, as the individualists argued, but was rather a form of association to which individuals belonged because if they did not they would have no rights. An individual had rights only as a member of society, not as a separate individual.[35] At the same time, in a passage that reflects the influence of the British liberal rights tradition on idealism in Canada, Watson argued that the common good could only be realized by assigning to each individual rights with which no other individual could interfere.[36]

As can be seen from the foregoing, although the political thinkers of the United States and Canada in the late 1800s were conservative in outlook, their conservatism expressed itself in different ways. The American thinkers adopted the individualism of Spencer. The objective world was composed of individual parts that formed the whole. Similarly, society was the result of a contractual agreement among discrete individuals to ensure that other individuals did not impose artificial barriers to the struggle for existence. Such extreme individualism fit well with the American individual tradition and justified the doctrine of laissez-faire in the industrialized nation.

Canadian thinkers, on the other hand, tended toward idealism tempered by liberalism. Individual parts of the objective world existed only in relation to the other parts of the whole. Individuals came together as a community because it was only through the community that they could achieve the higher good. The role of the state was to maintain social unity and to encourage, via institutions, the pursuit of the moral. This emphasis on the state over the individual fit well with the Canadian agrarian economy. The vast geography of the country and the limited population meant a reliance on communities for survival.

Despite these differing starting points—individualism versus idealism—the Canadian and American political thought shared a belief in the doctrine of laissez-faire as the proper government policy. The role of government was to protect individuals from the actions of others and to maintain order. Any attempts to equalize or reform society through legislation undermined both individuals and society. Although the intellectuals in the two countries used different justifications for these beliefs, the similarities can be attributed at least in part to some common influences. First, both countries were products of the British constitutional, liberal tradition, although they were influenced by that tradition to differing degrees. Second, in the late 1800s, the dominant mood in both countries was conservative, which meant a distrust of democracy and a desire to maintain the status quo. And third, evolution had become the dominant view of the history of mankind.

THE PROGRESSIVE ERA

The period from 1900 to 1920 is known as the progressive era. It is marked in both countries by a movement away from the doctrine of laissez-faire toward more government intervention. Reformers called for an increase in government authority to combat what were seen as abuses of individual liberty. In the United States, the dominant political thought was pragmatism, which rejected the extreme individualism of Spencer and called for practical responses to the problems facing society. Pragmatists continued to see individuals as autonomous but recognized that individuals existed in a community. The actions of individuals did not occur in isolation and necessarily had an impact on others. Individuals, therefore, had duties to each other. Government's role was to assist in satisfying those social duties by balancing the individual interests and societal interests and by implementing workable solutions to problems. Pragmatists were able to propose government intervention to solve social problems because they saw the evolution of society as a process that individuals could influence.[37] Truth was no longer an absolute but something that could be discovered through observation and the testing of alternatives. For the pragmatists, then, free discussion was necessary to determine the truth.[38]

In Canada, on the other hand, although there was a movement toward reform and government intervention, the dominant political thought remained idealism until near the end of World War I. Progressive thought manifested itself in the notion that individuals needed government assistance in achieving self-perfection, but individuals continued to be seen as a component part of society whose needs had to be subordinated for the greater good of society. That belief was sorely tested during the war when the government imposed ever greater restrictions on individual liberty for the sake of the society, resolving the tension between liberty and authority in favor of authority. By the end of the war, however, Canadian political thinkers were decrying the government's actions and calling for a movement back toward greater individual liberty. The progressive era ended for Canadian political thought with intellectuals reconsidering their notions of the individual, the state, and their relationship. The war produced a similar reaction in the United States although not to the same extent because the balance had not been tipped as far in the direction of authority.

Even before the turn of the century, criticism of the doctrine of laissez-faire had been mounting in the United States. The negative features of industrialization were beginning to make themselves clearly felt.[39] What had been a populist reform movement in the late 1800s, grew into the middle-class progressive movement as reform captured the imagination of many intellectuals by 1900.[40] These progressives challenged the notion of economic liberty.[41] The doctrine of laissez-faire had only succeeded in separating the haves from the have-nots, they argued.[42] The answer was to use the government to bring about positive reform in society, to encourage a return to the "virtuous community" of old. But that course of action required a shift in political thought from laissez-faire/individualism to interventionism. The rise of pragmatism in American philosophy helped that shift occur.

Pragmatism was described by philosopher William James in a series of lectures in 1906 and 1907 as a method of settling metaphysical disputes.[43] He suggested that in philosophical debates the question should be: What practical difference does it make if A is true rather than B? For example, instead of debating whether God in fact exists, the question should be: Does it make a practical difference to individuals if God does or does not exist? If there would be no difference, there is no dispute.[44] Pragmatism, thus, focused philosophical issues on the concrete and on empirical data. James offered pragmatism as a middle-ground between idealism and empiricism, although it had more in common with the latter than the former.[45]

While James suggested that pragmatism was really only a method, it was at the same time a theory of truth. The standard definition of truth in Spencer and Sumner's day was "the agreement of ideas with reality."[46] Truth with a capital "T" was considered ascertainable and absolute. James argued that truth was not absolute but was rather a process of verification and validation. Truth "*becomes* true, is *made* true by events," he argued.[47] He did not deny that there may be an absolute Truth, but he argued that society cannot verify it today and "we have to live to-day by what truth we can get to-day, and be ready to-morrow to call it falsehood."[48]

Although James is considered the father of pragmatism, it was John Dewey who brought pragmatism into the progressive fold. Dewey began his philosophic career as a devoted adherent of Hegelian idealism but had turned away from Hegel and increasingly toward pragmatism by the end of the nineteenth century.[49] Instead of a middle-ground, Dewey saw pragmatism in opposition to the older philosophies of empiricism and idealism.[50] He rejected empiricism for its emphasis on individuality and idealism for its tendency to reify the state.[51]

What Dewey considered most important about pragmatism was that it introduced responsibility into philosophic thought. By idealizing and rationalizing the universe, philosophers had absolved themselves of the responsibility of finding answers to concrete problems.[52] Philosophy must become, he argued, a method for dealing with the serious issues of life, "a method of moral and political diagnosis and prognosis."[53] Dewey's notion that intellectuals should be responsible for finding a solution to society's ills meant that individuals could no longer be blamed entirely for their misfortune. The doctrine of laissez-faire had been premised on the belief that individuals were responsible for their own destiny, and both empiricism and idealism fed into that belief. Those who got ahead did so because, in an ordered world, they were harder working and morally superior. Dewey challenged that belief by suggesting that intellectuals should deal with the here and now and not worry about the ordered world. They should not search for the one universal good as idealism suggested but rather converge "all the instrumentalities of the social arts, of law, education, economics, and political science upon the construction of intelligent methods of improving the common lot," he argued.[54] The purpose of government, then, was not to protect individual rights but to advance the interests of society.[55]

Truth, for Dewey, was relative to a society's particular circumstances and could be determined only through empirical study; hence, it is instrumental because the truth of a concept was to be measured by observation.[56] Instrumentalism, however, as historian Mark Graber has noted, was incompatible with the existing jurisprudential notion of "justice as derived from a set of eternally valid, deductively derived individual rights."[57] The result is that Dewey rejected outright the doctrine of natural rights and the ideal of natural law. Nature was not an unchangeable order; it was a process of becoming, as was society.[58] Laws were made by individuals acting as a society; they did not exist prior to society.[59]

Herbert Croly reiterated that sentiment in *Progressive Democracy* published in 1914. Society, he said, was the process of socializing; individuality was the process of individualizing.[60] Society was not simply an aggregation of individuals as had been believed in the nineteenth century. It had a reality of its own. The problem with the views of both the individualists and the idealists was that the result was a tendency to either sacrifice society to the individual or the individual to society.[61] But if individuals and society were considered as processes, then a relationship of interdependence between the two was established.[62] Both social and individual interests properly had to be taken into consideration in a democracy.

For Croly, America's commitment to the realization of the democratic ideal meant that it must be prepared to follow wherever that ideal led.[63] Traditionally, the promise of the United States meant economic independence and prosperity, which in turn had been associated in the American mind with free political institutions.[64] "The confidence which American institutions placed in the American citizen was considered equivalent to a greater faith in the excellence of human nature," he wrote.[65] The idea was that if individuals were given a fair chance, the natural goodness of human nature would lead to the betterment of society.[66] There was a sense that benefits would accrue automatically.

But the economic conditions had been profoundly altered from the days of the founders, and the political and social conditions had altered with them. As Croly described it, "Ugly obstacles have jumped into view."[67] The common people appeared not to be getting the "Square Deal" to which they were entitled.[68] Poverty was beginning to be seen not as an individual problem as was the case in the nineteenth century, but as a societal problem for which society had to take responsibility.[69] It was, in fact, Croly argued, the American democratic ideal that had made the social problem inevitable and "its attempted solution indispensable."[70] The democratic state had been conceived to secure individual rights and opportunities with the minimum of interference on the basis that the greatest individual happiness would harmonize with the public interest.[71] Under such a system, "unusually energetic and unscrupulous men were bound to seize a kind and an amount of political and economic power which was not entirely wholesome," he wrote.[72] The answer for Croly was clear: "Interference with the national course of individual and popular action there must be in the public interest."[73]

Croly's views on democracy were shared by future Canadian Prime Minister William Lyon Mackenzie King. King was a progressive who, as Minister of Labor, helped develop the Canadian government's labor policies in the first decades of the twentieth century. Firmly steeped in Hegelian idealism, he saw the individual as inseparable from the individual's relation to the community. Social control was essential to the well-being of the many, he argued, and he had a deep faith in the essential unity of society.[74] Like the rest of the Canadian idealists, he believed such social control was best achieved through voluntary moral reform. But King's progressivism made him willing to go the extra step of dictating social control through state action if the situation warranted it.[75] And he thought the situation in Canada in these early years of the twentieth century justified intervention. "In any civilized community, private rights should cease when they become public wrongs," he wrote.[76]

Canada continued to lag behind the United States in terms of industrialization, which had developed in the United States by 1880. In Canada, it was not until the economic boom of the late 1890s that there was a tremendous growth in industry.[77] The number of individuals employed in manufacturing increased some 350 percent in Canada between 1890 and 1910.[78] And intellectuals were taking notice, concerned that Canada was on the same path that the United States had taken.[79]

The doctrine of laissez-faire in Canada had been predicated on the belief that individuals had a degree of control over their lives and that society could ensure the transmission of the proper moral values through institutions, such as the church and schools.[80] When the vast majority of Canadians were farmers or lived in small communities, such beliefs were realistic. Protective legislation, such as welfare and unemployment insurance, was not needed in a society that was largely agrarian and would only serve to weaken the moral fiber of the society, it was believed. But city-dwellers did not have the same opportunities to become self-sufficient and to pull themselves up by their moral bootstraps. Therefore, Canadian intellectuals found it difficult to maintain their laissez-faire position in the face of a shifting societal structure.[81] The old system was not working in the new society.

Unlike in the United States, the doctrine of laissez-faire in Canada had never extended to all economic matters. The country was physically too big and the population too small for Canadians to rely solely on private investment for public works. Beginning with the building of canals after the War of 1812 and extending to the laying of railways in the nineteenth century, the federal government in Canada had been involved in several public works projects. The challenge for progressives in the early twentieth century, then, was to convince Canadians that the same kind of governmental involvement could apply to social and economic problems arising from industrialization. The state, they argued, was the only body in Canada that had sufficient resources and power to deal with the changing face of the societal landscape.[82]

The progressive movement in Canada was brought to an abrupt halt with England's declaration of war in 1914 because as part of the British Commonwealth, the declaration meant Canada too went to war.[83] The crisis of the war and idealism's organic conception of the state permitted the government to become stronger and more interventionist. The War Measures Act of 1914, passed with the support of the opposition, gave the federal government the power to effectively suspend individual rights.[84] And as the war progressed, the federal government found itself taking more and more control. At the beginning of the war, the language of the intellectuals remained largely idealistic.[85] But a change in thinking during the last two years of the war occurred among the intellectuals. There was growing concern that a war that was being fought for democracy was in fact eroding at home the very freedom for which democracy stood. The threat that democracy itself might be destroyed in the name of democracy became so strong that Canadian political scientist O.D. Skelton wrote in 1918, "All we can do is select our dictators."[86]

Intellectuals on both sides of the political spectrum in Canada felt the same: the means used to protect democracy threatened to destroy the end—democracy.[87] Although there remained a strong desire for the idealist notions of unity, social order, and stability, the war had brought into question many of the assumptions of idealism.[88] Idealism's organic conception of society elevated the state over the individual, requiring individual sacrifice for the good of society. For many in

Canada, Germany was an example of such statism taken to its logical extreme, and there was fear that statism was now entering the Canadian psyche. The war also challenged the assumption that reasonable men could work for the betterment of society.[89] By 1919, Canadian society had cause to doubt the supremacy of rationality and reason.[90]

Stephen Leacock, a political economist who is best known in Canada as a humorist, argued that liberation from all forms of governmental interference in the economy should be seriously questioned.[91] Although a conservative, he did not long to return to a golden past, but rather believed in progress.[92] As he put it, "In the history of every nation as of every man there is no such thing as standing still. There is no pause upon the path of progress."[93] In fact, Leacock was one of the first Canadian academics to fuse the insights of the American progressives with the Canadian conservative tradition.[94]

In *Elements of Political Science*, published in 1906, Leacock noted that the "position in which the individual stands to the state determines the proper province of the action of government."[95] There were, he said, two conflicting views on the relationship of the individual to the state. The first was the mechanistic or individualistic view of the state. Individuals were separate self-contained units who joined together to form a civil society. The state was merely the aggregate of these individuals and was not justified in interfering with the individual, except to prevent that individual from interfering with anyone else.[96] The second was the organic or idealist theory of society. The state and the individual were part and parcel of the social organism. Individuals could not exist separate from the society in the organic view.[97]

Both theories were flawed, according to Leacock. "Too great an amalgamation of the individual and the state is as dangerous an ideal as a too great emancipation of the individual will," he wrote.[98] The idealist view was impractical because it provided no guidelines for political conduct, and he could not accept the individualist argument that the sole duty of government was to protect the individual from other individuals.[99] It was against common sense, he argued, and went against what governments actually did. Providing education, running the post office, and minting currency were all examples of positive interference by government that would not be justified under the individualistic theory.[100]

In a series of articles for the *New York Times* in 1919, Leacock outlined his solution for what he considered "The Unsolved Riddle of Social Justice."[101] Writing just after the end of World War I, Leacock was troubled by what he saw in both Canadian and American societies. It was time for serious stock-taking of where society was and where it was going.[102] According to Leacock, individualism of the extreme kind was out of date, but the central problem facing society in the aftermath of the war was to determine how far from that principle it should deviate.[103] Socialism, which had a growing number of adherents in Canada, was not a viable alternative. Socialism, Leacock acknowledged, was a noble ideal; the problem was it would not work. And it would not work for the same reason that extreme individualism did not work. Both systems failed to take into account the selfishness of individuals.[104]

Having disposed of both extreme individualism and socialism as workable solutions for the modern state, Leacock proposed a middleground.[105] The modern state would be essentially individualistic, but it would blend a strong state control to curb excesses, regulate business in the public interest, and provide social welfare services.[106] He justified his position on the basis that the war had created new forms of social obligation. For the first time in history, individuals had been conscripted for democracy, not for a military tyranny. If every citizen now owed it to the state to fight and perhaps die for it in times of need, then that state owed every citizen the opportunity of a livelihood.[107] The war had made individuals realize that they stood or fell as a nation and that the welfare of each must be regarded as contributory to the safety of all.[108] He concluded that the natural order of society, based on natural liberty, did not correspond with real justice and real liberty, but worked injustice. Intrusive social legislation had to be used to remedy the situation and to prevent injustice.[109]

Canada was not alone in experiencing a growth in government intervention during the war and a fear of that tendency. As war clouds gathered in Europe, U.S. President Woodrow Wilson began instituting a policy of restriction on speech rights. The effect was to change the nature of free speech from one of interpersonal relations to one of government/individual relations.[110] The government's actions split the progressives. One group, concerned with the loyalty of second and third generation Americans, hailed the legislation as productive. These progressives saw the legislation as a way of encouraging community and promoting the national culture.[111] Croly, for example, had urged that becoming American required a certain kind of behavior.[112] Others, such as Dewey, decried the legislation as counterproductive. Free speech was necessary in a democracy, they argued. If society was going to be diverse, there needed to be diversity of opinion. This group of progressives saw free speech as a social right, not an individual right. They were able to decry legislation that restricted speech while advocating legislation in economic matters because they believed that the government had to ensure all citizens the resources necessary to participate in public life.[113] Thus, government intervention extended to the economy but not to expression.

Law professor Zechariah Chafee, Jr., argued that the controversy over freedom of speech was a conflict between two differing views of government. One viewed the government as master; the other saw the government as the servant, subject to the criticism of its master, the people.[114] The Espionage Act of 1917 was the product of the former view and to that extent was unconstitutional, according to Chafee, because it was contrary to the First Amendment on two counts. First, it violated the interests of individuals to express their opinions. And second, it infringed on society's interest in attaining the truth.[115] One of the most important purposes of society and government, Chafee argued, was the discovery and spread of truth on subjects of general concern. Truth could only be attained through unlimited discussion.[116]

Chafee recognized that there were times when the individual interest in free speech and the societal interest in other issues, such as protecting the nation in wartime, would clash. For that reason, he argued, it was useless to define free speech in terms of rights. Individuals assert their right to speak; the government asserts its right to protect the nation; and a deadlock ensues. The answer was to talk in terms of interests and to balance the two competing interests when they conflicted.[117] Even in wartime, he argued, the balance should be tipped in favor of free speech unless the public safety was really imperiled. The boundary line of free speech was to be drawn close to the point where words would give rise to unlawful acts.[118]

The Canadian Leacock also decried the bans on speech that had found their way into American and Canadian society. "Socialism, like every other impassioned human effort, will flourish best under martyrdom. It will languish and perish in the dry sunlight of open discussion," he wrote.[119] It was far better, Leacock argued, to let socialism be freely examined by all than to shroud it in mystery by locking it up. Then all would see that it was not capable of working.[120] Leacock set forth his point at which a Socialist's free speech could be proscribed:

> A man has just as much right to declare himself a Socialist as he has to call himself a Seventh Day Adventist or a Prohibitionist, or a Perpetual Motionist. It is, or should be, open to him to convert others to his way of thinking. It is only time to restrain him when he proposes to convert others by means of a shotgun or by dynamite and by forcible interference with their own rights. When he does this he ceases to be a Socialist pure and simple and becomes a criminal as well. The law can deal with him as such.[121]

The first twenty years of the twentieth century, then, saw a profound shift in political thought in both Canada and the United States. There was a general movement toward intervention on the part of the government to bring about social reforms, which was in response to a turn toward a sense of societal obligation. In terms of government intervention, that shift was greater in the United States given its starting point in extreme individualism. However, the perceived social crisis produced by industrialization and capitalism required drastic measures. The individual was no longer seen as a discrete being. It was recognized that individuals operated in a community and had duties to others. Government's role was to satisfy those social duties by implementing workable solutions. The proper solution—the truth—was to be found through open discussion, observation, and the testing of alternatives.

Implicit in this shift in attitude from limited and neutral government to active and positive government is a shift in the conception of the individual. Under the individualism of Spencer, the individual was rational and discrete. The pragmatists, however, were more skeptical of the rationality of individuals and their willingness to work for the betterment of society if left on their own. Abuses of liberty called for greater government authority to restrict individual actions for the public good.

Canadian thinkers with their idealistic focus on society accepted the concept of government intervention more readily; however, the experience of World War I caused many Canadian intellectuals to recoil from their earlier idealism. Idealism and its emphasis on statism were seen as responsible for the repressive government measures the Canadian government had taken during the war. Individuals were expected to subordinate their needs to the needs of the society under idealism, and in wartime, society's needs were perceived as great. Canadian thinkers questioned that relationship, seeking a way to balance the interests of both individuals and society. In many ways, Canadian and American political thought was closer by 1920 than it had been at the turn of the century as both idealism and individualism were tempered to meet the demands of the changing societies.[122]

POLITICAL SPEECH CASES

In the political speech cases in Canada and the United States from 1900 to 1920, a correlation can be found between the major trends in political thought and the judicial decision-making of the two countries. Although explicit references to political thinkers are rare,[123] implicit reference to the political thought is at times clear. Judges in both countries reflected the conservatism of the times through their distrust of the masses and their reliance on tradition, especially the rule of law, as a guiding principle. Speech critical of institutions of government was suppressed on the grounds that it threatened the peace, security, and order of society.

In the American cases, the majority of the judges tended to lag behind the political thought. Instead of implicit references to pragmatism, the majority reflected late eighteenth-early nineteenth century thought, predating the individualism of Spencer and Sumner. There was an assumption that a natural harmony existed between individuals and society, which the speech at issue in the cases threatened, and that society was formed via a social contract. Coinciding with this thought was a belief in an absolute truth that was readily determinable.

It is in the dissenting opinions that more contemporary thought can be found, first reflecting the influence of Spencer and Sumner—freedom of expression is an inalienable, natural right—and then, in the later cases, pragmatism—individual and social interests must be balanced, truth must be determined through open discussion, and freedom of expression is a social right.[124] In the 1920s cases, there was also present a questioning of the ability of individuals to act rationally.

In Canada, the judges rather consistently reveal the influence of idealism—individuals must obey laws because they are expressions of the majority will. But as in the political thought, the idealism of the judges is tempered by individualism. For example, freedom of speech was described as an inalienable right. Because idealism was the dominant political thought in Canada for a long time, it is difficult to gauge the extent of any lag between the thought and its appearance in the cases. However, as in the American cases, some judges did reveal the influence of more contemporary thought in their willingness to uphold freedom of expression against the wishes of the majority and in their questioning of the rationality of individuals.

In the United States, First Amendment law is said to be a twentieth- century phenomenon.[125] Freedom of expression prior to the 1900s was primarily a personal matter that was dealt with on a local level.[126] But as the United States become more industrialized and urbanized, the ability of communities to impose standards of behavior on individuals lessened.[127] Freedom of expression and its regulation became increasingly a national problem requiring governmental controls. The resulting Supreme Court political speech cases in the United States in the period 1900 to 1920 can be divided into three groups: pre-war cases, cases arising under the Espionage Act of 1917,[128] and cases arising under the Sedition Act of 1918.[129]

In the pre-war cases,[130] the Court reflected a conservative political spirit, as well as classical republicanism, which predated Spencer and Sumner's individualism. Conservatives place an emphasis on history and tradition as guiding principles. They also emphasize the role of institutions and the rule of law in providing social control and stress duty over rights.[131] American classical republicanism is primarily conservative in nature. It emphasized the importance of institutional checks and balances in a democracy because of an inherent distrust of the masses and equated citizenship with equal rights under the law.[132]

In these early cases, the Court stressed the duty of individuals to obey the law and the right of government to pass laws for its self-preservation.[133] Political scientist A. J. Beitzinger has argued that the judges of the Court in this period took a mechanical approach to jurisprudence, applying set legal principles to concrete facts, because they believed in the natural harmony of interests in society, an eighteenth century concept.[134] For example, in *Patterson v. Colorado* (1907)[135] the Court upheld the conviction of a Colorado newspaper for publishing articles and cartoons critical of the state's supreme court. The First Amendment, the Court said, prevented prior restraint by the government; it did not prohibit subsequent punishment of expression.[136] Freedom of speech and of the press were relative freedoms subject to whatever limitations society wished to place on them. In the case at hand, the integrity of the judiciary was to be protected even at the cost of such freedom. "When a case is finished," the Court stated, "courts are subject to the same criticism as other people, but the propriety and necessity of preventing interference with the course of justice by premature statement, argument or intimidation hardly can be denied."[137] The judicial institution was too precious a commodity in the American democracy to threaten its integrity during a legal proceeding.

The Court's protection of the institutions of democracy reached its height in these early cases in *Toledo Newspaper v. U.S.*, a case involving freedom of the press.[138] In upholding a contempt citation against a newspaper for publishing articles critical of the action of a trial court, the Court said: "The safeguarding and fructification of free and constitutional institutions is the very basis and mainstay upon which the freedom of the press rests, and that freedom, therefore, does not and cannot be held to include the right virtually to destroy such institutions."[139]

Another eighteenth-century notion reflected in the cases, although one that Sumner had advocated as well, was that of a social contract.[140] Freedom of expression, for example, belonged only to citizens of the United States; it did not extend to aliens, presumably because they were not party to the social contract. Therefore, according to the Court in *Turner v. Williams*, Congress was within its constitutional rights to restrict the entry of alien anarchists into the country.[141] Clarence S. Darrow had argued for the appellants that section 38 of "An Act to Regulate the Immigration of Aliens into the United States" violated the First Amendment because it discriminated against disbelief, which "is the same thing as abridging freedom of speech."[142] In support of his argument, Darrow cited Spencer and John Stuart Mill but without success. As the Court explained, "To appeal to the Constitution is to concede that this is a land governed by that supreme law, and . . . those who are excluded cannot assert rights in general obtaining in a land to which they do not belong as citizens or otherwise."[143]

Such was not the case in Canada, where social contract theory was never part of the political thought. Although no political speech cases reached the Supreme Court of Canada during this time period, the high courts in the provinces did address the issue of sedition, and those cases are analyzed here for purposes of comparison.[144] All but the earliest case arose from charges of sedition under the Canadian Criminal Code.[145] In the sedition cases, unlike in the American cases, there was no discussion of the government's right to self-preservation because the question before the courts was not one of constitutionality. In other words, the question before the courts was not whether the statute was constitutional, but whether the defendant in fact committed the crime of sedition. The Canadian cases, including the non-sedition case, however, do reflect a similar conservative spirit on the part of the judges in their emphasis on institutions and the rule of law.

What is different in the Canadian cases is the apparent trust in the will of the majority. In *The King v. Hoaglin*, for example, the defendant had been charged under a section of the Canadian Criminal Code that prohibited the spreading of false news damaging to the public interest.[146] The defendant, an American, had printed a placard stating that settlers from the United States were not wanted in Canada. Although the judge noted that the charge was very uncommon, in fact he had never known of a similar charge, it was, he wrote, the policy of Canada. The court in *Rex v. Bainbridge* gave a more elaborate explanation of the Canadian position, holding that,

> The subject has a right to free speech and a free press and before the measure is passed he has a perfect right to use every argument fair or unfair against it. But once an Act is passed and becomes the law of the land, no one has any right to urge or argue for resistance to it. The people of Canada have the right to vote for a Government to repeal any Act, they have a

right to urge for its repeal, but to urge resistance to it, unless and until it is repealed, is seditious.[147]

Such sentiments are in keeping with the Canadian idealist political thought that stressed the community over the individual. Once the community has spoken through majority rule, the individual must obey the community will. At the same time, however, freedom of speech was described by the court in natural rights terms as inalienable, reflecting, as did the political thought, that idealism in Canada was tempered by individualism.

In the American pre-war cases, only Justice John M. Harlan's dissent in *Patterson v. Colorado* referred to the freedoms of speech and the press as natural rights.[148] They were "essential parts of every man's liberty" for Harlan. He went on, reflecting Spencer and Sumner's individualism, to state that neither Congress nor any state could "impair or abridge the rights of a free press and of free speech whenever it thinks that the public welfare requires that to be done. The public welfare cannot override constitutional privileges."[149] Freedom of speech for Harlan would appear to be capable of restriction by government only to the extent that it infringed another's liberty.

Harlan's individualism was not adopted by the majority of the Court immediately, but the Court moved in that direction. In the 1919 case of *Schenck v. U.S.*, Justice Oliver Wendell Holmes, Jr., writing for a unanimous Court, enunciated the test for when Congress could constitutionally infringe on freedom of expression.[150] *Schenck* is the first in the line of cases resulting from the Espionage Act of 1917 and is considered the beginning of modern First Amendment case law.[151] Although the Court upheld Schenck's conviction for distributing a pamphlet urging men not to register for the draft, the case is seen as providing substantial First Amendment protection for expression. Congress cannot restrict speech unless the words "are used in such circumstances and are of such a nature as to create a clear and present danger that they will bring about the substantive evils that Congress has a right to prevent," Holmes held.[152] The boundary between protected and unprotected speech for Holmes was the point at which the individual's speech infringed on the rights of others. As he noted in *Frohwerk v. U.S.*, no one would suggest that making criminal the counseling of a murder would be an unconstitutional restriction on freedom of speech.[153] Even under Spencer's extreme individualism, the government is entitled to step in at that point to protect the rights of others.

In the three American cases following *Schenck*, the majority of the Court, although not using the clear and present danger test, did speak from a social Darwinist perspective.[154] One of Spencer's tenets was that individuals were responsible for their own destiny. In the cases, that is translated into the position that "men must be held to have intended, and to be accountable for, the effects which their acts were likely to produce."[155] The same principle is found in the Canadian cases, which is in keeping with the idealist view that individuals owe a duty to themselves as well as to others.[156] The position, regardless of the political basis, put speech at a distinct disadvantage, especially in wartime when emotions run high.

Some of the Canadian judges recognized the danger to speech the war produced and held that not all speech should be restricted for the good of the society. For example in *Rex v. Trainor*, Judge Stuart said he feared the defendant, who had commented during the war that British soldiers were killing as many women and children as German soldiers were, was being punished "for his mere opinions and feelings and not for anything which is covered by the criminal law."[157] It is not, he noted, "the disloyalty of the heart that the law forbids."[158] Sedition required something more, and "the Courts should not, unless in cases of gravity and danger, be asked to spend their time scrutinizing with undue particularity the foolish talk of men in bar-rooms."[159] A similar sentiment was expressed by Justice Holmes in *Abrams v. U.S.*, the last of the three Espionage Act cases. In *Abrams*, Holmes dissented, arguing that the speech in question did not constitute a clear and present danger warranting conviction.

There is some controversy among legal scholars over why Holmes apparently changed his mind between the *Schenck* case and *Abrams* and came out in favor of protecting speech. Some scholars suggest that Holmes had a change of heart because of criticism he received from his contemporaries over his failure to more forcefully protect free speech.[160] According to this view, he then used the *Abrams* case to clear the air and restate his position, although in his dissent, Holmes insisted that his position was consistent.[161] While it is not clear how much influence his contemporaries had on his reasoning in *Abrams*, it is clear that Holmes was influenced by progressive political thought and pragmatism.

In a passage reminiscent of both Dewey and James, Holmes referred to the Constitution as "an experiment, as all life is an experiment" and said that "we have to wager our salvation upon some prophecy based upon imperfect knowledge." Therefore "the best test for truth is the power of the thought to get itself accepted in the competition of the market."[162] Dewey and James had earlier called into question the notion of absolute truth. James had argued that truth was a process of verification and validation and that society must be prepared to discard its truths when new information shows them to be false.[163] And Dewey had suggested that society was a process and that solutions for its problems must be found through experimentation.[164]

The issue of the meaning of truth came directly before the Court with the last three cases in this time period. The difference between these cases and the earlier cases under the Espionage Act is that in the earlier cases, such as *Schenck*, the focus was on the intention of the defendants. In these cases, the question was whether the defendants knew or ought to have known the statements were false, thus forcing the Court to address the issue of truth directly.

The majority of the Court continued to believe in an absolute truth. Justice Mahlon Pitney in *Pierce v. U.S.*, for example, defined truth as common knowledge; therefore, anyone saying anything contrary to the common knowledge must know it to be false. In one of the pamphlets before the Court, it was stated that the entry of the

United States into the war was precipitated by the "certainty that if the allies did not win, J.P. Morgan's loans to the allies will be repudiated, and those American investors who bit on his promises would be hooked."[165] To which Pitney responded:

> Common knowledge (not to mention the President's address to the Congress of April 2, 1917, and the Joint Resolution of April 6 declaring war, which were introduced into evidence) would have sufficed to show at least that the statements as to the causes that led to the entry of the United States into the war against Germany were grossly false and such common knowledge went to prove also that defendants knew they were untrue.[166]

Justice Louis D. Brandeis, in his dissent, noted that what the majority was calling a fact—the declaration of the President that a state of war existed between the United States and Germany—was merely a conclusion from facts. For Brandeis, the statements in question were no different than those before the Court in an earlier case about which the Court had commented, "there is no exact standard of absolute truth by which to prove the assertion false and a fraud."[167] Brandeis went on to note that the "cause of a war—as of most human action—is not single." The allegedly false statements at issue before the Court were simply interpretations of public facts on matters of public interest, according to Brandeis, and no reasonable jury could have found them to be otherwise.[168]

The majority of the Court recognized the problem of dealing with emotionally charged issues but chose to put its faith in the reason of the law as the guiding principle. In *Schaefer v. U.S.*, the majority stated that "keeping free from exaggerations and alarms prompted by an imagination of improbable conditions, we bring this case, as it should be brought, like other criminal cases, to no other scrutiny or submission than to the sedate and guiding principles of criminal justice."[169] The statement reflects again the eighteenth century mechanistic view of jurisprudence in which set legal principles are applied to concrete facts.

But Brandeis and Holmes were not willing to leave the decision necessarily in the hands of criminal justice. Brandeis, joined in dissent by Holmes, noted that the clear and present danger test was a rule of reason and correctly applied would "preserve the right of free speech both from suppression by tyrannous, well-meaning majorities and from abuse by irresponsible, fanatical minorities."[170] What was needed was not the rule of law, but rather good judgment. "Certainly men judging in calmness and with this test presented to them could not reasonably have said that this coarse and heavy humor immediately threatened the success of recruiting," he wrote.[171]

Brandeis was essentially suggesting in *Schaefer* that judges should look at the case before them and determine the appropriate solution rather than rigidly apply the traditional law. His position reflects the pragmatist view that sought workable solutions to social problems.[172] In fact, he saw freedom of speech as a tool to be used by individuals seeking better conditions through legislation. In *Pierce*, he wrote that prohibiting opinions by declaring them false statements of fact would "practically deny members of small political parties freedom of criticism and of discussion in times when feelings run high and the questions involved are deemed fundamental."[173] Americans have, according to Brandeis, a fundamental right to strive for conditions through new legislation and new institutions. Freedom of speech for Brandeis was a social interest that needed protection for the betterment of society.

The American cases during the period from 1900 to 1920, then, run the gamut of American political thought, moving from late eighteenth-early nineteenth century thought and conservatism to the individualism of Spencer and finally to progressivism. Historian Mark Graber has argued that progressives, such as Dewey and Brandeis, failed to provide a strong theoretical framework for protecting speech in this time period.[174] From an examination of the language used by the justices in these cases, however, it appears to have been the progressive

The Progressive Era: 1900-1920

questioning of truth that provided Holmes and Brandeis with their basis for dissent, combined, in the case of Brandeis, with a classical republican fear of the irrationality of the masses. The Canadian cases in the lower courts reveal less divergence, reflecting a less varied political thought. Essentially, the cases reflect idealism tempered by individualism. But they also show that idealism is not necessarily averse to the notion of freedom of speech. In the nine sedition cases, freedom of speech prevailed twice, while in the United States, freedom of speech did not succeed in any of the twelve cases. It must be noted, however, that the cases before the U.S. Supreme Court involved either public speeches or pamphlets. The cases in the Canadian courts involved speakers in small, unorganized settings and pamphlets of small distribution. It cannot be argued that these cases presented the same threat as those in the United States did, and it may in part account for why those cases were not appealed to the Canadian Supreme Court. They simply did not warrant the time and expense of a further appeal.

But what became clear in both countries by 1920 was that there was a growing tendency on the part of some judges to distrust the rationality of individuals. That individuals are rational creatures and would act accordingly was the basis of eighteenth century Enlightenment thought[175] and very much played a role in the Jeffersonian notion of democracy in the United States and in Canadian idealism. There was also a greater willingness on the part of the judges in both countries in the later part of the period to balance the interests of the society with those of the individual. World War I had seriously challenged the belief in the rationality of individuals, causing intellectuals to rethink the relationship of the individual to the state and some judges to cast about for greater protections for freedom of expression.

SUMMARY OF FINDINGS AND CONCLUSION

During the progressive era from 1900 to 1920, the political thought of Canada and the United States underwent a shift toward more government intervention. In the last half of the nineteenth century in the United States, the major trends in political thought emphasized individualism and the doctrine of laissez-faire. Individuals were seen as discrete, rational beings who were locked in a struggle with nature to survive. Society was simply an instrument for the protection of individuals from the actions of others. During the progressive era, however, extreme individualism came under fire. Pragmatists continued to see individuals as autonomous but recognized that individuals existed in a community and that their actions impacted on others. The role of government, then, was to assist in promoting the betterment of society through the implementation of workable solutions to what were now seen as social problems. Truth was no longer an absolute but was discoverable through observation, discussion, and the testing of alternatives.

The American cases in the period 1900 to 1920 reflect a conservatism on the part of the judges and a reliance on late eighteenth-early nineteenth century political thought in which the law involves the application of eternal, abstract principles to concrete facts. In terms of freedom of expression, this meant favoring the rule of law and the preservation of government institutions over the freedom of the individual. The dissenting judges, however, at the beginning of the period used Spencer's individualism and the doctrine of natural rights to uphold freedom of expression. By the end of the period, pragmatism and progressive thought could be found in the dissenting opinions. These judges called for a balancing of the interests of the individual and society and questioned the notion of an absolute truth. They saw freedom of expression as a social right necessary to further the betterment of society.

The Canadian cases also reflected nineteenth century thought, specifically idealism. The needs of the individual were subordinated to the needs of the society, and once the society had decided on its needs, the individual had no choice but to obey. Idealism saw the individual as a component part of society that had no separate existence from the organic whole. The duty of individuals was to seek a higher, moral life through self-identification with the good of the society. Such self-identification would ultimately lead to freedom through self-perfection. Idealism was used to restrict the individual's right to freedom of expression on the basis that the restriction was required by society. At the same time, early in the period, the courts described freedom of expression as an individual right, reflecting the influence of the British constitutional, liberal tradition on Canadian thought.

It was idealism, however, that had permitted the government to curb individual liberty in the name of public safety and welfare during World War I. Some of the Canadian judges recognized the danger to speech the war had produced. These judges reflected the progressive thought in Canada, which called for a balancing of individual and societal interests and upheld freedom of expression on the grounds that not every statement against society warranted restriction. The political thinkers in Canada from 1900 to 1920, while initially following idealism, had turned first toward greater government intervention and then toward greater liberty for individuals.

From 1900 to 1920, then, the tension between liberty—the desire of individuals to freely express themselves without fear of government interference—and authority—the desire of the state to restrict expression to protect public safety and welfare—was resolved in favor of authority. The reliance on late eighteenth-early nineteenth century political thought on the part of the American judges and idealism on the part of the Canadian judges meant that speech critical of government institutions was suppressed because it threatened the peace, security, and order of society. Under these philosophies, the individual was subordinated to the right of government to protect society and other individuals.

Determining the influence of the dominant political thought on judicial decision-making in this period is confounded somewhat by World War I. The war was an extraordinary event, and the courts have usually granted greater deference to the government in times of military crisis than in times of peace. At the same time, however, the reaction of individuals to the war caused judges influenced by progressive thought to uphold freedom of expression. In the United States, it was the notion of truth as a process that worked to the advantage of freedom of expression. In Canada, it was the progressive notion that social interests should be balanced with individual interests that protected speech. The war also made judges in both countries, as well as the intellectuals, question whether the masses were able to act rationally, a question that continued to be asked in the next decade.

CHAPTER 3
Disillusionment with Democracy: 1921 – 1945

Canadian political scientist Stephen Brooks has described modern politics as the search for the good society, and that description is particularly apt for the time period from the early 1920s until the end of World War II.[1] It was a time of social unrest in Canada and the United States, and the political thought in both countries reflects that instability. World War I had left a legacy of doubt among intellectuals. The war had been fought to save democracy, but many intellectuals wondered whether the price had been too high. And following hard on the heels of the war was the Great Depression, for which both capitalism and democracy were blamed. The disillusionment with and the questioning of democracy produced by the war and the Depression necessitated a reconceptualization of the individual, the state, and their relationship.

Because it was a period of questioning old values, no one political thought appears dominant over others. Common themes in the political thought of each country do emerge, however. In the United States, the focus was on individuals and their relationship to the state. The political thinkers were reacting to how individuals responded to the war and the Depression. These thinkers modified their conception of the individual as a rational being and the relationship of the individual to the state, but they did not change the pragmatic conception of the state that had prevailed in the progressive era ending in 1920. The state continued to be seen as a mechanism to balance individual and societal interests and to implement workable solutions to social and economic problems.

The Canadian political thought made a more significant break with the past. Idealism had been the dominant political thought in Canada until 1920. But after World War I, the Canadian intellectuals sought to limit the power of the state and give greater autonomy to the individual, which meant a corresponding change in the relationship between the two.

Despite these differences in focus, three themes common to the thought of both countries emerged: the notion that the democratic state was based on coercion and emotion as opposed to reason, the traditional basis of democracy; the idea of social unity and its importance to a democracy; and the concept of the state as a corporation, limited in function but capable of intervention to promote social welfare. All three were products of the social unrest brought on by World War I and the Great Depression.

POLITICAL THOUGHT FROM 1921 TO THE GREAT DEPRESSION

The traditional liberal faith in democratic theory appeared shattered in the period after World War I by a new realism, especially in the United States. Democracy was premised on the assumption that individuals were capable of rational thought. But World War I, the nativism exhibited by some Americans during the war,[2] and the Red Scare after the war, all challenged the notion of the rationality of individuals and shook the foundations of American democracy. If the individual were no longer rational, then in order to preserve the democratic state a new conceptualization of individuals was needed. It was to this task that the American political thinkers turned their attention after the war.

Canadian intellectuals, on the other hand, were not as troubled by the apparent irrationality of individuals. Canada experienced occasional bouts of nativism during the war but not to the same extent as did the United States.[3] More troubling for Canadians was the extent of government intervention in their lives under the pretext of protecting national security during the war. The federal government had gained power in Canada during World War I and appeared reluctant to give up that power in peacetime. The political philosophy of idealism, in which the individual is subordinated to the state, had justified the state's intrusions into previously private areas during the war. The question confronting the Canadian political thinkers was how to reconceptualize the state and its relationship to individuals to limit the state.[4]

Although Canadian intellectuals sought to move away from idealism because of its tendency to turn into authoritarianism, they did not want to shift too far in the opposite direction toward individualism either. During the final years of World War I, civil conflicts seemed to be on the rise in Canada, as evidenced by the Winnipeg General Strike of 1919, the formation of the One Big Union, and the coalescing of various farmers' movements in the West.[5] Not surprisingly given these circumstances, the watchwords of the intellectuals in the 1920s and early 1930s were the same as they had been under idealism—unity, social order, and stability.[6] Borrowing from idealism, nineteenth-century utilitarianism, and pragmatism, the Canadian intellectuals fashioned a new concept of the role of the state that social worker F. N. Stapleford described as "socialized individualism."[7] Socialized individualism permitted state intervention not in the name of a collective social goal, as was the case in idealism, but in the name of the potential of the individual in whose behalf the intervention was taking place.[8]

An expression of this view of the state can be seen in the work of Canadian political economist R. M. MacIver. MacIver's goal in *The Modern State* was to establish a new political philosophy to replace idealism, which he thought outdated and no longer viable in the Canada of the 1920s. Idealism, the dominant Canadian political thought since the late 1800s, subordinated the individual to the state. Society and the state were essentially one, an organic whole composed of individuals. Individuals were by their very nature social and formed part of the organism of society in which the good of each was bound up with the good of all. Taken to its logical extreme, idealism resulted in idolatry of the state and the submersion of the individual into the state; it was this aspect of idealism that troubled MacIver.

MacIver was faced with two tasks. The first was to establish the individual as autonomous, and the second was to separate the state from society so that he could justify limiting the state. MacIver began by arguing that the state was not organic. It was not an organism unto itself; rather, it was similar to a business corporation.[9] And like all associations, the state had a defined sphere in which it operated. It was to be restricted to legislating in those areas that could reasonably be considered of universal interest.[10] Therefore, the state could not favor one religion or one culture over others, for example. It was to remain universal or neutral. "The state must stand for what is recognized by the political consciousness of the times as the common concern of the people," MacIver wrote, although he noted that such determination could be perverted by dominant interest groups.[11]

The state created rights, not in its own right, but as the agent of society. In its service to society, the state functioned as a guarantor of rights, and its powers were to be limited just as its function was limited.[12] For example, the state was not permitted to control expression. The justification for denying the state the right to control expression was not to be found in the traditional notions of liberty, MacIver argued, or because opinion was personal and therefore outside the competence of the state, nor because opinion could not be separated from action.

> The true reasons are found when we appreciate the pitiful irrelevance of force in the control of opinion.... Force allies itself as easily with falsehood as with truth, so that its mere invocation in support of an opinion is a blasphemy against truth. Opinion can be fought only by opinion. Only thus is it possible for truth to be revealed. Force would snatch from truth its only means of victory. Force can suppress opinion

but only by suppressing the mind which is the judge of truth.[13]

The law could force one to act in a certain way but never to think in a certain way, he contended.[14] The state was permitted, however, to control expression in the case of incitement to break laws or defy authority because such incitement went beyond mere expression of opinion.[15] An individual could use any means of peaceful persuasion to convince others that a law was unjust or illegitimate and urge constitutional challenges, MacIver argued, "but to urge law-breaking is to attack the fundamental order, the establishment of which is the first business of the state, and for the preservation of which it is endowed with coercive power."[16] The state was entitled, therefore, to stop an individual from advocating overthrow of the government by force because ultimately an attack on the state was an attack on the community that sustained the state.[17] As defined by MacIver, then, the state was an association that maintained the social order of a community through laws.[18]

For MacIver, the maintenance of social order was necessary for the protection, conservation, and development of society.[19] The state's duty was to maintain social order because it was through the social order that individuals could more freely and more fully seek fulfillment, a sentiment that reflects his idealist roots.[20] MacIver's individuals, then, were still social beings whose nature sought unity, as they had been under idealism, but now they were also autonomous and self-legislating.[21] Individuals did not live within the state, but only by means of the state, MacIver wrote, which is fundamentally different from idealism.[22] Under idealism, the individual could not exist separate from the state. Now, the state was seen as merely providing the means to enable existence; it was a mechanism to assist individuals in their quest for fulfillment. The state was "an expression of the social sense, the sense of solidarity, the sense of common interest."[23] As such, it was the root of the unity of society and the form through which that unity was expressed. But, MacIver wrote, no structure, no form of government, can assure social unity. The final unity lies in the solidarity of men not in the power of the state. There is social unity just in so far as the sense of common interest or common nature is stronger than that of dividing interests.[24]

Political commentator Walter Lippmann in the United States would have agreed that unity was important in society but would have denied that a common interest could be achieved in a nation as heterogeneous as the United States. Lippmann was not concerned necessarily with the state but with the individual.[25] The difference in focus between the Canadian and American thinkers in this period can be explained in part by the reaction of individuals in the respective countries to the war. American society reached a level of hysteria during and after the war that many intellectuals found troubling. The United States had been the site of a propaganda war between Great Britain and Germany for American support, and the U. S. government itself used propaganda to bolster support for the war effort.[26] The result of all the propaganda was a nativistic fervor that appeared to the political thinkers in hindsight to be highly irrational. Individuals, it appeared, were capable of being swayed by propaganda. Public information had not led to the truth and rational decision-making but instead had allowed interest groups to control majority opinion. It was this aspect of propaganda that most concerned Lippmann.

In his 1921 work, *Public Opinion*, Lippmann challenged such fundamental assumptions of democratic theory as the rationality of individuals, the inherent ability of all individuals to govern, the ability to achieve a common will in a diverse nation, and that the end of democracy was self-governance.[27] Underlying these assumptions was the notion that truth could be determined and arrived at through open discussion, he argued. But, for Lippmann, knowledge could only be gained through the physical senses.[28] Individuals could only know what they could experience directly. For the most part, individuals only indirectly experienced the environment in which they lived.

Lippmann conceded that in small, homogenous communities, it was possible to have direct knowledge about many facets of life. And it was only in such communities that democracy would work, according to Lippmann, reflecting a classical republican view of democracy. "If democracy is to be spontaneous," as was supposed in the doctrine of laissez-faire, then "the environment must be confined within the range of every man's direct and certain knowledge," he argued.[29] In addition, the community had to maintain a homogenous code of morals because then the only differences of opinion would be the result of a faulty application of logic to the facts. It followed that "an error in reasoning would be quickly exposed in a free discussion."[30]

But America was not a small, homogenous community, Lippmann argued. Americans could not possibly have direct knowledge of everything affecting them or their country. They had to rely on others, such as politicians and journalists, for their information. Instead of seeking out the truth, people sought out the most trustworthy source of information even though they had no independent means of assessing trustworthiness. It became, wrote Lippmann, a matter of seeking out those with whom they agreed. In such a situation, individuals were left vulnerable to propaganda.

Propaganda, for Lippmann, was not necessarily an evil for it could be used to reach a consensus in a diverse electorate, but it did open individuals up to exploitation by interest groups, something the Constitution was written to prevent. The Founding Fathers were aware that democracy would never work on a national scale, according to Lippmann, and so they drafted the Constitution not on a theory of democracy, but on the classical republican theory that men could be governed if special interests were kept in equilibrium by a balance of power.[31]

Lippmann, then, challenged the foundations of democratic theory in suggesting that truth could not be determined without direct knowledge, something that was impossible in a nation the size of the United States. Individuals could not know everything and, therefore, depended on information from others to make their way in the world. That dependence, however, opened them up to exploitation by interest groups because individuals neither had the means of testing the information they received nor the capacity of reason to do so. Sounding very much like a British Tory, Lippmann wrote that "the mass of absolutely illiterate, of feeble-minded, grossly neurotic, undernourished and frustrated individuals, is very considerable, much more considerable there is reason to think than we generally suppose."[32]

Despite having such a view of the great unwashed, Lippmann sought to leave the concept of the state as it was. He accomplished that goal by interposing experts between the individual and "the vast environment in which he is entangled."[33] Lippmann's solution was a network of intelligence bureaus in each government department and in industry. Intellectuals working in these bureaus would have access to all information and would provide administrators with expert, objective opinions.[34]

Other American political thinkers, such as Reinhold Niebuhr and T.V. Smith, held a more positive view of the individual, while acknowledging that individuals were not necessarily rational. Neibuhr, for example, argued that there was a distinction between the moral and social behavior of individuals and groups.[35] Individuals had a natural empathy with and compassion for others, which he characterized as a rational faculty. Aided by education, this rationality allowed individuals to view a social situation with some measure of objectivity. But such objectivity was next to impossible for groups. In groups there was "less reason to guide and check impulse, less ability to comprehend the needs of others, less capacity for self-transcendence."[36]

Thus for Neibuhr, the solution to society's ills was neither more experiments to control behavior as the social scientists proposed, nor more education as educators proposed.[37] According to Neibuhr, what was lacking in these propositions was "an understanding of the brutal character of the behavior of all human collectives, and the power of self-interest and collective egoism in all intergroup relations."[38] Social conflict was an inevitability, he argued, and the relations between groups were determined on the basis of power, not on ethics or morals.[39]

According to Neibuhr, society was in a perpetual state of war and even democracy was a product of coercion.[40] Those in power maintained their position by cloaking their actions in political, moral, or economic theories. For example, when the state used its police power to shut down rebellions, it justified its suppression of liberties on the basis that it was necessary to preserve peace.[41] Individuals bought into the theory because they were connected at the national level, by emotion.[42] "In other words, the nation is a corporate unity, held together much more by force and emotion, than by mind," he wrote.[43] It was the public's emotional attachment and unqualified devotion to the nation that was the basis of the state's power.[44] But Lippmann's bureau of experts was not the solution. The suggestion that society needed trained specialists merely revealed the prejudice of the intellectual, Neibuhr argued.[45] Instead, society had to acknowledge the inevitability of group selfishness and work to cultivate individual moral discipline and an "uncompromising idealism."[46]

Smith, on the other hand, following in the tradition of pragmatism, was concerned with equality and what the new view of the individual would do to that concept.[47] Originally, the natural rights doctrine justified the notion of equality—everyone was born equal.[48] Individuals were born with a soul, or "fixed self" as Smith put it, that was God-given. But thanks to Charles Darwin and pragmatists such as William James and John Dewey, human nature was no longer viewed as fixed, and if there were no fixed self or soul, there was no inherent equality.[49] Despite such conceptual changes, Americans accepted equality in principle, Smith noted. His goal, then, was to fashion a new basis for the claim of equality.

In doing so, Smith took a more optimistic view of individuals than did Lippmann. True, humans were not primarily rational, he wrote, but they were secondarily so. They did on occasion have ideas; they were not simply animals. Smith summarized the then current view of individuals: selves were organisms capable of self-direction; the mechanism of this self-direction was direct observation; and the self-direction arose out of ideas that on occasion transformed an impulse- or habit-guided individual into an end-guided one.[50] For Smith, the notion of self-direction implied that humans were dynamic, not static, and in the process of becoming. He acknowledged that individuals were not equal, but for him the question was whether they, "as dynamic centers of activity, ought to be treated equally."[51] The answer for Smith was yes, because "men work better together when they regard themselves as substantially equal."[52] The spirit of cooperation, then, was Smith's justification for equality. And equality would only be achieved through "bold experimentation" with education and with the promotion of an active citizenry.[53]

Smith and the other American intellectuals during the 1920s seemed preoccupied with the individual and with the need to reconceptualize the individual to fit within democratic theory. On the whole, American thinkers appeared to be more disenchanted with democracy than their Canadian counterparts. The realization that individuals were not necessarily rational troubled the Americans and struck at the heart of democratic theory because in many ways democracy stood for America itself. The question for the political thinkers was how to maintain the democratic state in the face of the irrationality of individuals. Solutions proffered included the use of experts to advise the public, the education of the public in rational-thinking skills, and the promotion of individual morals. Through such solutions, these thinkers sought to maintain the concept of the state as it had been at the end of the progressive era. The state's role under the pragmatic thought of that period was to balance individual and societal interests and to implement workable solutions to social and economic problems.

Canadians, on the other hand, were more concerned with the excesses of government power during the war than they were with the irrationality of individuals. No doubt that stems at least in part from their idealist roots. Under idealism, individuals were not the basic unit of society; they were merely a component part of the greater whole.

The irrationality of individuals did not affect the existence of the state. But the lack of concern in Canada can also be attributed to the fact that the Canadian state was never theory-driven. The Canadian parliamentary democracy, meaning essentially majority rule, had been inherited from Great Britain and adapted to fit the practicalities of the Canadian political and cultural landscape. Democracy was not a symbol to Canadians in the way it was to Americans.

Canadian intellectuals, however, were troubled that the state had gained power during World War I and appeared reluctant to give up that power in peacetime. The political philosophy of idealism, in which the individual is subordinated to the state, had justified the state's intrusions into previously private areas during the war. A new way of looking at the state and its relationship to individuals was needed; one that did not extend too far in the opposite direction toward individualism. MacIver, then, sought to redefine the state by limiting its sphere of action and increasing the autonomy of the individual. The result was socialized individualism. The state was seen as just one more association, along with family, work, church, and school, affecting the life of an individual. State intervention was permitted, not in the name of a collective social goal, but in the name of the potential of the individual in whose behalf the intervention was taking place. It necessarily followed that individuals were autonomous, but they were not discrete. They were, by nature, social beings who sought harmony with each other.

All of these writers were reacting to the war and its aftermath. But the Great Depression and the rise of totalitarian systems in Europe soon created a new threat. Democracy and capitalism had developed almost hand in hand, but the Depression had the potential to bring both to their knees, especially as the political/economic ideologies of fascism, communism, and socialism gained strength in Europe.

POLITICAL THOUGHT FROM THE GREAT DEPRESSION TO 1945

American political thinkers continued to be concerned with the individual during and after the Great Depression. They adopted the 1920s view and saw individuals as not necessarily rational, but as at least capable of reason. The problem produced by the Depression was that individuals had failed to recognize their relationship to the state had changed. They were reluctant to let go of the concept of the negative state, a state limited in function, and embrace the positive state, a state active in setting social policy. The political thinkers sought to explain why that was the case.

In Canada, despite the writing of MacIver, idealism still existed during the 1920s, but it had fragmented into a left reform wing and a right paternalistic wing. Both stressed social stability and government authority and advocated government planning and intervention to right the ills of society, especially as it became clear that business and government, as constituted, lacked the means to deal with the Depression.[54] The state was viewed, based on the concept expressed by MacIver, as a mechanism to be used to promote social well-being that was increasingly defined in terms of practicalities and efficiency.[55]

According to Canadian conservative H. M. Cassidy, for example, the state had a duty to provide social assistance that was based on the need to preserve the status quo. "Conservatives hold it just and proper that those with property, acquired or inherited, are entitled to superior rank and station to those lacking in property," he wrote.[56] However, he argued, radicalism would be less likely to grow and, therefore, less likely to challenge the status quo in a society that provided some social services.[57]

Other Canadian political thinkers drew on utilitarianism to justify state intervention.[58] For example, Alexander Brady noted that the happiness of the individual was sought in combination with other persons and that the purpose of the state was the "production of the means of happiness through a host of public authorities."[59] William

Price argued that the principal duty of a government founded on the popular will was to protect itself and to ensure that no minority, however well organized or armed, could usurp its powers.[60] Price took the position that the Canadian system was designed so that a numerical majority of the people had to approve of what was to be done, on the theory that the minority should be content with what suited most of the people. Those who advocated violent means of change did so because they could not convince a majority of the worthiness of their position. "They thus want to substitute the government of a minority, a tyranny, for the government of the greatest number, a democracy," he wrote.[61]

The left reform wing of the Canadian political thinkers advocated government planning of the economy on the basis that only through such planning could individuals achieve true freedom. Many of these left-leaning intellectuals came together in a group known as the League for Social Reconstruction (LSR), formed in 1932. The principal work of the LSR, a book titled *Social Planning for Canada*, combined idealist, utilitarian, pragmatist, Socialist, and even individualist thought in an attempt to achieve the good society.[62]

In the preface to its book, the LSR wrote that if democracy were to be real, two things had to be present—complete freedom to criticize the existing institutions, "provided that factual grounds are given for this criticism," and public knowledge of the faults and deficiencies of the economic system.[63] The LSR argued that economic domination carried over into the law when the state insisted that order was of higher social value than justice because in doing so the state was siding with those who had vested property interests. Order, in that situation, was simply the maintenance of the status quo, which perpetuated injustice and inequality.[64]

There was always a conflict between the demands of personal liberty and the necessities of order and organization, the LSR noted. But the conflict was superficial. "Order is itself a necessary condition for the full realization of personal freedom; willing cooperation in concerted social action is a prerequisite of the enlargement of individual liberty in the fullest sense."[65] True freedom, which the League defined as "opportunities for unfettered personal development," could only be enjoyed by individuals who were secure in their employment and who could afford a decent life.[66]

One member of the LSR, social worker Charlotte Whitton, noted that average citizens sought from the state the assurance of their ability to maintain a certain level of material well-being.[67] Whitton agreed that the state should provide the general framework and the safeguards, but the actual attainment of individual well-being resided with the individual, she concluded.[68] Thus, Whitton, despite her desire for social services, reflected the influence of the idealist thought of the turn of the century that advocated the doctrine of laissez-faire at the same time that it subordinated the individual to the state. Both Whitton and the early idealists saw individuals as morally responsible for their own well-being.

In the province of Quebec, corporatism was seen as the answer to the Depression.[69] Under corporatism, the state was not only the guardian of law and order, but also worked through laws and institutions to promote the economy. Corporatism harkened back to feudalism when society was organized into guilds.[70] The key social unit under corporatism was not the individual, but the group—families, guilds, associations. It was through these multiple groups or associations within society that the individual could lead a satisfactory life, according to Quebec corporatist Fr. Desrosiers. Desrosiers also argued that secular society was not the sum of its individuals, but the synthesis of its component parts.[71] Although Desrosiers sounds very much the idealist, he was actually revealing his ultramontanist roots in the statement.

Ultramontanism was the dominant political thought in Quebec in the late 1800s. For the ultramontanists, the religious sphere was bound to the secular as intimately as the soul was bound to the human body.[72] It was not possible, according to ultramontanism, for a society to exist without religion, specifically Catholicism. The political ideal was an officially Catholic state that was subject to the pressure of public opinion.[73] By the 1930s, ultramontanism had evolved into corporatism, which provided for class co-operation, profit-sharing, and social harmony. The state's main role was to restore order in a society that was considered damaged by economic liberty.[74]

Along with corporatism, the political thought in Quebec in the 1930s expressed a fear of industrialization, urban growth, and anything new.[75] The result was the spread of antisemitist and antiCommunist messages by Quebec's intellectuals that made the province a fertile ground for fascism.[76] Quebec nationalists were openly impressed by the authoritarian regimes of Europe. Lionel Groulx even wrote in *L'Action Nationale*, "Happy the peoples that have found their dictators."[77]

At the opposite end of the political spectrum from Quebec was the United States. Thurman Arnold, in *Folklore of Capitalism*, argued that because Americans were tied to the state through emotion and not reason, they could not accept government intervention in the economy during the Depression.[78] Such intervention was viewed by Americans as leading to the destruction of individual initiative, the national character, and capitalism and permitted Americans to ignore the realities that had produced the need for intervention in the first place.[79] Every practical scheme for social betterment had to be tested for tendencies leading to the systems of capitalism, communism, or fascism rather than for their immediate effect on society.[80]

Arnold was different from the writers of the 1920s who had focused on the irrationality of individuals. He, too, was concerned with the individual, but it was the individual's relationship to the state that he found troubling. He implicitly accepted the concept of the individual as not necessarily rational but capable of reason that came out of the political thought of the 1920s. But those less than perfectly rational individuals were unable to see the reality of the Depression because they viewed their relationship to the state in individualistic terms, according to Arnold. They continued to think of themselves as discrete individuals and the state as limited in function to the protection of themselves and their property from the actions of others. Individualism was no longer a reality in the United States, if it ever had been, Arnold contended, but it had nevertheless taken on the stature of a myth to which Americans held steadfast.

For Arnold, it was through a belief in absolutes that the idea of systems of government took on a mythology of its own.[81] To absolutists, communism was the same no matter the country, the leader, or the social and historical context. Absolutism ignored the reality that politicians simply adapted their creed to fit public opinion regardless of their professed doctrine.[82] Democracy was no longer an ideology, according to Arnold; it had become simply a political fact, meaning a government that operated through emotion and not force.[83] Arnold argued that social creeds, laws, economic theories, and social philosophies had no meaning whatever apart from the organization to which they were attached.[84]

Like the Canadian MacIver, Arnold noted that it was the social organization of a nation that was the unifying force binding the people together.[85] Individuals had various social organizations in their lives—government, business, social.[86] "We have reached a time when men are beginning to realize their complete interdependence, when the personality of the individual is submerged in the personality of the organization," he wrote.[87] Arnold was not troubled by the idea of a society where principles and ideals were more important than individuals, but he warned that "the greatest destroyer of ideals is he who believes in them so strongly that he cannot fit them to practical needs."[88]

For Arnold, then, the state's role, as it was in pragmatic thought, was to assist in promoting the betterment of society through the implementation of workable solutions to social and economic problems. Therefore, the relationship of the state to the individual was to remain as it had been in the progressive era. The problem, as Arnold saw it, was that individuals were not accepting that relationship. They were, instead, viewing democracy and their role in it in mythological terms that prevented them from seeing the reality and the need for intervention.

While Arnold was concerned with what he perceived as the American propensity to lose sight of practicalities in its fear of fascism and communism, Erich Fromm sought to explain the attraction of the totalitarian ideologies of the 1940s. Fromm's thesis was that modern man, "freed from the bonds of pre-industrialistic society, which simultaneously gave him security and limited him, has not gained freedom in the positive sense of the realization of his individual self."[89] Freedom, while bringing individuals independence and rationality, had made them isolated, anxious, and powerless. Instead of uniting themselves "with the world in the spontaneity of love and productive work," individuals sought to escape the burdens of freedom in the security of authoritarianism.[90]

Americans, Fromm reasoned, had been too preoccupied with gaining freedom from outside influences to realize that individuals were subject to inner restraints as well. The right to freedom of expression, for example, "means something only if we are able to have thoughts of our own; freedom from external authority is a lasting gain only if the inner psychological conditions are such that we are able to establish our own individuality."[91] For Fromm, the true individual existed as an independent self that was at the same time united with other individuals and nature. Therefore, positive freedom was achieved when individuals were simultaneously autonomous and united in harmony.[92] Positive freedom implied that there was no higher power than the individual self and that the individual was the center and purpose of that person's life.[93]

From the Depression until 1945, then, American political thinkers continued to be concerned with the individual. They accepted the premise of the 1920s that individuals were not necessarily rational but were capable of reason. But now they were concerned with the relationship of the individual to the state. The Depression had forced the pragmatic concept of the state into a political reality. The federal government, through President Roosevelt's New Deal legislation, became a player in the economic and social spheres to an unprecedented extent. That change in role promoted a change in the relationship between the individual and the state. The concern among the political thinkers was that Americans continued to think of themselves as individualists and of freedom in negative terms, meaning that the state's role was to be limited to the protection of individuals from the action of others. Any greater intervention on the part of the state was seen as a movement toward fascism or communism. Such thinking blinded Americans from seeing the need for practical solutions to social and economic problems.

In Canada, both the left- and the right-wing thinkers agreed on the need for government planning and intervention to right the ills of society. They adopted MacIver's concept of the state as a mechanism to serve society and reinforced his notion of the individual as both autonomous and social. Their concern was how best to use the state to right what were seen as flaws in the capitalistic and democratic system.

Throughout the period from 1921 to 1945, then, a general disillusionment with democracy permeated the political thought of the United States and Canada. The political thought in both countries discussed the democratic state's power in terms of coercion and emotion. The Canadian MacIver, for example, referred to the state as having been endowed with coercive power. And Neibuhr, in the United States, argued that democracy was a product of coercion and that the state was held together by force and emotion, not reason. For Arnold, democracy meant a government that ruled, not by force, but by emotion. Such sentiments suggest traditional liberal notions of democracy had given way to a more jaded view of both individuals and the state.

The theme of unity or harmony appears in the political thought of both countries, and given the social unrest of the time, it is probably not surprising. Intellectuals in both countries argued that individuals achieved self-fulfillment through society. In the United States, individuals were at the center or the core of the thought and were personally responsible for seeking self-fulfillment. In Canada, on the other hand, society was at the center, and the state had a duty to help individuals achieve their potential as part of that society. The difference reflects the countries' roots in individualism and idealism respectively.

Although the Canadian intellectuals dealt more with the concept of the state than the Americans did, thinkers in both countries referred to the state as a corporation. As a corporation, the state had a limited function, but its limitations were different than those previously imposed on the state by the doctrine of laissez-faire. The state under laissez-faire was limited in its scope to the preservation of order. The state as a corporation had a limited sphere within which it could act, but it was free to act within that sphere. MacIver described it as being restricted to matters of universal concern. Therefore, in Canada, the state was free to intervene in the economy and provide social services to ensure a minimum standard of living, for example. In the United States, Arnold intimated that the state ought to be given the same powers when he argued that the Depression required practical solutions by government.

The political thought of the two countries, then, continued to move closer together in this period. Intellectuals progressively sought a middleground between individualism and idealism in their search for the good society. Individuals were considered both autonomous and social, rather than one or the other. And the state was given a greater role in providing social services to individuals.

POLITICAL SPEECH CASES

The tension between liberty—the desire of individuals to freely express themselves without fear of government interference—and authority—the desire of the state to restrict expression to protect public safety and welfare—finds its expression in the period from 1921 to 1945 in the governments' attempts to silence the voices of those disenchanted with democracy, such as Communists and the unemployed. Governments in both countries used the law to control expression in the name of public safety and welfare. How individual judges decided a case involving political speech depended in part on their conception of the individual, the state, and their relationship.

Again the judges tended to lag behind the political thought. In the United States, the majority of the Supreme Court justices in the early 1920s combined aspects of classical conservatism and classical republicanism to deny speech rights and find in favor of the government. As conservatives, the justices placed an emphasis on history and tradition as guiding principles. Change to the status quo was to come from slow evolution rather than sudden break. They also emphasized the role of institutions and the rule of law in providing social control.[94] As classical republicans, they emphasized the importance of institutional checks and balances in a democracy because of an inherent distrust of the masses and saw active participation in politics as a duty of citizenship.[95] But in the 1930s, the Court began to support speech rights, and the shift coincided with the appointment of justices exhibiting a pragmatic political philosophy. As pragmatists, the justices saw freedom of expression as a social right that was essential to the democratic process and to the discovery of truth. They also called for a balancing of social and individual interests in the quest for a better society and for practical solutions to social problems.

In the final years of the period, when virtually all of the justices were pragmatists, the differences in opinion in political speech cases arose from a split between those justices with liberal tendencies and those with conservative tendencies. The conservative pragmatists, such as Justice Felix Frankfurter, thought the legislature was the branch of government that ought to determine social policy and was hesitant to change that policy. The more liberal pragmatists saw free speech as the most important social right in a democracy, a right that needed special protection from legislative infringement.

In Canada, the early cases involved the issue of unlawful assembly and incitements to violence. The judges followed the earlier idealism in upholding social order as paramount. One political speech case reached the Supreme Court in this time period, and the case marked the first time the Canadian high court addressed the issue of freedom of expression. The opinion reflects both the earlier idealism and the then contemporary socialized individualism of the Canadian political thought. The language used by the justices shares many similarities with that of the American justices concerning the purpose and value of freedom of expression in a democracy.

American Political Speech Cases

The early 1920s cases in the United States came out in favor of authority over liberty primarily because the majority of the justices conceived of the individual and the state in classical republican and conservative terms. For example, in *Milwaukee Publishing Co. v. Burleson*, a 1921 case involving a newspaper denied a second-class postal rate by the Postmaster General because of its pro-German stance during the war, the majority upheld the government's position.[96] Justice John H. Clarke, in his opinion, noted, "Freedom of the press may protect criticism and agitation for modification or repeal of laws, but it does not extend to protection of him who counsels and encourages the violation of the law as it exists."[97] The Constitution was created to preserve the government, he continued, not to protect those who sought to destroy it. Maintenance of public order and the existing system of government was very important for Clarke. Implicit in his denial of protection for those who advocated violation of the law was his fear of the ability of these individuals to sway others. The Milwaukee Publishing Company posed a threat to the status quo that Clarke was seeking to protect.[98]

Similarly, Justice Edward T. Sanford, in *Gitlow v. New York*, wrote that the state unquestionably was entitled to use its police power to punish those who abused freedom of speech and of the press "by utterances inimical to the public welfare, tending to corrupt public morals, incite to crime, or disturb the public peace."[99] The state was permitted to punish statements that threatened the "foundations of organized government" and threatened its overthrow by violence because "these imperil its own existence as a constitutional State."[100] The state for Sanford, then, was an organism separate from society and had a "primary and essential right of self preservation."[101] Therefore, the state was not required to wait to determine the effect of the speech before taking action to protect itself.

Sanford's state, with its right of self-preservation, was a far cry from the conception of the state enunciated in the Declaration of Independence. For the drafters of that document, the people, as sovereigns, had a right to revolt and overthrow a state that was no longer legitimate in their eyes.[102] For Sanford, revolution was never an option for the people, in part because he had no faith in the masses. He saw them as easily swayed.

The distrust of the masses on the part of these classical conservative and classical republican justices comes through clearly in Justice Willis Van Devanter's dissent in *Herndon v. Lowry*.[103] Herndon was convicted under a state statute that forbade the solicitation of members for a political party that advocated overthrow of the government by force. In upholding the conviction, Van Devanter noted,

> It should not be overlooked that Herndon was a negro member and organizer in the Communist Party and was engaged actively in inducing others, chiefly southern negroes, to become members of the party.... The literature placed in his hands by the party for that purpose was particularly adapted to appeal to negroes in that section.[104]

The effect of the literature that Herndon was distributing was not to be tested against a reasonable person standard, according to Van Devanter, but with "regard to the capacity and circumstances of those who are sought to be influenced."[105]

Against the classical conservative and classical republican justices in the early 1920s stood only Justices Louis D. Brandeis and Oliver Wendell Holmes, Jr. Although Brandeis reflected features of classical republican thought and Holmes reflected features of individualism, they shared a pragmatic outlook that led them to dissent in the early cases. Brandeis, like the pragmatists, saw freedom of expression as a social right, essential to the democratic process. Restricting expression short of imminent and immediate danger to the state imperiled the "discovery and spread of political truth," he wrote.[106] He was able to support freedom of expression because of his strong classical republican notions that "the greatest menace to freedom is an inert people" and "that public discussion is a political duty."[107] What made Brandeis different from his fellow classical republicans on the bench was his liberal belief in reason. As was seen in the cases prior to 1920, Brandeis did not always have faith in the rationality of the masses, but he did believe that free discussion would afford "ordinarily adequate protection against the dissemination of noxious doctrine" and "free men from the bondage of irrational fears."[108]

Holmes, on the other hand, was a more complex individual. Holmes was protective of speech, not because he believed in the rationality of individuals, but because he distrusted absolute truth. Like the pragmatists, Holmes saw truth as relative. The best test of truth was whether it was accepted in the marketplace. Truth was a process, not an absolute. Society, for Holmes, was locked in an evolutionary struggle to survive in which the most powerful groups win out. It was a natural evolution that could not be tampered with by the state. Under such an individualist position, the state was only entitled to restrict expression when the words used presented a clear and present danger to the state. Holmes, then, was able to write in *Gitlow v. New York* that "if in the long run the beliefs expressed in proletarian dictatorship are destined to be accepted by the dominant forces of the community, the only meaning of free speech is that they should be given their chance and have their way."[109]

In many ways, Brandeis and Holmes were transitional figures who combined the older political philosophies of classical republicanism and individualism with the more contemporary pragmatism. But it was not until the addition of Justices Charles E. Hughes and Owen J. Roberts to the Court in 1930 that the majority shifted from the conservatives and classical republicans to the pragmatists, and freedom of expression began to win the day.[110]

Chief Justice Hughes was a strong supporter of freedom of expression. In almost identical wording in two separate opinions, he noted that the right of free speech was necessary "in order to maintain the opportunity for free political discussion, to the end that government may be responsive to the will of the people and that changes, if desired, may be obtained by peaceful means."[111] It was essential, in other words, to the democratic process. The state could only restrict speech in limited circumstances, and in determining the constitutionality of any such restriction, the Court was to test the statute's practical effect on speech.[112]

Justice Roberts also saw freedom of expression as necessary for a democracy. "Citizenship of the United States would be little better than a name if it did not carry with it the right to discuss national legislation," he wrote.[113] But at the same time, freedom of speech was a social right that was to be balanced against other social rights. Thus, the use of parks "for communication of views on national questions may be regulated in the interest of all," he wrote. Free speech had to be exercised in "subordination to the general comfort and convenience, and in consonance with peace and good order."[114] But that did not mean the state had free reign to regulate speech as it saw fit. Speech could be limited only when the limitation had an "appropriate relation to the safety of the state."[115]

Justices appointed to the bench in the years following Justices Hughes and Roberts all had a pragmatic political outlook, which meant strong support for freedom of expression. Justice Robert H. Jackson, for example, in the case of *Thomas v. Collins*, held that, while the state had an interest in shielding the public from untrustworthy business practices, it had no such duty to protect the public from false doctrines.[116] The First Amendment foreclosed the state from assuming guardianship of the public mind. "In this field, every person must be his own watchman for truth, because our forefathers did not trust any government to separate true from false for us," he wrote.[117] Freedom of expression was protected in the Constitution because the founding fathers "knew no other way by which men could conduct a representative democracy."[118]   Implicit in Jackson's opinion is the liberal faith in individuals and in reason.

Not all of the justices on the bench in the thirties and early forties were liberal, however, although virtually all were pragmatists. As pragmatists, the justices agreed that the state could be involved in setting social policy, but they disagreed on whose job it was to set that policy. The more liberal pragmatist justices saw their role as determining the validity of the policy set by Congress. The conservative pragmatists thought Congress the appropriate branch of government to determine policy because it could devote the time and public discussion to the issues. It was this difference in the tendencies of the justices that led to differences of opinion in speech cases.

As a pragmatist, for example, Justice Wiley B. Rutledge argued that the line indicating where the individual's freedom ended and the state's power began was to be drawn based not on generalities, "but on the concrete clash of particular interests and the community's relative evaluation of them and of how one will be affected by the specific restriction, the other by its absence."[119] But Rutledge was conservative in holding that the decision on where the line was to be placed rested in the first instance with the legislature.

The difference between the liberal and conservative pragmatist justices can be seen clearly in the 1941 criminal contempt case of *Bridges v. California*.[120] The issue before the Court was the extent of the power of state judges to hold individuals in contempt for publishing out-of-court criticisms of the judicial handling of a pending case. The liberal pragmatist Justice Hugo L. Black, speaking for the majority, wrote that the Court must begin its discussion "by considering how much, as a practical matter," liberty of expression would be affected by the contempt finding.[121] The Court was not to assume that the publications in question would threaten justice. Instead the Court needed to assess the degree of likelihood that they would in fact do so.[122] Speech was a personal right and was to be restricted only to avert some serious, substantive evil. The evils to be averted in the case at hand—disrespect for the judiciary and the unfair administration of justice—did not warrant restriction, according to Black. Judges ought to expect criticism and should not be affected by it.

Black is most often noted for his absolutist stance on the First Amendment. But in many ways his position reflects an individualist philosophy. Speech was a personal right for Black that the state could infringe only to maintain public order. He combined individualism with pragmatism in requiring the Court to examine the actual effect of the state's action on speech.

Justice Felix Frankfurter, on the other hand, argued in his dissent that the majority opinion deprived the state of California of the means of securing for its citizens justice according to law.[123] "The power of the people of the States to make and alter their laws at pleasure is the greatest security for liberty and justice," he wrote. "Under the guise of interpreting the Constitution we must take care that we do not import into the discussion our own personal views of what would be wise, just and fitting rules of government."[124] The function of the Court, rather, was to mediate between competing social policies. In the case at hand, the right of free press had to be weighed against California's right to safeguard the system of justice.[125]

According to Frankfurter, freedom of expression was essential to the enlightenment of a free people and to the restraining of those in power. And judges were not to be free of criticism. But justice was the right of all other rights in an organized society and the very foundation of orderly government. Judges had to be free from threats of intimidation to ensure that the people maintained confidence that justice was being distributed fairly. Addressing Justice Black's absolutist position, Frankfurter wrote that while freedom of expression was indispensable to the democratic process, it was not absolute. "By a doctrinaire overstatement of its scope and by giving it an illusory absolute appearance, there is danger of thwarting the free choice and the responsibility of exercising it which are basic to a democratic society," he wrote.[126]

Frankfurter, then, was pragmatic in seeing freedom of expression as a social right that had to be balanced against other rights such as the right to a fair trial. But he was conservative in viewing the government, the elected representatives of the people, as the body to set social policy, not the courts.

The justices in the early cases of this period were concerned by threats to the status quo and sought to protect society and themselves from that danger. In the five political speech cases heard before the addition of Justices Hughes and Roberts in 1930, the speaker lost in four.[127] But as more pragmatic justices were appointed to the bench, speech began to prevail, winning thirteen of the next fourteen cases.[128] Freedom of expression was seen as a social right that was essential to the democratic process and the discovery of truth.

Canadian Political Speech Cases

In 1938, the Supreme Court of Canada got its first chance to speak out on freedom of expression. The case was a reference involving three acts of the Alberta legislature. In Canada, either a provincial or the federal government may refer legislation to the Supreme Court for a determination of its constitutionality. The issue for the Court on references is only whether the legislation is within the enumerated powers of the enacting government under the British North America Act.[129] Albertans had elected a Social Credit government, and the acts were to implement the complex system of credit created by the Social Credit party. The purpose of the credit system was to increase the purchasing power of Albertans by tying it to the productive capacity of the province. Individuals received both a dividend payment from the provincial government and a rebate on purchased goods.[130] Although two of the acts involved banking and taxation, one was "An Act to Ensure the Publication of Accurate Laws and Information," dubbed the Press Bill. Section 3 of the act essentially provided for a right of reply, in that the government could require a newspaper to publish a government-prepared statement correcting or amplifying any statement relating to any policy or activity of the government published by that newspaper.[131]

The authority of the Canadian Supreme Court in hearing this case was limited to deciding whether the act came within the jurisdiction of the province, that is, whether it came within one of the enumerated provincial powers under the BNA Act. The province argued that the act came within the category of "property and civil rights," a provincial power. The federal government, on the other hand, argued that the "pith and substance" of the act went beyond civil rights. The Court concluded that the province had indeed exceeded its constitutional bounds in enacting the statute. The Canadian system of government derived its "efficacy from the free public discussion of affairs, from criticism and answer and counter-criticism, . . . from the freest and fullest analysis and examination from every point of view of political proposals," the Court held.[132] Freedom of expression was of course subject to legal restrictions and open to abuse, but "it is axiomatic that the practice of this right of free public discussion of public affairs, notwithstanding its incidental mischiefs, is the breath of life for parliamentary institutions," wrote Chief Justice Lyman P. Duff for the majority.[133]

Justice Cannon also held that freedom of discussion was essential to the formation of public opinion in a democracy. And it could not be curtailed without affecting the right of the people to be informed by an independent source on matters of public interest. Such a right could not be abrogated by the provinces because it was a right that belonged to Canadians as citizens of Canada. Therefore, it could only be curtailed by the federal government if expedient and in the public interest.[134]

The Canadian Court, then, in its first political speech decision, reflected in many ways the contemporary socialized individualism, or at least an idealism heavily tempered by individualism. The justices spoke eloquently about freedom of expression as the foundation of democracy. But at the same time, they considered freedom of expression to be a social right that could be abrogated for the public good.

SUMMARY OF FINDINGS AND CONCLUSION

Political thought in the period from 1921 to 1945 involved, in many ways, a search for the good society. World War I and the Great Depression had profoundly affected Americans and Canadians. They had produced a disillusionment with democracy that called for a reconceptualization of the individual, the state, and their relationship. Because it was a period of questioning old values and of social unrest, no one political thought was dominant in either country, although common themes emerged. There was a tendency in the political thought of both countries to view democracy less idyllically than in the past. The democratic state was seen as maintaining power through coercion and emotion, rather than by reason. The theme of social unity ran through the political thought in both Canada and the United States, as did the concept of the state as a corporation.

The focus of American thought was the individual and the relationship of the individual to the state. American intellectuals were troubled by what they had considered irrational behavior on the part of many Americans during and shortly after World War I. Because democratic theory had been based on the rationality of individuals, the preservation of democracy required a new conceptualization of the individual. Some intellectuals, such as Lippmann, took a classical republican elitist approach, arguing that because individuals were not rational, social science experts would have to provide the masses with the information necessary to make democracy work. Others, such as Neibuhr, countered that individuals themselves were rational but collectively were irrational and that the answer was strengthening the moral integrity of individuals.

The Depression produced a concern about the relationship of the individual to the state for the American political thinkers. Arnold was troubled that Americans still thought in terms of individualism and the limited state, which prevented them from taking a practical approach to the problems the Depression created. Fromm, too, saw Americans as being preoccupied with the concept of "freedom from" external restraints. Thus for Fromm, the issue was how to make individuals secure in their individuality and hence in their relationship to the state.

Canadians during this period were not as concerned with the rationality of individuals. Canadian intellectuals were more troubled by the intervention of the state into private areas during the war. They sought then to reconceptualize the state and give greater autonomy to individuals. The answer was socialized individualism, as expressed by MacIver. Under MacIver, the state was a corporation that operated within society as an agent of society to maintain its unity and cohesiveness. But the unity of society depended ultimately on the individual, who by nature was both autonomous and a seeker of harmony. Other Canadian intellectuals, both conservative and left-wing, used MacIver's conception of the state to promote their own solutions to the problems brought on by the Great Depression.

First World War I and then the Great Depression created a disillusionment with democracy that permeated not just the political thought, but society in general. The social unrest produced a tension between the desire of individuals to speak about public issues in the hopes of resolving them and the desire of the state to restrict expression to protect public safety and welfare. The majority of political speech cases in this time period pitted the disenchanted, such as Communists and the unemployed, against governments that sought to preserve the status quo.

The judges, however, did not express the same disillusionment with democracy as exhibited by either the political thinkers or the speakers in the cases. In the 1920s and early 1930s, the justices in the United States revealed a classical conservative and classical republican political philosophy dating from the previous century in which the maintenance of social order was paramount. For American judges, social order was necessary to preserve the status quo. Implicit in the position is an assumption that without organized society there would be anarchy.

From the early 1930s on, the American justices revealed a pragmatic political philosophy. The lone Supreme Court case in

Canada suggested that by 1938 the justices were moving toward the then contemporary notion of socialized individualism. Both high courts saw freedom of expression as a social right that was essential to the democratic process. Implicit in both positions is faith in the individual and in reason. Thus despite the difference in their political philosophies—pragmatism versus socialized individualism—the justices reached similar results in political speech cases using similar justifications.

Although in Canada there was a suggestion that the justices were beginning to adopt contemporary political thought, for the most part the justices in both countries lagged behind the political thought by at least a decade. Yet despite the lag, political speech was protected as a social right in both countries in the later part of the period, permitting greater information and discussion on issues affecting democracy.

From 1921 to 1945, then, the tension between liberty and authority was resolved increasingly in favor of liberty. Underlying the movement toward liberty was a fundamental faith in the individual and in reason. Accordingly, as the justices moved from conservatism and classical republicanism to pragmatism in the United States and from idealism to socialized individualism in Canada, the greater the protection for political speech grew.

CHAPTER 4
The Consensus Years: 1946–1962

World War II ended with the United States at the height of its power and influence internationally. At home, it was a time of prosperity, and Americans took advantage of the economic boom. Canadians also were benefiting from economic growth and, with Great Britain virtually bankrupt after the war, the country was coming into its own on the international scene. In both countries, the disenchantment and discontentment of the twenties and thirties were replaced by feelings of consensus and contentment as the political thinkers reacted against the pre-War pessimism.

POLITICAL THOUGHT FROM 1946 TO 1962

In the United States, the dominant political thought in the period was pluralism. Pluralism was the product of relativistic thought, itself an evolution from pragmatism. The philosophies of relativism and pragmatism were both ways of knowing. Relativists, like their pragmatic forerunners, argued that truth was relative. Only propositions capable of empirical testing could be verified as true. Because there was no way to verify ethical or value judgments, they had no substantive meaning. Even classical democratic theory was challenged by the relativists as incapable of proof. Instead, relativists sought to create a new theory of democracy based on empirical observation—pluralism.[1]

Relativists assumed that underlying democracy was a particular type of culture, specifically a culture that "denied absolute truths, remained intellectually flexible, critical, valued diversity, and drew strength from innumerable competing subgroups."[2] At the same time, however, this diverse democratic culture was held together by a foundation of homogeneity. Not surprisingly, the relativists saw American society, with its diversity and shared values, as the prime example of a pluralist democratic culture. Relativists began the postwar era, then, with a heavy emphasis on shared values and beliefs and a determined refusal to acknowledge that there were any political or social questions remaining to be answered in the United States.[3]

Relativists, although considered liberal, were a far cry from their classical liberal forerunners. Under relativism, as it had been under pragmatism, the state was no longer seen as needing to be strictly limited. In the course of the first four decades of the twentieth century, the state had increasingly been given the role of promoting and furthering equality, a process that was accelerated by the Great Depression.

At the same time, the classical liberal conception of the individual had come under attack on a number of fronts. Thanks to a combination of such factors as Darwinism, Sigmund Freud's psychoanalysis, and scientific naturalism,[4] individuals were no longer considered born with a fixed nature but were now seen as socially constructed. And if individuals were socially constructed, then they could be behaviorally engineered or conditioned to act in certain ways. The success of totalitarian ideologies in Europe appeared to provide empirical evidence of the irrationality of individuals, and at home there was fear that the new mass media were turning the public into a mass society.

The belief that individuals could be manipulated, combined with the presence of communism in the Soviet Union, produced a second intellectual movement, called new conservative. The new conservatives questioned the ethical and social relativism produced by the pragmatic and positivistic thought of the previous decades.[5] They argued for morality and ethics in politics and thus were considered absolutists.

These intellectuals began to reconsider the liberal idea of inevitable progress and the inherent goodness of individuals.[6] The same split along relativist/absolutist lines among intellectuals occurred in Canada although not to the same degree. Left-wing intellectuals argued after the War that there was agreement on Canadian values, which looked very much like those of the United States. Conservative intellectuals, on the other hand, like their American counterparts, questioned the idea of a mass society and social relativism. For the most part, however, intellectual life in Canada was relatively quiet during this period, with little political thought being written. Both conservatism, expressed in a desire to hang onto traditional Canadian values, and the socialized individualism of the 1930s, expressed in a new focus on civil liberties, were present. Although these two can be considered absolutist and relativist respectively, the relativist/absolutist debate was not as important in Canada as it was in the United States because the academic community had not embraced scientific naturalism as had American scholars.

As indicated, the stress in the United States on the word "science" in "social science" led to the belief that the behavior of individuals could be conditioned. An example of the kind of behavioralism, or social planning, that many American intellectuals were reacting against in this period can be found in B.F. Skinner's 1948 novel *Walden Two*. The book detailed how individuals, conditioned by behavioral engineering, could live together in a benevolent, noncompetitive, and tolerant society. Skinner, the noted behavioral psychologist, assumed in his work that individuals were by nature neither good nor bad but were socially constructed. It followed then that their behavior could be scientifically modified and conditioned to permit them to live together peacefully and happily.[7] For Skinner, democracy was not the best system of government because it was based on an unscientific conception of individuals as basically good and failed to take into account that individuals were socially constructed. Instead, Skinner proposed a system whereby a committee of experts would determine what was best for the community as a whole by taking into account everyone's desires and needs. It was fear of this kind of thought, especially in light of the real experience of totalitarianism in Europe in which social engineering was an integral part of the political plan, that moved many intellectuals to examine the American democracy. In the early 1940s, absolutists and relativists blamed each other for the rise of totalitarian regimes in Europe. Absolutists argued it was the relativist belief that morality and ethics had no meaning that allowed the Hitlers of the world to gain power. Unable to distinguish between good and evil, the relativists unwittingly were conformists, according to the absolutists. The relativists, on the other hand, argued it was the absolutist belief in an absolute truth that permitted totalitarian ideologies with their party line to take control. By the 1950s, relativists had won the day, aided by the rise of the absolutist Senator Joseph McCarthy.[8] Diversity and plurality came to be seen as shared American values and representative of a democratic culture.

Characteristic of the relativist thought in the first fifteen years post-World War II was the "consensus" interpretation of American society.[9] Daniel Boorstin, for example, argued in his *The Genius of American Politics* that because Americans were "born free" they had never felt the need to articulate a political theory.[10] They had been given a political theory, in fact "a perfect and complete political theory," at the country's inception, and their duty from then on was to preserve that "preformed theory."[11] Hence, he argued, Americans had no interest in and no need of producing a political theory. The "American experiment" was a matter of proving those values that had clearly been in the minds of the founding fathers.[12] "Our mission, then, is simply to demonstrate the truth—or rather the workability—of the original theory," he wrote.[13]

Combined with this belief in a preformed theory, Boorstin argued, was the American belief that "what is" was "what ought to be."[14] "We believe in *American* equality, *American* liberty, *American* democracy, or, in sum, the *American* way of life," he said.[15] The result, for

Boorstin, was that virtually everyone in the United States shared the same values. American politics was a disagreement over means, not ends.[16] Even public debate was simply a matter of stating what everybody already thought.[17] For Boorstin, these shared values helped explain the tendency of Americans to undertake witch-hunts against individuals who held different values. The "heresy-hunts," such as the Red Scare after World War I and McCarthyism after World War II, were not so much directed against espionage as "against acts of irreverence toward that orthodox American creed believed to have been born with the nation itself," he wrote.[18] Boorstin was concerned, however, that people were losing touch with these shared values. There was a growing call among Americans for a new theory of democracy.[19] The problem, as Boorstin saw it, was not to create a new theory but to conserve the unique American democratic institutions and ideals.

The concept of the United States as unique also comes through in Louis Hartz's *The Liberal Tradition in America*. Hartz argued that American liberalism was unique because it did not develop in response to feudalism as classical liberalism had in Europe. The principles of classical liberalism were adopted in the United States but not its revolutionary spirit.[20] The founding fathers were already living in a free society when they created the country on the basis of classical liberalism. They may have revolted against England, but they were not revolutionary in the sense that there was no real change in colonial life after the American Revolution.

In the "free air" of American life, individuals thought of themselves not as parts of a community but as sharing a uniform way of life.[21] According to Hartz, sharing a way of life meant sharing values and ideals, which allowed Americans to declare certain truths to be self-evident because they were accepted by everyone.[22] That uniformity, however, was deceptive. It looked individualistic, Hartz wrote, and in part it was. But it was also profoundly anti-individualistic because it demanded conformity.[23] Any deviation from the norm was alien and a threat to the shared way of life. It was this aspect of liberalism in the United States that troubled Hartz.

Freedom in the fullest sense, Hartz argued, implied both variety and equality. History had separated the two, leaving variety or diversity with classical conservatives and giving equality to the classical liberals. The tragic flaw of the United States was that it had never had a classical conservative tradition to balance classical liberalism and preserve diversity, he argued.[24] The result was that in the United States of the 1950s there was an emphasis on conformity to the point of irrationality, as evidenced by McCarthyism, according to Hartz.[25]

Like Boorstin and Hartz, Daniel Bell saw Americans as basically in agreement on public policy matters. In fact, he wrote, "there is today a rough consensus among intellectuals on political issues: the acceptance of a Welfare State; the desirability of a decentralized power; a system of mixed economy and of political pluralism."[26] For Bell, the apparent consensus meant the end of ideology because the old battles had been won.[27] "What gives ideology its force is its passion," he wrote.[28] But the passion was gone. A distinguishing feature of modern society was the separation of ethics and politics.[29] And it was the ethics, the morality, that gave politics its passion. Everyone was satisfied with life and the status quo, Bell argued, so there was no need for ideology.

Although Bell claimed there was no need for ideology, the relativists sought to create a new theory of democracy based on empirical observation. One of the most influential advocates of the empirical theory of democracy was Robert A. Dahl. In *Preface to Democratic Theory*, Dahl rejected traditional theories based on checks and balances and popular sovereignty. The United States had succeeded, he argued, because it combined a unique consensus with a widespread number of minority interest groups.[30] The making of government decisions in the United States was not a matter of majority rule, he wrote, but "the steady appeasement of relatively small groups" or "minorities' rule."[31] America was a pluralist society, and pluralism was the basis of its democracy.[32]

Although pluralism was widely accepted by political scientists in the 1950s, not everyone agreed with its premises. Challenging the empiricism, consensus, and relativism of the period were the new conservatives, a group of classical conservatives and classical liberals who were united in their anti-Communistic views and their desire to blame the pluralists and relativists for what they perceived as society's problems. Classical conservatives believed in an organic society that existed separate from the individuals within it. Society was seen as having a long tradition and history. The obligation of the individuals of the present was to conserve society for the individuals of the future. Change to society had to be consistent with the tradition and to be change for which society was ready. Unlike classical liberals, classical conservatives believed that most individuals were ruled more by their emotions than by their reason. Therefore, society was best governed by those few individuals who were capable of civic responsibility.[33]

In the United States, classical conservatism has never been a significant force. In the twentieth century, when Americans speak of conservatism, they are referring to the classical liberals who seek to conserve the liberal-capitalist principles of individualism and laissez-faire.[34] Therefore, the new conservatives, a blend of classical conservatives and classical liberals, sought to conserve the tradition and history of the American society, which meant a focus on individualism, property rights, and the rule of law.

One of the new conservatives was Russell Kirk. In *The Conservative Mind*, Kirk reacted to what he called the social planners of the 1930s and 1940s such as Skinner. These pragmatists, and later relativists, had promoted a belief in the perfectibility of the individual and the limitless progress of society.[35] But in doing so, he argued, they had reduced the wants of individuals to materialism and created a "mass-mind."[36] For Kirk, the social planners looked on society as "a homogeneous mass of identical individuals, with indistinguishable abilities and needs."[37] The only hope for society's salvation lay in conservatism, Kirk argued. Society had to recognize its moral nature and acknowledge that diversity was more important than uniformity.[38] Democracy would endure, he knew, but whether it was to be a democracy in which individuals were degraded into a mass-mind or elevated into true individuality depended on the new conservatives.[39]

Peter Viereck sounded a similar note in his *Conservatism Revisited: The Revolt Against Revolt, 1815–1949.* "The fate of mankind may depend on whether the sober, rigorously national appeal of liberty can inspire as much unity as the romantic, emotional appeal of its enemies," he wrote in reference to both communism and the anticommunism that had produced McCarthyism.[40] Viereck blamed the relativists, with their emphasis on shared values and conformity, for destroying liberty in the United States. Conformity, according to Viereck, had produced McCarthyism, which was just one step away from totalitarianism. True liberty, for Viereck, depended on order, and he acknowledged that the just state had to limit freedom to preserve order.[41] But it had to do so by virtue of a "nonarbitrary, nondespotic system of law."[42] Clearly, Viereck was questioning laws such as the Smith Act of 1940 and the Internal Security Act of 1950.[43] Viereck suggested that the question to be asked whenever a law restricting freedom was proposed was whether the law would endanger civil liberties more than the evil it sought to prevent would. For Viereck, so long as that question existed and was pondered by society then freedom still existed.[44]

Alexander Meiklejohn would have argued in response that any speech going toward public policy was protected absolutely by the First Amendment. Writing in 1948, Meiklejohn contended that the Constitution protected two different freedoms of speech. One was open to restriction by government; one was not. The First Amendment protected absolutely the freedom to speak on all matters of public policy. The Fifth Amendment protected private rights of speech from abridgement without due process.[45] The absolutism of the First Amendment stemmed from the necessities of self-government, "from the basic American agreement that public issues shall be decided by universal suffrage."[46] But, he argued, "when self-governing men demand freedom of speech they are not saying that every individual has an unalienable right to speak whenever, wherever, however he chooses. . . . What is essential is not that everyone shall speak, but that everything worth saying shall be said."[47]

The purpose of the First Amendment was to protect thinking that furthered the general welfare. It made no difference, argued Meiklejohn, whether the individual was advocating conscription or opposing it, for example, so long as the topic was a matter of public policy.[48] According to Meiklejohn's reasoning, then, the question posed by Viereck—would the law endanger civil liberties more than the evil it sought to prevent—need not be asked because "substantive evils which, in principle, Congress has a right to prevent, must be endured if the only way of avoiding them is by the abridging of that freedom of speech upon which the entire structure of our free institutions rests."[49]

C. Wright Mills questioned both the new conservatives and the relativists with their pluralist democracy. He agreed with Hartz that American society had never passed through a feudal era, but, he argued, that did not mean the United States did not have social classes. The classical liberals who came to America entered society as a virtually unopposed bourgeoisie. From the beginning, there were prominent families who had social, cultural, and political influence at the local level. By the 1950s, however, the local elite had achieved the status of a power elite.[50] There was an increasing interdependence between the economic, political, and military structures in the United States, which meant the major players in business were now major players in politics on the national level, he argued.

But Americans did not see what was happening, according to Mills. They continued to cling to the idea that government was a machine, regulated by the balancing of competing interests.[51] The checks and balances imposed on the government by the founding fathers were considered to be the chief mechanism by which economic and political freedom was guaranteed.[52] But the notion of "balance," Mills noted, implied the status quo was satisfactory. It was rather a "hopeful ideal" that often "masquerade[d] as a description of fact."[53]

Checks and balances, he continued, only worked in a society that was itself balanced. That is, one that had an upper class and a lower class that pivoted around a stable middle class. Checks were in place to act as restraints on the passions of individuals and to maintain society in an equilibrium. The theory, he argued, rested on two assumptions: that a natural harmony in society existed or could be achieved and that the classes operated independent of one another because if they did not, society could not adjust itself to maintain the balance.[54] Neither assumption was valid for Mills. He denied that a natural harmony could ever exist in society, and he denied that classes operated independent of one another because he said there were no strict divisions among classes in the United States.

According to Mills, in addition to the belief in a system of checks and balances, Americans were prevented from acknowledging the existence of a power elite because of their belief that the "Great American Public" was the holder of legitimate power.[55] Under classic democratic theory, it was assumed that individuals were rational and shared a harmony of interests.[56] Freedom of expression was essential to the formation of public opinion because it was believed that free discussion would lead to a rational, just decision.[57] Public opinion was thus the "infallible voice of reason."[58] This classic image of the public was still used as the justification for power in American society, Mills argued. But, like the notion of balance, it was just an ideal, not a fact.[59]

The classic democratic assumptions had been challenged by the discovery that individuals were not necessarily rational and that their behavior could be socially conditioned, Mills argued.[60] The result was the transformation of the public into the masses and the collapse of the liberal optimism that had fueled the democratic theory of the public.[61] The importance of this result for Mills was that publics were no longer acting autonomously to influence political decisions. Now they were masses being manipulated by interest groups, essentially the negative side of pluralist democracy.[62] As Mills put it, "the idea of a mass society suggests the idea of an elite of power. The idea of the public, in contrast, suggests the liberal tradition of a society without any power elite."[63]

Canadian political philosopher George P. Grant was as concerned as Mills about the apparent movement toward a mass society. The mass scientific society was, Grant considered, "the great fact of Canada today and of the modern world."[64] The result of living in a mass society was that individuals were both more dependent on large institutions and less related to them. Grant saw this as leading inevitably to a dying away of the individual's participation in politics because the individual would feel increasingly unable to influence institutions.[65] A mass society, then, called into question the possibility of democratic government founded on individual participation.[66] Modern Western liberalism had turned economic expansion into an end, when the end of human existence was freedom, Grant argued. And a free individual was "not ruled by fear or passion—or the world around him—but by the eternal world of truth and goodness," he wrote, revealing his absolutism.[67]

Canadians had emerged from World War II with a new sense of Canada as a nation. Although their allegiance was still with Great Britain, Canadians now saw themselves as Canadian first and only secondarily as British subjects. The optimism was fueled in part by the largest economic boom in Canada's history. At the same time as it moved toward greater independence as a country, Canada was becoming more dependent culturally on the United States. The growth of American mass media had a profound influence on Canada as radio and television programs and movies flowed easily across the border.[68] Perhaps because of the increasing cultural connection with the United States, there was an increasing interest in Canada in civil liberties and the idea of a written bill of rights, culminating in passage of the Canadian Bill of Rights in 1960. And it was in this context that the relativist/absolutist debate can be found in Canada.

Canada's parliamentary democracy had been set up by the British North America Act in 1867. The Act divided powers between the federal and the provincial legislatures and made no mention of civil liberties. Protection for civil liberties was left to the common law as inherited from Great Britain. By its nature, the common law is relativistic. It evolves slowly over time in accordance with changing circumstances. There are no legal absolutes. But a written bill of rights is a codification of values and therefore can be considered absolute; at least comparative legal scholar Edward McWhinney saw it that way.

McWhinney was not sold on the idea of a bill of rights for Canada.[69] "Comparative constitutional law literature is littered with the wreckage of Bills of Rights and similar sounding declarations of rights of man, professed at their inception to be perpetually immutable," he noted.[70] The spirit of a constitution rested with its day-by-day efficacy and not by the fact that it was written, he argued. He continued,

> If the new Canadian Bill of Rights happens to correspond to deeply-felt popular sentiments, no legislative majorities in the future are likely to interfere with it: if it does not so correspond, then no amount of "entrenchment" or any other type of constitutional concretisation can save it and put teeth into its paper guarantees. In the latter case, like the cardinal provisions of the American Bill of Rights over significant time periods, it will remain no more than a pious affirmation ignored or openly flouted by those who do not choose to agree with its principles.[71]

The problem, as McWhinney saw it, was that belief in the idea of progress and scientific naturalism had been shattered by the Cold War. Individuals sought new orthodoxies to replace the old; they wanted a "value-oriented jurisprudence." The result was a revival of natural law thinking.[72] But, he argued, natural law thinking was only possible in a homogeneous society in which there was agreement on the fundamentals. Otherwise, there would be no way of defining the new absolutes. And a bill of rights, which essentially codified the law, required an element of precision, not just on the values to be protected, but on the direction of the future development of the society. "Otherwise the code, instead of assisting societal growth in the future, will fetter and confine it," he argued.[73] McWhinney concluded that the desire for a Canadian bill of rights was misplaced because Canada was undergoing rapid growth and change. "Any government might well be commended to exercise caution as to jelling contemporary pressure group demands in this area as timeless absolutes of constitutional law," he wrote.[74]

Constitutional legal scholar Frank R. Scott, on the other hand, took the absolutist position, arguing that the changing nature of society and the growth of the government called for an explicit guarantee of civil liberties. Canada had adopted the British method of protecting civil liberties, he noted, which was based on three assumptions: parliamentary restraint in legislation, bureaucratic restraint in administration, and a strong tradition of personal freedom among individuals generally.[75] Unfortunately, these assumptions did not apply to Canada. First, while England had one legislature to watch over, Canadians had eleven, one federal and ten provincial. And those eleven possessed almost unlimited sovereignty within their spheres, he argued.[76] Although the British North America Act was drafted with a strong federal government in mind, judicial decisions had given the provincial legislatures increasing autonomy over their territories. Especially in Quebec, he argued, provincial autonomy had come to be synonymous with cultural particularism.[77]

Secondly, he argued, there had been enormous growth in government activity, in both administration and authority, at all levels since 1867. "Collectivism is creeping upon us with every increase of population and automation, and its coming is reflected in the almost total covering of our society by group activity, be it public or private," he wrote.[78] "We are all civil servants or organization men today." And finally, Canada had a very mixed population. Its citizens did not necessarily share a tradition of parliamentary democracy as did the majority in England. In addition, Canada was "working out the co-existence of two cultures [French and English] with very different concepts of relationships of individual and church to state."[79]

Despite these features, Canadians had only in recent years, Scott wrote, begun to concern themselves with civil liberties. The first cases arose around questions of minority rights and were dealt with on a case-by-case basis without benefit of a theory of freedom.[80] The courts had only two ways to protect civil liberties, he noted. One was to use the established rule that all statutes were to be strictly interpreted if they limited or reduced the rights of individuals. This rule was based on the assumption that Parliament always intended the least interference with freedom. The second way to protect civil liberties was simply to find the law outside the powers or jurisdiction of the enacting legislature.[81]

In arguing that the common law system inherited from Great Britain was insufficient to protect civil liberties in 1950s Canada, Scott was not necessarily lamenting the growth of government. He was not advocating a return to the doctrine of laissez-faire, for he wrote, "We have learned from bitter experience that the satisfaction of basic human needs is essential for the survival of any form of orderly government, and in a highly industrialized society, the state cannot leave this task to unregulated private enterprise."[82] But, he concluded, to ensure proper protection for civil liberties, given the changing nature of the Canadian demographic landscape and the necessity of a bureaucratic government, a written bill of rights was needed.

At the heart of the debate over a written bill of rights was the conception of the individual and the state. The relativist McWhinney saw no need for a written bill of rights because he had faith in both the state's and the individual's ability to exercise restraint in the area of civil liberties. And a written guarantee of civil liberties was not going to stop the state from infringing rights if it saw fit to do so. The absolutist Scott, on the other hand, sought to control the state's potential to encroach onto civil liberties, given its expansion and the diversity of the Canadian population. It was not that he necessarily feared the state because he agreed with the state's involvement for the betterment of society, but he did not have faith that Canadians were all equally capable of exercising rational thought.

The same tensions appear in American political thought. The relativists promoted the idea of pluralism and diversity, while celebrating consensus. On the surface, they appeared to have faith in the state and in individuals because empirical observation showed

American democracy was working well. But their demand for conformity would suggest that the relativists in fact lacked faith in individuals. True diversity was not welcomed because it threatened the consensus and the American democratic culture. The new conservatives, on the other hand, sought to protect diversity through order. Left alone, they argued, individuals would be ruled by their emotions, as evidenced by the attempt to purge the United States of un-American ideas in the 1950s. The new conservatives had faith that the state would be just in putting limits on freedom to preserve order and promote true diversity.

POLITICAL SPEECH CASES

In the political speech cases in Canada and the United States from 1946 to 1962, a correlation can be found between the major trends in the political thought and the judicial decision-making in the two countries. The period saw a burgeoning of political speech cases in the United States. The McCarthyism of the late 1940s and early 1950s produced a spate of state and federal statutes, clashing head on with the right of freedom of expression. In terms of their conception of the individual, the state, and their relationship, the justices reflected the relativist/absolutist debate of the period and for the first time were ahead of the political thought in discussing American society as a consensus and the "genius" of the Constitution.

All the American justices exhibited a liberal political philosophy, either classical liberal, pragmatic, or relativist. The classical liberals were more skeptical of government attempts to control freedom of expression in the name of public safety or welfare than were the pragmatists. The pragmatists and relativists called for a balancing of social and individual interests in the quest for a better society and for practical solutions to social problems. The more conservative pragmatists and relativists exercised judicial restraint, arguing that the initial balancing of interests was the job of Congress, not of the Court.

In Canada, all of the justices appeared more conservative than their American counterparts in their focus on order, which revealed their idealist roots. However, there was a recognition of the importance of freedom of expression in a democracy and a willingness to accept diversity. Those justices favoring freedom of expression seemed to have adopted the political philosophy of socialized individualism. These justices expressed no fear of the state as is found in the American cases.

American Political Speech Cases

The Cold War and McCarthyism in the United States produced a spate of federal and state laws that clashed head on with freedom of expression. The result was a burgeoning of political speech cases before the Supreme Court. There were fifty-two political speech cases in this period, forty-two involving what legal scholar Harry Kalven, Jr., called subversive speech,[83] five involving the press, and five involving a variety of other issues. Of the fifty-two cases, speech won in twenty-seven. And of the forty-two cases involving subversive speech, speech won in eighteen. The subversive speech cases concerned the speech of Communists and the advocacy of violent overthrow of the government. The cases included not just issues of speech, but also of assembly, immigration, and loyalty. These cases will be considered together because they all raise the issue of the state's right of self-preservation versus the individual's right of free expression. The five cases addressing freedom of the press will then be examined.

But first, the relativist/absolutist debate reflected in the cases will be discussed. An examination of the debate within the cases is important because it places the justices within the intellectual discussion of their time. And although their position in the debate was not the deciding factor in determining the outcome of political speech cases, it was important when combined with a justice's conception of the individual, the state, and their relationship. Of the eighteen justices on the bench from 1946 until 1962, six can clearly be identified from the language used in their opinions as relativists and two as absolutists.[84] The remaining ten did not write enough decisions for a determination of their position to be made.

The dominance of the relativists on the bench until 1962 corresponds with the use of the balancing approach in First Amendment cases because relativists rejected the existence of an absolute truth and called for openness and the testing of alternatives. Balancing competing interests on a case-by-case basis was a technique employed by the pragmatist justices and first appeared in political speech cases in the 1930s, but it suited the relativist rejection of the application of rigid, formulaic standards. Relativist Justice Felix Frankfurter, for example, argued that the tension between the state's right of self-preservation and the individual's right of free expression could not be resolved "by a dogmatic preference for one or the other, nor by a sonorous formula."[85] Some saw both interests as absolute, he noted, but "absolute words would lead to absolute exceptions." The demands of free speech in a democratic society were better served by a candid and informed weighing of competing interests rather than by the application of inflexible dogmas.

Frankfurter concluded that focusing attention on constitutionality tended to make constitutionality synonymous with wisdom. Frankfurter agreed that the language of the Constitution did not change but argued that changing circumstances in a progressive society yielded new and fuller meanings of the Constitution.[86] Reflecting his pragmatist roots, Frankfurter noted that social development was the result of trial and error, in which what was once official truth was displaced as error. The true savior of democracy was an open mind and an open society.[87]

Justice Hugo L. Black, on the other hand, was clearly an absolutist. He repeatedly criticized his fellow members of the bench for applying a balancing test in First Amendment cases. For Black, "balancing and elastic concepts reduce the absolute commands of the Constitution to mere admonitions."[88] The majority's application of balancing to the First Amendment made the amendment not the rigid protector of liberty it was drafted to be but a poor, flexible imitation, he wrote.[89] Whether political speech was to be protected in any given case depended, under the balancing approach, on the emphasis a particular judge gave the competing social values. Balancing should be applied, Black argued, only where the law incidentally affected speech. In pure speech cases, balancing violated the "genius" of the Constitution, making freedom of expression relative—dependent on the mood of the justices, the times, the context.

Four years before Louis Hartz published *The Liberal Tradition in America* in which he criticized the consensus liberals and their relativism for producing conformity, Justice Black wrote that laws restricting the speech of Communists resulted from a tendency to mold people into a common intellectual pattern.[90] Loyalty oaths, for example, which the majority consistently upheld in the 1950s, tended to stifle unorthodox thought, producing a stultified conformity.[91]

The relativist Justice William O. Douglas, on the other hand, blamed absolutism for standardized thought. Like Justice Black, he argued that loyalty oaths required individuals to follow the "party line" of orthodoxy, of the accepted and conventional approach. But loyalty oaths were the product of absolutism, not relativism, according to Douglas. Orthodoxy worked against versatility, which was America's greatest asset, he argued. Allowing openness and free discussion encouraged the "testing of our own preconceptions," a relativist position.

Chief Justice Fred M. Vinson revealed his relativism when he wrote that the Court's interpretations of the Constitution should not be reduced to the status of mathematical formulas. The considerations that gave rise to the clear and present danger test, for example, should be taken into account, not the phrase itself, he argued.[92] The clear and present danger test was not a hard and fast rule. In fact, "nothing is more certain than the principle that there are no absolutes. All concepts are relative," he wrote.[93]

Although Vinson employed the balancing test in political speech cases, he consistently found in favor of the government's right to restrict speech. It was Justice Frankfurter who took relativism to heart, perhaps because of his pragmatism, taking a case-by-case approach. Therefore, he sometimes upheld restrictions on political speech and other times held that the government had overstepped its boundary.

The justices from 1946 to 1962 reflected the relativist/absolutist debate going on in intellectual circles. Although relativism resulted in a balancing approach to the First Amendment, it was not the decisive factor in determining the level of protection for freedom of expression. Nor was absolutism. However, relativism and absolutism were important when combined with a justice's conception of the individual, the state, and their relationship.

As indicated, the majority of the cases in this period involved advocacy of violent overthrow of the government. At issue in these political speech cases was the state's right of self-preservation versus the individual's right of free expression. Those who had faith in the individual were more willing to allow free expression than were those who were skeptical of the ability of individuals to separate the false from the true. For example, classical liberals such as Justices Black and Douglas, with their belief in the rationality of individuals and their fear of government intervention, were willing to allow the speech of Communists because they believed that free expression would keep the nation strong. National security was not to be found in government suppression of speech, but in the First Amendment.

Justices with a more conservative outlook, such as Justice Robert H. Jackson, were not as willing to leave the country's well-being in the hands of individuals. The state had the right to preserve itself because individuals were capable of being manipulated by Communists. Because Communists themselves did not value freedom of expression, they ought not to be permitted to use that freedom to gain the power that would allow them to deprive Americans of their constitutional rights, the argument went.

Justices Black and Douglas saw freedom of speech as the best protection against the destruction of freedom and took a strong stand against curtailing any speech, whether that of Communists or ordinary

Americans. In *Dennis v. United States*, for example, Justice Black argued that charging Dennis and the others under the Smith Act with conspiring to organize the Communist Party and teach Communist doctrine was not the way to preserve the state. Justice Black acknowledged that a policy of unfettered speech entailed dangers for the state. In fact, "this freedom is too dangerous for bad, tyrannical governments to permit."[94] "To the Founders of this Nation, however, the benefits derived from free expression were worth the risk," he argued.[95]

As seen earlier in the section on political thought, Meiklejohn had argued that the First Amendment was an absolute guarantee for political speech—speech that furthered democracy. Justice Black was the greatest proponent of what is now considered the Meiklejohnian theory of the First Amendment. In the 1957 case of *Yates v. United States*, Justice Black in his dissent explicitly adopted the Meiklejohn approach, arguing that the First Amendment forbade any punishment for discussing public affairs, even if it incited action, legal or illegal.[96] The reason for such a strict standard was that First Amendment freedoms were "absolutely indispensable for the preservation of a free society in which the government is based on consent of informed citizenry."[97] The same sentiment was expressed by Justice Douglas in *Dennis*. The philosophy of the First Amendment was that "violence is rarely, if ever, stopped by denying civil liberties to those advocating resort to force," he wrote.[98] Freedom of expression was essential to the preservation of a democratic government.[99]

Both justices saw the First Amendment as protection for the state because they had faith the American people would never choose communism. The justices described that faith in terms later echoed by such consensus political thinkers as Boorstin, Hartz, and Bell. Americans were assumed to share a set of values against which communism appeared alien; the "genius" of the Constitution was in its recognition of those shared values. Justice Black, for example, noted that abridgement of liberty on the part of Congress in the 1950s was based on the fear that the American people could be alienated from their allegiance to their democratic way of life by the talk of zealots.[100] But, the fear was groundless because, he wrote, "our free way of life enlists such respect and love that our Nation cannot be imperiled by mere talk."[101] Communism was wholly foreign to "our habits and our instincts," he argued.[102]

Similarly, Justice Douglas held that books espousing the Communist doctrine should be freely available because then the "ugliness of Communism" would be revealed. The First Amendment reflected the founders' trust in the common sense of the people to choose the doctrine "true to our genius and to reject the rest."[103] Americans might have been tempted by communism in earlier days, but not in 1951. He wrote:

> In days of trouble and confusion, when bread lines were long, when the unemployed walked the streets, when people were starving, the advocates of a short-cut revolution might have a chance to gain adherents. But today there are no such conditions. The country is not in despair; the people know Soviet Communism; the doctrine of Soviet revolution is exposed in all of its ugliness and the American people want none of it.[104]

The consensus interpretation of the American way of life also comes through in the opinions of Justice Robert H. Jackson. Jackson appears to have been a classical liberal with conservative overtones. As a classical liberal, he agreed with Justices Black and Douglas and the relativists that Americans shared a way of life and a democratic culture. For example, he noted that democracy worked because people generally agreed on the larger issues.[105] But communism could not work in the United States because however gifted the Communist Party's founders may have been "not one of them ever lived in America, experienced our conditions, or imbibed the spirit of our institutions."[106] Communism was an ideology born of European history, not American.[107]

But Justice Jackson differed from Justices Black and Douglas in that he was not as optimistic that Americans were capable of resisting communism on their own. Communists worked through sabotage and infiltration, and Jackson had no faith in the American people's ability to combat such tactics with speech alone. Jackson saw them requiring the assistance of the state to fight communism. While Black and Douglas sought refuge in the First Amendment, Jackson questioned the rationale of applying a constitutional principle—devised under different circumstances to strike a balance between authority and liberty—to communism, a worldwide conspiracy. When the Constitution and the First Amendment were written, he noted, the antagonists in the struggle between authority and liberty were the state and the individual. Individuals, it was believed at the time, could take care of themselves if the state were limited in scope. In more recent times, the struggle between authority and liberty had been complicated by the intervention "of permanently organized, well-financed, semisecret and highly disciplined political organizations" between the state and the citizen.[108] The Communist Party was not simply another political party; it was fundamentally different in its ideology and should be treated as such, he argued. Those who believed otherwise assumed, he wrote,

> that the First Amendment allows Congress to make no distinction between advocating change in the existing order by lawful elective processes and advocating change by force and violence, that freedom for the one includes freedom for the other, and that when teaching of violence is denied so is freedom of speech.[109]

The 1949 case of *Terminiello v. Chicago* clearly sets out the philosophical differences between Justices Douglas and Jackson in their attitude toward the state.[110] Terminiello was a far-right activist who spoke before an invited audience at a private hall in Chicago. Outside, Socialists and Communists protested the speech, causing a disturbance. Terminiello was charged and convicted of breaching the peace. Justice

Douglas, writing for the majority, found in favor of Terminiello on classical liberal terms. The vitality of civil and political institutions depended on free discussion, he argued. It was in fact the right to speak freely and to promote diversity that set America apart from totalitarian regimes. Speech was often provocative, he noted, as it pressed for acceptance, and it served a purpose in inviting a condition of unrest. The state had no right to step in and silence a speaker under such circumstances.

Justice Douglas was prepared to permit Terminiello's speech because he saw the alternative—government intervention—as causing greater harm. His position, which he enunciated more clearly later in *CBS v. Democratic National Committee*,[111] was that the struggle for liberty had been a struggle against government. "Experiences have shown that unrestrained power cannot be trusted to serve the public even though it be in government hands," he wrote.[112] The fear for classical liberals who conceived of the state in limited terms as Douglas did was that local authorities would become censors.

Justice Jackson, in his dissent, however, presented the conservative view of the state's role in such cases. The majority's conception of free speech was so rigid, he argued, it made no concession to society's need for public order. Terminiello was not a lone soap box orator who had incensed a crowd. He was part of something larger that was, he wrote, "a local manifestation of a world-wide and standing conflict between two organized groups of revolutionary fanatics, each of which has imported to this country the strong-arm technique developed in the struggle by which their kind has devastated Europe."[113] And the technique appealed not to reason, but to fears and mob spirit. The only obstacle to the "mastery of the streets" was the authority of local governments, which represented the free choice of the people. Free speech existed only under law, not independent of it, he argued. If it were to have any meaning, affirmative and immediate protection was required.

Justice Jackson reminded his brethren that mobs did not form without some speech. And once formed, mobs did not protect anyone's liberty. The "crowd mind" was never tolerant of any idea not conforming to its "herd opinion." In fact, the law was more tolerant of discussion than most people were. The choice, he concluded, was not between order and liberty but between liberty with order and anarchy without either.

Justice Jackson had special reason to fear communism and totalitarian ideologies. After his 1941 appointment to the bench by President Roosevelt, Jackson was asked by President Truman to negotiate the final arrangements for the Nuremburg Trial and act as the chief American prosecutor of Nazi war criminals.[114] A "man of urgent idealism"[115] who believed in equal justice for all members of society, he had been profoundly affected by his experience at Nuremburg.[116] In his opening address at the trial, he promised to show the Nazi war criminals "to be living symbols of racial hatred, of terrorism, of violence, and of arrogance and cruelty of power."[117] Based on his experience, then, Jackson was willing to invoke government intervention to protect against Communist infiltration.

It could be argued that Jackson's experience should have aligned him more firmly on the side of Black and Douglas rather than with the conservatives advocating government intervention. But Jackson was troubled that Hitler had come to power in Germany legitimately through the ballot. That at least fueled his conservative lack of faith in individuals and his corresponding faith in the American government's ability to protect the country.

Joining Jackson in voting to uphold legislation restricting the political speech of Communists were Justice Frankfurter and Chief Justice Fred M. Vinson. Both were pragmatists in that they sought workable solutions to social problems and attempted to balance social and individual interests. But they were conservative or judicial restraintists in arguing that social policy was to be set in the first instance by Congress or state legislatures. The role of the Court was to determine whether the ensuing law was constitutional, not to determine the validity or merit of the policy itself. Vinson could then rule in *Douds*[118] that the Court was in no position to substitute its judgment for that of Congress and in *Dennis*[119] that the societal value of free speech must be subordinated to other values on occasion. Similarly, Frankfurter, in his concurring opinion in *Dennis*, held that it was the job of Congress to balance the interests involved. The Court should decide constitutional issues, he wrote, only when they inescapably came before it. Until then the Court's duty was to refrain from marking boundaries of congressional power by deciding cases.[120] The sole question for the Court was whether the effects of any statute were constitutionally permissible. The Court was not to engage in an enquiry into the motives of Congress. Justices Frankfurter and Vinson could rely on Congress because they had faith in the ability of the state to work for the betterment of society.

At the heart of the arguments of Justices Black and Douglas, on the other hand, was the classical liberal fear of the state. Justice Black, for example, argued that taking away the liberty of groups whose views most people detested jeopardized the liberty of all.[121] The threat of communism had to be tolerated, in part, because any incursions by the government into the sphere of individual liberty protected by the First Amendment opened the door to greater incursions, essentially the slippery slope argument.

In addition, Black argued that government restrictions had a chilling effect on speech. Society should never forget, he cautioned, that laws stigmatizing and penalizing unpopular thought and speech tended to silence more people than originally intended.[122] Therefore, he held that requiring identification on handbills would tend to curtail expression. Douglas also noted the chilling effect of government restrictions, arguing that no true freedom of mind existed if thoughts were secure only if pent up.[123] The First Amendment stood as a barrier to state intrusion into privacy.[124]

Two traditional First Amendment arguments against government legislation, then,—the chilling effect and the slippery slope—result from the classical liberal fear of the state. Those arguments are not found in the opinions of justices who are more conservative in their views about individuals and more optimistic about the state's ability to work for the betterment of society. For example, Justice Jackson challenged the notion of the slippery slope, arguing that liberty would not be made more secure by saying abuses of liberty could not be separated from its enjoyment.[125] And Justice Tom C. Clark questioned the efficacy of the chilling effect, arguing that freedom of speech did not mean freedom of anonymity, which would encourage irresponsibility.[126]

What appears to have been the decisive factor in whether the individual's right to free speech won out over the state's right to self-preservation in subversive political speech cases from 1946 to 1962 was the justices' faith in the state. The justices who were consistently on the side of the government in this period were conservative in the sense that they wished to preserve social order and the status quo and saw the state as the mechanism to accomplish that. For these justices, individuals were not autonomous and rational, but they were an integral part of society. And society had to be preserved or anarchy would result. The justices who consistently found in favor of freedom of expression saw the state as the ultimate threat to individual liberty. Individuals were rational and capable of making their own decisions. The state's role was to be limited to the protection of individuals from the actions of others.

The same split between conservative justices who view individuals as not rational and therefore have no faith in their ability to separate out the true from the false and the liberals who do see individuals as rational and have faith in them is found in the freedom of the press cases in this period. From 1946 to 1962, five press cases came before the Supreme Court, and the press won in all five. Three of the cases involved contempt charges resulting from criticisms of pending court cases, and two involved libel.

At issue in the contempt cases was the state's right to protect the administration of justice and the individual's right to freedom of expression. The classical liberal Justice Frank Murphy argued in *Craig v. Harney*, a case involving an editorial about a pending case, that freedom of the press was at the heart of democracy and its preservation was essential to the survival of liberty.[127] Any inroad on that freedom by the state undermined the freedom of all individuals to print and read the truth. Again the slippery slope argument was used to support freedom of expression. Murphy wrote, "Any summary suppression of unjust criticism carries with it an ominous threat of summary suppression of all criticism."[128]

The more conservative justices, such as Frankfurter and Jackson, while acknowledging the importance of freedom of the press for a democracy, argued that the right to a fair trial was the most important right of all. Jackson criticized the majority for sponsoring "the myth that judges are not as other men are, and that therefore newspaper attacks on them are negligible because they do not penetrate the judicial armor."[129] And Frankfurter revealed his lack of faith in individuals when he wrote,

> Judges are also human, and we know better than did our forbears how powerful is the pull of the unconscious and how treacherous the rational process. While the ramparts of reason have been found to be more fragile than the Age of Enlightenment had supposed, the means for arousing passion and confusing judgment have been reinforced.[130]

While the split between the liberals and the conservatives is clear in the contempt cases, it is not as clear in the two libel cases. In both, the justices sought to promote the free flow of information. For example, in *Farmers Educational and Cooperative Union v. WDAY*, the issue was whether the Communications Act of 1934 under its equal opportunity rule barred a radio station from removing defamatory statements contained in speeches broadcast by legally qualified candidates for public office and in doing so granted the station immunity from liability.[131] Justice Black for the majority held that permitting a broadcaster to censor allegedly libelous remarks would undermine the basic purpose for which the equal opportunities rule existed—full and unrestricted discussion of political issues by legally qualified candidates. Because the Communications Act denied broadcasters the right to censor the speech of such candidates, it was natural that it also granted immunity to the broadcaster for anything the candidates said, Black held. It was this issue that caused Justice Frankfurter to dissent.

Justice Frankfurter's position was that the federal act could not unilaterally make changes to a state's libel laws, and declaring broadcasters immune from libel suits in these circumstances did just that. It was up to the state court to determine the issue, Frankfurter argued.

The second libel case involved a press release issued by a government agency in which a former employee of the agency was defamed. The issue was whether the official in charge of the agency had an absolute privilege against a civil suit brought by the former employee. The conservative justices John M. Harlan, Frankfurter, Clark, and Charles E. Whittaker upheld the plea of absolute privilege. Justice Harlan, for the majority, wrote that "officials of government should be free to exercise their duties unembarrassed by fear of damage suits in respect of acts done in the course of their duties."[132]

Justice Black, the classical liberal, concurred but took a different point of view. "The effective functioning of a free government like ours depends largely on the force of an informed public opinion," he wrote.[133] And that public opinion depended in turn on the information getting out to the public. Justice Black, then, appears to have been consistent in his reasoning in that he sought to protect the flow of information rather than the ability of government officials to fulfill their duties.

The other classical liberals on the bench, however, dissented, arguing that an absolute privilege was not justified and that the press release was not in the course of the official's line of duty. Although classical liberals would later argue that individuals ought to have an almost absolute privilege against libel actions for criticizing public officials, they were not willing to extend the same privilege to government officials themselves. The two positions appear inconsistent but actually are not. Classical liberals are distrustful of government and presumably seek to make government officials accountable to the people. Extending their existing absolute privilege to things said outside of the legislature would presumably remove the officials from the reach of the courts and reduce their accountability.

These freedom of the press cases are different from the subversive cases of the period because they do not pit the individual's right to freedom of expression against the state's right to self-preservation. As a result the split between the liberal and conservative justices is not as great although it is still present. In contempt cases, the conservative justices seek to protect the right of the state to preserve the administration of justice because social order is necessary for the preservation of society. Because individuals are not rational, the maintenance of social order is extremely important. Liberal justices, on the other hand, see contempt of court as a method of depriving individuals of the right to decide issues for themselves. Individuals are rational and autonomous, and the state must be limited to the protection of individuals from the actions of others.

In the libel cases, the difference in conceptualization of the individual and the state is not as clear because all of the justices favored the free flow of information. But the classical liberal justices were more inclined to find against the state, a position consistent with their fear of the state.

World War II ended with a liberal bloc in the majority on the Court. All of the justices were either classical liberal, pragmatic, or relativist, although some of the pragmatic and relativist justices had conservative overtones. As the period progressed, more conservative justices were appointed, shifting the majority. The classical liberals, such as Justices Black and Douglas, consistently found in favor of freedom of expression, based on their fear of government and faith in individuals. The relativist justices were less consistent, finding in favor of freedom of expression on occasion and in favor of the government at other times, although consistent with their political philosophy. Relativism supported a balancing approach, which meant a case-by-case analysis and left more room for inconsistency of outcome.

Canadian Political Speech Cases

In Canada, six political speech cases reached the Supreme Court in the period from 1946 to 1962. Four of those cases involved subversive speech, and two involved libel law. When comparing the opinions of justices who supported freedom of expression in both the United States and Canada, the most striking feature is what is missing in the Canadian cases. Although the justices discuss the importance of freedom of speech and the press to a democracy, there is no mention of the marketplace of ideas or the chilling effect of government restrictions. Nor do the justices employ the slippery slope argument. And they refer to the attainment of truth only briefly. What is found is an acknowledgement that Canadians will espouse a diversity of ideas and beliefs and that diversity must be permitted in a democracy. Overall the Canadian justices revealed their idealist roots with their emphasis on society and the state over the individual. Freedom of expression is seen as a social right to further democracy. The cases dealing with subversive speech will be analyzed first, followed by those dealing with libel.

While the late 1940s and early 1950s are in many ways a dark period in American free expression history because of McCarthyism, the same cannot be said for Canada. Certainly there were curtailments on Communist speech and abuses of freedom of expression and of assembly but not to the same extent as in the United States. In a 1959 law review article, Canadian W.F. Bowker wrote,

> It is not unfair to point out that we have had no loyalty oaths, no loyalty programmes, no elaborate plan to withhold passports, no section in the Criminal Code proscribing advocacy of overthrow of government by force. These are examples of government action that have troubled responsible men like the late Professor Chafee and Professor Gellhorn. As the former once said, schemes like these are a case of "Give me the hammer Suzy, there's a fly on the baby's head." We are

better off without them and can take satisfaction in having refrained from them.[134]

Bowker's comments explain at least in part the difference in the number of cases between the United States and Canada in this period, although it must be noted that he got a little carried away singing Canada's praises. The Canadian Criminal Code did contain at the time a section outlawing advocacy of overthrow of the government. Section 133(4) provided:

> Everyone shall be presumed to have a seditious intention who publishes, or circulates any writing, printing or document in which it is advocated, or who teaches or advocates, the use, without the authority of law, of force, as a means of accomplishing any governmental change within Canada.[135]

In 1936 a subsection was added that specifically removed criticism from the meaning of seditious intention if the person intended in good faith "to point out, in order to their removal, matters which are producing or have a tendency to produce feelings of hatred and ill-will between different classes of His Majesty's subjects."[136]

It was under section 133 of the Criminal Code that the first two subversive political speech cases came before the Supreme Court. Both cases arose from the same fact set, involving a pamphlet printed in the province of Quebec that accused government officials and judges of being controlled by Catholic priests. The first time *Boucher v. The King* came before the Court, it was remanded back to the trial court for reconsideration.[137] One year later it came back before the Court on appeal.[138]

On its first appearance, the majority of the justices held that incitement to violence was not a necessary ingredient for conviction under the section. A conservative Justice Taschereau acknowledged that such a holding could "to a certain extent curtail the liberty of the press and the right to free speech,"[139] but the Court's powers did not extend beyond the interpretation of the laws as enacted by Parliament.

Justice Rand in his dissent took a strong stand for freedom of expression. Seditious libel, he noted, arose from the belief that rulers exercised authority via a divine mandate. But constitutional changes in the nineteenth century necessitated a modification of the legal view of public criticism. Rulers were now seen as servants of the people. Freedom of thought and speech and disagreement in ideas "are of the essence of our very life," he wrote.[140] Controversy and discontent "are part of our living which ultimately serve us in stimulation, in the clarification of thought and, as we believe, in the search for the constitution and truth of things generally."[141] The test, then, for seditious intention was "good faith by legitimate means toward legitimate ends."[142]

When the case came back before the Court one year later, the majority had shifted, and Rand's dissenting position was accepted. The intention needed for seditious libel was incitement to violence against constituted authority. An intention to bring the administration of justice into hatred or contempt was not seditious without also an intention to incite to violence against it.

One of the majority, Justice Kellock reviewed the history of seditious libel, noting that the ruler was now seen as the agent and servant of the people. Under this view, there could be no such thing as sedition, he argued. "Every member of the public who censures the ruler for the time being exercises in his own person the right which belongs to the whole of which he forms a part," he wrote.[143] Therefore, nothing short of incitement of violence could constitute seditious libel. Interestingly, Kellock described the right to criticize the government as a right belonging to the whole. As in the United States, then, freedom of expression was seen as a social right, necessary for democracy.

But in the American cases, the right was seen as the individual's right that is used to further society. Here Kellock described it as society's right that the individual merely exercises for the time being. The difference clearly reveals Kellock's idealist roots. The political philosophy of idealism had elevated society over the individual and combined society and the state into one. Although, as was seen in Chapter Three, there was a movement away from idealism toward greater individual autonomy in Canada, the concept of society was still very strong.

Despite the emphasis on society or perhaps because of it, the majority justices were cognizant that diverse viewpoints were to be found in any society and appeared willing to permit those viewpoints to flourish. Justice Rand argued that the clash of opinions on political, social, and religious subjects had become the "stuff of daily experience" and mere ill-will as a product of a discussion was not sufficient to render the speech criminal. He wrote,

> Controversial fury is aroused constantly by differences in abstract conceptions; heresy in some fields is again a mortal sin; there can be fanatical puritanism in ideas as well as in morals; but our compact of free society accepts and absorbs these differences and they are exercised at large within the framework of freedom and order on broader and deeper uniformities as bases of social stability.[144]

Justice Locke, focusing on the charge of sedition, argued that the people had a right to freely criticize the government subject only to the restraints of civil and criminal libel and contempt of court.[145]

What can be seen from the Canadian supporters of freedom of expression is an emphasis on freedom and order, or as one justice put it, freedom prescribed by law. The connection between liberty and order is only found in the American cases in the opinions of the more conservative justices, such as Justice Jackson. That even the more liberal justices in Canada are essentially conservative is not surprising given the history of idealism and its focus on society and the conservative political thought of the period. There has always been a conservative emphasis on law and order in Canada.

It should also not be surprising that the dissenting justices in the second *Boucher* case were even more conservative than the majority, requiring greater order. Chief Justice Rinfret, for example, argued that interpreting freedom as license, as apparently the majority had done, was dangerous. "Obviously pure criticism, or expression of opinion, however severe or extreme, is, I might almost say, to be invited," he wrote. But, he continued, there was a point at which individual freedom had to be restricted on "the grounds of reason, or on the grounds of the democratic process and the necessities of the present situation."[146] Individuals did not have the right, according to Justice Rinfret, to say what they wanted and when without regard to the consequences of their speech. Ironically, Rinfret cited John Milton for support—"License they mean when they cry liberty."[147] Milton, of course, is cited in American cases to support protection of freedom.

At the heart of the issue in *Boucher* was not overthrow of the government or even criticism of the government, but the creation of divisions among groups in Canadian society. Boucher got himself into trouble because his pamphlet had the potential to create a rift between Catholics and non-Catholics in Quebec. Ethnic, religious, and community group rights have always been important in Canada because Canada's nationhood was formed through an alliance of groups, the most obvious ones being the English and French. Deliberately fostering hostility among any of these groups, then, carries within it the seeds for the destruction of the alliance and the nation itself. The United States, although it could be considered an alliance of groups, was formed on the basis of a shared way of life, at least that was the vision put forward by the political thinkers in the 1950s.[148]

These differences between Canada and the United States help explain in part the difference in the political philosophies of the two countries, with one focusing on society, the other on the individual. They also help explain why Canada was less concerned with communism than was the United States. Communism was a political ideology that did not threaten the Canadian sense of nationhood. That is not to say that Communists met with no opposition in Canada.

They did, especially in the provinces. But the Supreme Court reined in the provincial governments' excesses in terms of freedom of expression for Communists in the two cases it heard in this period involving Communists.

In *Smith v. Rhuland Ltd. v. R.*, the Court struck down an order of the Labor Relations Board of Nova Scotia rejecting the application of the shipbuilders' union for certification as a bargaining agent on the grounds that the secretary-treasurer of the union was a Communist.[149] The board had found, like Congress had in the United States, that Communists worked by deceit, treachery, and revolution to subvert democracy. Therefore, the union could not have a Communist in a key position.

Again, Justice Rand, for the majority, came out in favor of freedom of expression. He acknowledged the consequences of the successful propagation of Communistic doctrines but argued there was no law against holding Communist views or being a member of a Communist party. "This man is eligible for election or appointment to the highest political offices in the province," he continued. "On what ground can it be said that the legislature of which he might be a member has empowered the board, in effect, to exclude him from a labor union?"[150] Like Justice Black in the American cases, Justice Rand put his faith in the people to reject communism. He wrote,

> The dangers from the propagation of the Communist dogmas lie essentially in the receptivity of the environment. The Canadian social order rests on the enlightened opinion and the reasonable satisfaction of the people as a whole. . . . [T]he security of the state itself resides in their solidarity as loyal subjects. To them, . . . we must look for the protection and defense of that security . . . .[151]

What is missing in Justice Rand's opinion that was found in Justice Black's is the idea that communism would never be acceptable because it was alien or un-Canadian. Rand did say that communism was repugnant to the Canadian political traditions, but it was clearly not the same kind of threat to Rand as it was to the American justices. The dissenting Canadian justices were more in line with the American justices, arguing that the board had reason to fear the presence of the Communist in the union and validly exercised its discretion.

The final Communist case of the period involved a Quebec statute that made it illegal for anyone to use a house to propagate communism by any means.[152] Because the attorney general for the province was ordered to close any such house, the law became known as the Padlock Act. The case arose when a landlord sued for cancellation of a lease on the ground that the tenant had violated the act. The tenant argued that the statute was outside the jurisdiction of the provincial legislature. Under the British North America Act, provinces had jurisdiction over property, civil rights, and local matters. The federal government had the sole power to enact criminal laws.

The majority of the Court found that the "pith and substance" of the Act was criminal law and therefore within the enumerated powers of the federal Parliament. Justice Nolan, for example, held that the act's "true nature and purpose" was to suppress communism by creating a new crime.[153] The sole dissenting justice argued, on the other hand, that the act was not criminal, but dealt with property. It was calculated to suppress conditions favoring the development of crime and to control property to protect society from illegal uses that might be made of it. Although the case was disposed of on this narrow point of law as were most cases that came before the Court, Justices Rand and Abbott went on to speak out about freedom of expression.

Justice Rand noted that there had been a steady removal of restraints on expression over the past 150 years in the United Kingdom and Canada. Apart from sedition, obscenity, and criminal libel, the public law, he argued, left "the literary, discursive, and polemic use of language in the broadest sense, free."[154] The object in the case at hand was the suppression of Communist propaganda, but it could have been as easily the suppression of any political, economic, or social theory. "The aim of the statute is, by means of penalties, to prevent what is considered a poisoning of men's minds, to shield the individual from exposure to dangerous ideas, to protect him, in short, from his own thinking propensities," he wrote.[155] But freedom of expression was a "condition of social cohesion and its ultimate stabilizing force."[156]

As was found in the American cases, Justice Rand argued that freedom of expression was essential to a democracy. Parliamentary government was based on the concept that individuals, "acting freely and under self-restraints," were capable of governing themselves. As a result, freedom of expression had a national significance that could not be within the power of a province to curtail. He wrote,

> This constitutional fact is the political expression of the primary condition of social life, thought, and its communication by language. Liberty in this is little less vital to man's mind and spirit than breathing is to his physical existence. As such an inherence in the individual it is embodied in his status of citizenship.[157]

Rand, however, left open the issue of whether the federal government was in a position to regulate freedom of expression.

Justice Abbott, on the other hand, was willing to take the extra step and commit himself. Having argued that the right of freedom of expression on matters of public policy, whether it be social, economic, or political, were essential to the working of a parliamentary democracy, Abbott concluded that "as our constitutional Act now stands, Parliament itself could not abrogate this right of discussion and debate."[158]

There were two libel cases in this period, although only one was an action against the press. Both involved political candidates and reflect a difference in attitude toward libel and politicians among Canadian judges from that of the American justices.

In *Douglas v. Tucker*, a 1952 case, the premier of the province of Ontario was sued for libel by the leader of the opposition party.[159] During a provincial election campaign, the premier alleged in public that the plaintiff had been involved in fraudulent farm loans. The plaintiff had responded in a speech that the allegation was without foundation. To justify his claim, the premier, in turn, responded during a campaign event that the plaintiff was facing a fraud suit. A reporter covering the event printed the allegations. The premier argued that the statements were true and subject to a qualified privilege. The Court, however, said that the fraud suit was not in itself evidence that the plaintiff committed fraud. Anyone could file a civil fraud suit, the Court noted. Nor were the statements subject to a qualified privilege.

The reasoning behind the decision in *Douglas v. Tucker* becomes clearer when considered with the case of *The Globe and Mail Ltd. v. Boland*.[160] *The Globe and Mail*, a national newspaper, ran an editorial criticizing a candidate in a federal election. The editorial accused Boland of attempting to mislead the new Canadian vote by putting forward an ex-Communist as evidence that the Liberal Party was soft on communism. The newspaper claimed qualified privilege in response to Boland's libel action.

Justice Cartwright, writing for the majority, acknowledged that the press had a right, in common with all the people, to report truthfully and comment fairly on matters of public interest, which would give rise to a defense of qualified privilege. But to hold that any defamatory statement could be made during an election and protected by qualified privilege would be contrary to the "common convenience and welfare of society," which is the underlying principle on which the rules of qualified privilege are founded. "It would mean every man who offers himself as a candidate must be prepared to risk the loss of his reputation without redress unless he be able to prove affirmatively that those who defamed him were actuated by express malice," Cartwright held.[161] Ultimately, it would do more harm than good because it would keep honorable men from seeking office. Implicit in Cartwright's opinion is the conservative belief that the people will best be served by an elite.

In the six political speech cases that came before the Supreme Court in this period, all of the justices were more conservative than their American counterparts, stressing law and order. However, those justices who spoke out in favor of freedom of expression did so from a socialized individualism political philosophy.

SUMMARY OF FINDINGS AND CONCLUSION

The period following World War II was one of relative prosperity for Americans and Canadians. Political thinkers in the two countries emerged from the disenchantment and pessimism of the 1930s and 1940s with a new optimism. In the United States, the dominant political thought was pluralism, grounded in relativism. Relativists saw the pluralism of American democracy, based on competitive minority interest groups, as the democratic ideal because it worked. Underlying American democracy was a culture that valued diversity and openness and that was held together by a foundation of homogeneity. There was a heavy emphasis on shared values and beliefs. Like the pragmatists before them, the relativists saw the state as a mechanism to promote and further equality. They also continued the pragmatic elitist approach to individuals, believing them to be malleable and susceptible to social engineering.

Reacting against the relativists with their pluralism were the new conservatives, a combination of classical conservatives and classical liberals. The new conservatives questioned ethical and social relativism, arguing that it led to a stultified conformity. They sought to reaffirm diversity and true individuality through the preservation of order and the maintenance of the status quo.

Conservative thinkers in Canada also sought a return to the notion of the individual from the concept of the mass society. The prevalence of associations and organizations in individuals' lives was reducing individual participation in government and destroying the basis of parliamentary democracy. Unlike classical conservatives, the Canadian conservatives in this period believed in the goodness of individuals, revealing their idealist roots.

Also present in Canada was the socialized individualism of the 1930s. Socialized individualism saw the state as a mechanism to promote the betterment of society, while granting individuals a degree of autonomy. The philosophy was expressed in this period by those seeking a written bill of rights in Canada to protect civil liberties. Those advocating a bill of rights tended to be absolutists, while those rejecting the idea of a codification of rights were relativist in outlook. The Canadian justices tended not to reflect the relativist/absolutist debate in their opinions, but the American justices did. Many of the American justices in the period could be clearly identified as relativist or absolutist in their opinions. The importance of the debate to freedom of expression is that relativism supported the use of a balancing approach to First Amendment cases, meaning less protection for speech. While the majority of the justices in the period held a liberal political philosophy, either classical liberal, pragmatic, or relativist, only the classical liberals, with their fear of the state and their faith in individuals, were consistently in favor of freedom of expression. Pragmatists, with their questioning of absolute truths, had been supportive of freedom of expression in the 1920s and 1930s. But their belief in balancing interests, along with the addition of pragmatists and relativists who had conservative outlooks, led to less support for freedom of expression in this period. The more conservative justices were willing to defer to Congress when it came to subversive speech or speech that threatened the overthrow of the government. Freedom of the press, however, had greater success with the Court. The media were seen as fulfilling a vital function in the working of a democracy. The media were to be protected when they sought to criticize the government and get information to the people.

Interestingly, the Canadian cases reflect the opposite result. The Canadian Supreme Court was less supportive of press rights, at least in libel cases, than it was of speech rights. Criticism of politicians threatened the democratic process because it would keep the best from seeking office, essentially a conservative position that reflected the Court's idealist roots. On the other hand, the Court strongly supported freedom of expression even for Communists in this period. Of course, it must be recognized that the number of Canadian cases was significantly smaller and the threat of communism in Canada was never as great as in the United States.

Missing from the Canadian Court's speech opinions, however, were the traditional American justifications for freedom of expression—the marketplace of ideas, the slippery slope argument, and the chilling effect. Freedom of expression was a social right, in that it was essential to a working democracy, but the nature of that right was different from its conception in the United States. In the United States, freedom of expression was a social right belonging to the individual but used to further society. In Canada, it was a social right belonging to society as a whole and only exercised on occasion by the individual. The Canadian conception of freedom of expression fit with the political philosophy of socialized individualism because it granted a certain level of individual autonomy but only within the parameters of an ordered society.

The Canadian justices, then, were in line with the contemporary political thought. They were either conservative or subscribed to socialized individualism. The American justices were also on a par with their political thought contemporaries. And in the cases of the early 1950s, the American justices were even ahead of the political thinkers who would a few years later discuss the "genius" of the Constitution and the consensus in American society.

Unlike the previous period, the United States resolved freedom of expression issues in favor of authority. The primary reasons were the balancing approach used by the Court and the fear of communism. The positive aspects of the period, however, were the establishment by the classical liberals of such justifications for freedom of expression as the slippery slope and the chilling effect arguments. In Canada, the cases were split, and it cannot be said that the tension was resolved in favor of either liberty or authority. But the Court established strong precedents for the protection of freedom of expression in the future. Underlying the positive features in both countries was a fundamental faith in the individual.

CHAPTER 5
Change versus continuity 1963 – 1974

The 1960s and early 1970s were a time of tremendous social change and instability. They called into question old values and pitted change against the status quo. In the United States, the civil rights demonstrations, the women's movement, and the anti-war protests stood out in stark relief against the conformity and consensus of the 1950s. And in Canada, Quebec's Quiet Revolution ushered in the modernization of that province, strengthening the identity of the Quebecois and threatening the new found sense of nationhood acquired by the rest of the country in the postwar period.

POLITICAL THOUGHT FROM 1963 TO 1974

The 1960s and early 1970s were a turbulent time in the United States. As historian Edward A. Purcell, Jr., described it,

> By the mid-sixties American society had begun to look significantly different to many citizens. The dashing of hopes created by the Kennedy enthusiasm, an increased awareness of poverty and racism, the sharpening identification of a military-industrial complex, ever growing governmental mendacity, and an apparently endless, pointless, and destructive war all

combined to create a profound disillusion with the realities of America.[1]

The result of the disillusionment, as one scholar put it, was "an authentic and widespread reaction against the complacent conformism, rigid authoritarianism, and narrow rationalism of the organizations—corporations, military services, universities—that controlled Americans' lives as the 1950s ended."[2] The new conservatives who had argued for a reaffirmation of the role of the individual in society in the 1950s became more vocal and gained more support. A new left also arose, advocating the American ideal of equality and seeking change within the existing system. Members of the new left, such as Students for a Democratic Society (SDS), found passion in the very shared values Daniel Bell had said in the 1950s had produced the end of ideology.[3] While the new conservatives sought a return to old values, the new left sought change, albeit within the confines of the existing constitutional framework. But both targeted their criticism at the pragmatic and relativist liberals and their continued advocacy of pluralism as the basis of American democracy.

In Canada, a similar connection arose between the left and the conservatives. Both sought a return to the dignity of the individual but advocated different methods of achieving it. The conservative George Grant, for example, argued for a return to moral values, while the left-wing C.B. MacPherson argued for a new democratic theory.

Canada did not experience the social upheaval in this period that the United States did. But that did not mean there was no social change. The effect of American mass media on Canadian values and culture was especially troubling for the conservatives and left wing political thinkers who feared the liberals were selling out the country to the Americans. That fear was heightened when Canadian students began mimicking their American counterparts, staging sit-ins and protesting for social reform. In Quebec, there was a conscious movement to modernize the province that involved the rejection of the authoritarianism of the Catholic Church and an adoption of liberal-democratic values. While conservatism remained strong in the province, the young developed a new sense of identity of themselves as Quebecois and began calling for political independence.

Despite the Quebecois in Quebec and the pluralists in the United States, the focus of the dominant political thought in both countries was on the individual. The political thinkers reacted against the behavioralist concept of the individual as socially constructed and sought to re-establish the primacy of the individual and the notion of self-fulfillment found in the earlier political thought of individualism and idealism. The change in the conception of the individual produced a corresponding change in the conception of the state. The change from the 1950s was that the new left and the conservative thinkers saw the state as a mechanism to assist the individual in achieving self-fulfillment rather than as an association through which interest groups sought power, as the pluralist liberals saw it.

In the United States, the pluralist liberals continued to identify pluralism as the basis of American democracy. For example, Robert Dahl in 1967 argued that there were two kinds of democracy. The first involved decision-making by a sovereign majority. For this kind of democracy, a high degree of consensus among all citizens as to what the government's policies should be was required and was virtually impossible to achieve in a heterogeneous country like the United States.[4] The second was pluralism, in which there was no single center of sovereign power. Instead there were multiple centers of power, none of which was wholly sovereign.[5] These multiple centers of power, Dahl argued, helped tame power, secure the consent of all, and settle conflicts peacefully. It was this form of democracy that was found in the United States and that was provided for by the Constitution, he said.

The Constitution had established the principles of limited authority, balanced authority, and political pluralism, Dahl argued.[6] What allowed pluralism to work in the United States was the ideological nature of Americans. All Americans had the same democratic ideology, and it was this consensus that united the country, making it possible for both freedom and diversity to flourish.[7] As can be seen from his argument, Dahl continued to see American society in terms of consensus. Of course, without some kind of basic agreement on values, the pluralistic society described by Dahl could not support democracy because there would never be a majority. The new conservatives were not convinced of the merits of pluralism or its application to American society. These intellectuals were a mixture of classical liberals, classical conservatives, and neoconservatives, the latter being former Communists and Socialists. One neoconservative was Frank S. Meyer. Meyer had held responsible positions in the Communist Party in Great Britain and the United States in the 1930s. But World War II and Stalin's international revolutionary aims after the War led him to reject communism. He turned to conservatism and in his 1964 book *What is Conservatism?* attempted to bring together the existing divergent views of conservatism.

According to Meyer, classical liberals and classical conservatives in the twentieth century shared a common conservatism. Although classical liberals continued to stress freedom and the individual, and classical conservatives emphasized virtue and order, they really were dependent on each other, he argued. Without virtue and order, freedom would lead to anarchy. And conversely, a belief in virtue implicitly recognized the necessity of freedom to choose. The modern conservative, Meyer argued, combined the best of both traditions, classical liberal and classical conservative.[8] For modern conservatives, the end of civil society was "to guarantee freedom, so that men may uncoercedly pursue virtue."[9] And their goal, according to Meyer, was to vindicate "the true nature of man, free and responsible, against the arid, mechanistic, collectivist denial of man's nature which transitorily prevails," under the name of "collectivist Liberalism."[10]

Members of the new left, such as Students for a Democratic Society, would have found much in Meyer's book with which they could agree. Drawing on the writings of C. Wright Mills in the 1950s and his description of the power elite,[11] the SDS criticized the pluralists for failing to bring American ideals into reality, pointing out the lack of racial and gender equality in society. The SDS opposed what it described as the depersonalization of individuals. It was this reduction of individuals to mere objects that had permitted the atrocities of the twentieth century, the group argued. The members also opposed the idea that individuals were incapable of directing their own affairs because they saw this incompetence as a product of manipulation, not of nature. For the SDS, individuals possessed unfulfilled capacities for reason, freedom, and love and were capable of meeting the complexities of modern society, provided "society is organized not for minority, but for majority, participation in decision-making."[12] It was the goal of individuals and society to provide the means whereby individuals could achieve human independence in the sense of having a way that was one's own, as they described it.

Society, then, was to be governed by two aims: that individuals share in social decisions affecting the quality and direction of their lives and that society be organized to encourage independence. It followed from these that matters of social consequence were to be decided by individuals in a participatory democracy. Politics was to be seen "as the art of collectively creating an acceptable pattern of social relations." The SDS concluded with a call to action for students and universities to "complete a movement of ordinary people making demands for a better life."[13]

Consistent with the SDS's emphasis on the dignity of the individual was the broadening of freedom of expression values to include individual self-fulfillment. Unlike the pragmatists and Alexander Meiklejohn who saw freedom of expression as purely a social right, constitutional legal scholar Thomas Emerson, drawing on earlier theories, argued it was both a social right and an individual right. It was a social right for three reasons. First, it furthered the attainment of truth. The search for truth was a continuous process, for Emerson, requiring "a rethinking and retesting of the accepted opinion" through open discussion.[14] Second, free discussion allowed for participation in political and social decision-making, which "embraced the right to participate in the building of the whole culture." And third, it acted as a social safety valve because individuals were able to release their frustrations before they erupted in violence. Ultimately, however, freedom of expression was an individual right because the proper end of individuals was the realization of their characters and potentialities as human beings, according to Emerson. Individuals had the right to form their own beliefs and opinions and to express them. Suppression of that right was an affront to the dignity of the individual, he argued.

Respect for the individual also comes through in *Elements of Democratic Government*, written by Canadian constitutional law professor J. A. Corry and Henry Abraham of the University of Pennsylvania. Corry and Abraham acknowledged that individuals were neither solitary nor self-sufficient. In fact, all history testified to their need for society, which these authors defined as the entire network of social relationships among individuals.[15] Social relationships were established by custom and habit and existed prior to the state. The state, however, was necessary because "the history of human societies is a history of conflict as well as of voluntary cooperation." The primary role of the state, then, was to maintain order and suppress violence by coercive power.[16] Corry and Abraham described the state as a mutual insurance association that was limited to specific purposes—promoting the common interests and common purposes of its members.[17] As such, the state was an instrument of society.[18]

Democracy, according to Corry and Abraham, was a manner of governing and of being governed, and it was based on a number of ideals, with the highest being respect for individual personality. From that value all others, such as freedom, equality, and the rule of law, followed.[19] The ultimate aim of democratic politics was to provide the necessary conditions for the full realization of individual personality, which included an ordered society and individual freedom within limits.[20]

Individual freedom, of course, included freedom of expression. But, according to Corry and Abraham, before individuals could make fruitful use of freedom of expression, they had to be conscious of an underlying unity that transcended differences of opinion. They had to believe in one another's reasonableness and have some measure of agreement on what amounted to proof of the truth. If the differences among individuals on these points were too vast, then discussion would not bring them closer together.[21] And freedom of expression was not absolute. The maintenance of public order and security came first, for Corry and Abraham. The test a liberal democracy should apply before restricting speech was: "Will the forbidding of such talk further or hamper the realization of liberal democratic ideals?"[22] A society that chose repressive measures was losing its faith in its ability to win and keep loyalty, Corry and Abraham argued.[23]

Canadian political philosopher George P. Grant was also concerned about the potential deterioration of democracy. Reacting to the relativism and behavioralism of the 1950s, Grant noted that freedom was in knowing the truth about things.[24] But social scientists had opted out of trying to decide what was true and good, spending their time instead on discovering techniques for adjusting people to the existing system.[25] "The liberal society keeps itself going above all by propaganda, by submerging people with propaganda. A society that feeds on propaganda soon cannot tell the difference between lies and truth," he wrote.[26] Grant feared that a society based on the claim that social sciences could build a society of free and equal men would not result in human excellence, but would devolve into tyranny.[27] Grant defined human excellence as the realization of those virtues that would allow individuals to live together well in communities and to think.[28]

But even more troubling for Grant was the loss of "local cultures." In *Lament for a Nation*, Grant described how the social sciences were moving individuals ever closer to membership in a universal and homogenous state, by which he meant the United States, that would make local culture, or Canada, anachronistic.[29] Ironically, in Quebec, the flood of American culture through the mass media was being welcomed. The United States was a symbol of liberation to the young Quebeckers who sought to get away from the stultifying authoritarianism and rigidity of the dominant ideology in the province.[30]

The Quiet Revolution, consisting of a series of reforms carried out by the provincial administration in the years 1960 to 1966, fueled the new Quebec nationalism that flourished by the end of the sixties. Quebec society was essentially democratized and revitalized, while the old doctrine of laissez-faire promoted by the Catholic Church was replaced by state interventionism. The state actively pushed the modernization of the economy, the education system, and the concept of democracy in the province. As political scientist Denis Moniére put it, "in the ruling ideology, the age-old focus on spirituality was giving way to a more rationalist, materialistic social philosophy."[31]

As the state in Quebec brought in social and political reforms, the culture of the province changed. The young people threw out the old morals and adopted the liberalizing attitudes sweeping the United States. Moniere wrote, "Quebec entered the world cultural revolution proclaiming its own national specificity. Its people no longer defined themselves as French Canadian, but as Québécois."[32] This new sense of nationalism spawned independence movements, most notably the Parti Quebecois. The PQ wanted control over the political, economic, and social agendas of Quebec to ensure the future of the Quebecois. The PQ saw the state as "a neutral, objective arbiter, above interests of class; the centre for demands to be lodged and regulations meted out; a device to serve the common good."[33]

What is most noticeable about the Quebec political thought of this period is its emphasis on society as opposed to the individual. It should not, however, be surprising that the focus was on the collective rather than the individual because the political thought was seeking to establish Quebec as a distinct culture within a larger whole. Thus despite its Socialist leanings, the Quebec political thought was different from the left-wing thought in the rest of Canada. Thinkers on the left in Canada, such as C. B. Macpherson, were, like the conservatives, more concerned with the individual than with society.

Macpherson, for example, wanted to put the dignity of individuals back into democratic theory. According to Macpherson, the existing liberal-democratic theory rested on two claims: that it maximized individual satisfaction and that it maximized individual powers.[34] The first claim was that a liberal democracy provided a wider freedom of individual choice and thereby maximized individual satisfaction in an equitable fashion, which was essentially the liberal utilitarian theory. But, Macpherson argued, using the maximization of satisfaction as the ultimate justification for society meant viewing individuals as consumers.[35] The second claim was that a liberal democracy maximized the potential of individuals to use and develop their human capacities. This view, Macpherson argued, was older than ulititarianism and saw individuals as actively creating and developing their attributes.[36]

For Macpherson, the two principles were essentially inconsistent. Utilitarianism saw individuals as basically passive. The other saw individuals as active. This inconsistency resulted in a weakness in the liberal-democratic theory, according to Macpherson.[37] That weakness had been aggravated by technology in that it was continually creating new goods for consumers to consume and was permitting consumers to consume by making their jobs easier and freeing up their time. But technological change, he argued, also made possible "the rejection of the concept of man as essentially an infinite consumer and appropriator of men's essence,"—the market concept.[38] Technology had provided society with the means to finally free individuals from compulsive labor and give them time to further their own capabilities.[39]

Macpherson criticized the relativist political theorists of the 1950s, such as Robert Dahl, for furthering the market concept of the state while at the same time distinguishing politics from economics. Classical theorists, he argued, saw power in terms of power over other individuals, which included the power of wealth. But the empirical theorists looked to the source of power. They were interested in the state's monopoly on coercive power and how that power was maintained, according to Macpherson. "What is lost sight of is that political power, being power over others, is used in any unequal society to extract benefit from the ruled for the ruler," he wrote.[40] Focusing on the source of the power ignored the purpose of the power. The empirical view was based solely on the first claim of maximizing satisfaction.⁴¹ Democracy was simply a means by which individuals could register their wants "as political consumers in a political market," he argued.⁴² Democracy was treated as a mechanism to maintain equilibrium, divorced from the liberal moral ideal.

Macpherson's solution was to see democracy, not as a political system, but as a kind of society.⁴³ He wrote,

> As soon as democracy is seen as a kind of society, not merely a mechanism of choosing and authorizing governments, the egalitarian principle inherent in democracy requires not only "one man, one vote," but also "one man, one equal effective right to live as fully humanly as he may wish."⁴⁴

Any democratic theory, he argued, must assume that the essentially human capabilities may all be used and developed without hindering the use and development of all the rest and without preventing others from using and developing theirs.⁴⁵

At the heart of the political thought of the period, except that of the pluralist liberals and the Quebecois, then, was a reaffirmation of the individual, a movement away from the socially constructed, mass individual toward an active, dignified individual. Correspondingly, the state was seen for the most part not as one more association in the lives of individuals, but as a mechanism designed to assist individuals in their quest for self-fulfillment.

POLITICAL SPEECH CASES

In the political speech cases in the United States and Canada from 1963 to 1974, a relationship can be found between the major trends in the political thought and the judicial decision-making in the two countries. The majority of the justices in the United States exhibited either classical liberal or pragmatic philosophies although more conservative, classical republican justices were appointed in the last five years of the period. Given the dominance of the classical liberals and pragmatists on the bench, it is not surprising that speech prevailed in the majority of cases. The greater number of wins for freedom of expression from 1963 to 1974 than in the previous periods corresponded to a movement away from balancing toward the preferred position approach, in which freedom of expression is given extra weight when balanced against other important rights, and a broadening of the values of freedom of expression to include individual self-fulfillment.[46]

The nature of the claims and claimants coming before the United States Supreme Court also changed in this period. Although there continued to be cases involving subversive speech and Communists, the fear reflected by the Cold War and McCarthyism had subsided. The cases before the Court now included the mainstream press and Americans, often students, and the issues involved speakers seeking American values.

There were only two political cases that came before the Canadian Supreme Court in this period, making it difficult to establish a definite correlation between judicial decision-making and the dominant political thought. But the justices did emphasize the individual over the state, reflecting the focus on the individual in the political thought, and they continued to be more conservative than their American counterparts.

American Political Speech Cases

From 1963 until 1969, the majority of the justices in the United States exhibited either classical liberal or pragmatic philosophies. During this period, there were thirty-one political speech cases, and freedom of expression won in twenty-six. Of those thirty-one cases, nineteen involved subversive speech,[47] and freedom of expression lost in only two. Six cases involved reflexive speech,[48] and six were press cases.

In the last five years of the period, the three justices appointed—Lewis F. Powell, Jr., William H. Rehnquist, and Warren E. Burger—exhibited a more conservative, classical republican political philosophy; however, the majority of the Court continued to favor freedom of expression.[49] From 1970 to 1974, there were thirty-one political speech cases, and freedom of expression won in twenty-six. There were only six subversive speech cases in these years with speech winning in five. Fifteen cases were reflexive speech cases, and six involved freedom of the press. The press cases will be examined first, followed by the reflexive speech cases. The subversive speech cases will not be discussed because they add little to the analysis already set out in Chapter Four.

Until the 1960s, the First Amendment was seen by the United States Supreme Court as protecting a social right—freedom of speech that was essential to the democratic process. Such a view led Alexander Meiklejohn in 1948 to argue that the First Amendment protected political speech absolutely. In 1964, the majority came close to adopting the Meiklejohnian view of the First Amendment, holding in *New York Times v. Sullivan* that the media were free to criticize public officials provided they did not do so with actual malice—knowledge of falsity or reckless disregard for the truth.[50] Justice William J. Brennan, speaking for the majority, based his decision on what he described as a "national commitment to uninhibited, robust, and wide-open debate" on public matters.[51] While agreeing with the outcome, Justices Hugo L. Black and Arthur J. Goldberg would have gone even further and given absolute immunity for criticism of the government in line with Meiklejohn.

After the Court's 1964 landmark decision in *New York Times v. Sullivan* in which defamatory speech was brought under the protection of the First Amendment for the first time, the Court consistently applied the same principles to the eleven press cases[52] that came before it. What is perhaps most interesting about the press cases is the amount of consensus on the bench. For example, Justice Abe Fortas was the sole dissenter in *St. Amant v. Thompson*, a case in which a political candidate defamed an individual during a radio broadcast.[53] The majority, per Justice Byron R. White, held that the people's stake in the conduct of public officials was so great that some erroneous statements had to be protected to ensure the ascertainment and the publication of the truth. Justice Fortas disagreed, arguing that the First

Amendment was not so fragile that it required the Court to "immunize such a reckless, destructive invasion of private life."[54] The consensus seems to have stemmed from what Justice Black described as the "practically universal agreement that the major purpose of the First Amendment was to protect free discussion of government affairs."[55] Americans had, Black concluded, an unconditional freedom to criticize the way public functions were performed, and it was the duty of the press to keep government officials responsible to the people.[56] Justice Douglas agreed that individuals had a basic right to express views on matters before the electorate.[57]

What becomes clear from the justices' opinions is that freedom of the press, at least, was a social right, first and foremost. Its purpose was the furtherance of the democratic process and the attainment of truth. As Justice Brennan put it, where criticism was of public officials and their conduct, the interest in private reputation was overborne by the larger public interest in the dissemination of truth. Speech concerning public affairs was more than self-expression; it was the essence of self-government.[58]

Relying on the chilling effect argument, the justices agreed that inaccurate but honest utterances had to be protected to ensure a free interchange of ideas and the ascertainment of truth. Justice White, in *Ocala Star-Banner Co. v. Damron*, for example, argued that misinformation had no merit in itself, but if misinformation were suppressed, then too often truth would be suppressed as well.[59] The sole reason for protecting misinformation was to ensure access to the truth.

Despite the relative consensus among the justices in the press cases, they did have different conceptions of the state and of individuals, as can be seen in *CBS v. Democratic National Committee*.[60] The question in the case was whether a broadcaster's general policy of not selling advertising time to individuals or groups wishing to speak out on issues they considered important violated the Communications Act of 1934. Chief Justice Burger, for the majority, argued that Congress intended to give the widest journalistic freedom to broadcasters.

Broadcasters were not the government for the purposes of the First Amendment, as the Democratic National Committee had argued, and were entitled to exercise considerable journalistic discretion.[61] The basis of Justice Burger's argument was not freedom from state intervention, but freedom from the influence of the masses. Burger, who had classical republican tendencies, made reference to Meiklejohn's statement that "what is essential is not that everyone shall speak, but that everything worth saying shall be said."[62] The question for Burger was who should decide what issues were to be discussed by whom and when. Broadcasters knew best, not the masses, he argued. Thus his conservative distrust of the masses comes through. He did not like the thought of the masses controlling what was said over the airwaves.

Justice Potter Stewart, on the other hand, from his classical liberal stance, argued that the First Amendment and the public interest standard under the Communications Act were not co-extensive. The Democratic National Committee had argued that the public interest standard under the Communications Act required broadcasters to accept the ads in question. Justice Stewart disagreed. The Communications Act required broadcasters to do certain things in the public interest that the First Amendment would not require if broadcasters were the government. What was happening, he argued, was that individuals were attempting to pursue the values protected by the First Amendment and in doing so were losing sight of the amendment itself. Fairness was too fragile to be left to government bureaucracies to accomplish, he concluded. Justice Douglas, another classical liberal, agreed. The struggle for liberty had been a struggle against government, he argued, and experience had shown that unrestrained power could not be trusted to serve the public even when in government hands.

At the opposite end of the spectrum in terms of the conception of the state, was the pragmatist Justice Brennan. For Brennan, the principle at stake in the case was the people's right to engage in and hear vigorous public debate on the broadcast media. The reliance on the Fairness Doctrine[63] advocated by the majority misconceived and underestimated the public's interest in receiving ideas and information without the imposition of journalistic middlemen. If individuals were to be honestly and forthrightly apprised of views then opponents needed to speak for themselves. The "genius" of the First Amendment was that it had always defined what the public ought to hear by permitting speakers to say what they wished. Brennan stressed not the ascertainment of truth as the most important value of freedom of expression, but self-fulfillment. The First Amendment had to safeguard the right of the public to hear debate and also the right to participate. "Individual self-fulfillment through experience and individual participation in public debate are central to liberty," he wrote.[64] Citing Thomas Emerson, Brennan noted that freedom of expression granted individuals some measure of control over their lives.

Justice Brennan was not alone in seeing freedom of expression as an individual right although the majority of the Court stressed its importance as a social right in the press cases. The seeds of the broader notion of freedom of expression as enunciated by Emerson in the middle of the 1960s can be seen in the opinions of Justices Douglas and Frankfurter in the 1950s. For example, Justice Frankfurter, who had described freedom of expression as a social right in the 1930s and 1940s, seemed to be moving toward its protection as an individual right when he wrote in 1950:

> The cardinal article of faith of our civilization is the inviolate character of the individual. A man can be regarded as an individual and not as a function of the state only if he is protected to the largest possible extent in his thoughts and in his beliefs as the citadel of his person.[65]

And Justice Douglas in *Dennis v. United States* argued that the airing of ideas released pressures, suggesting Emerson's notion of freedom of expression as a social safety valve.[66] By 1966, Douglas was writing that protected speech should not be restricted to speech addressed to larger public matters. It should be applicable to speech at lower levels of science and the humanities. And in the early 1970s, he cited Emerson directly in his opinions upholding freedom of expression.[67]

Coinciding with Emerson's broadening of First Amendment values was the movement in the political thought in the 1960s toward recognizing the dignity of the individual. Such intellectuals as members of the Students for a Democratic Society reacted to the notion of the mass society coming out of the late 1930s and 1940s by focusing anew on the individual. The political thought of the 1960s can be found in the cases in the late 1960s and early 1970s. Justice Stewart, for example, in the 1966 libel case of *Rosenblatt* argued that the right of individuals to protect their reputation reflected "no more than our basic concept of the essential dignity and worth of every human being, a concept at the root of any decent system of ordered liberty."[68] And Justice John M. Harlan in his majority opinion in *Cohen v. California* wrote that the constitutional right of freedom of expression was based on the belief that "no other approach would comport with the premise of individual dignity."[69]

But viewing freedom of expression as an individual right or as both a social and an individual right did not in itself determine how the tension between liberty and authority would be resolved. The notion that freedom of expression was important for individual self-fulfillment caused justices to differ in their view of the state's role in fostering that value, which became clear in the reflexive speech cases in this period.

Reflexive speech, to use legal scholar Harry Kalven's term, is speech that causes the audience to take immediate steps to silence the speaker.[70] At issue in these cases is the state's right to maintain order versus the right to speak, peacefully assemble, and petition the government for redress of grievances. It includes for the purposes of this discussion symbolic speech because the issue remains the same. The fear was not that the audience would be attracted to the ideas of the speaker, the demonstrators, or the symbolic expression, but that the audience would become hostile and violence erupt. The assembly cases will be discussed first, followed by symbolic expression cases.

From 1963 to 1974, there were twenty-one reflexive speech cases. Of those, the speaker lost in four. One of the determining factors in the cases was the justices' conception of the state. The strong protection afforded reflexive political speech in this period reflects the number of classical liberals and pragmatists on the bench. It also no doubt reflects the nature of the claimants.

Legal scholar Vincent Blasi has argued that during the 1960s and 1970s there was a change in both the claims and the claimants coming before the United States Supreme Court.[71] The civil rights and anti-war movements brought with them new tactics, such as mass demonstrations, sit-ins, and symbolic expression. The First Amendment issues raised by such new tactics could no longer be analyzed in the traditional terms of individual autonomy, the commitment to the marketplace of ideas, and a belief in self-government, he argued. The new claims "presented questions not of compassion or symbolic participation but of power—power to unleash latent social forces, to discredit persons and institutions, and to disrupt routines."[72] The claimants were no longer powerless alien groups who could be granted freedom of expression because they were not likely to succeed. Now the groups were decidedly American, seeking to bring reality in line with American values and ideals.

Blasi was correct that the claims and claimants in the 1960s and 1970s political speech cases were different from those in the 1950s. But the justices continued to analyze the cases in traditional First Amendment terms although broadening their understanding of the values protected by the First Amendment. Therefore, the justices' attitudes toward the state and its role remained an important factor in their decisions, suggesting that regardless of the type of claim and the nature of the claimant, the political philosophy of a justice will continue to be an important influence on the outcome.

Conservative justices, such as Clark and Burger, were concerned in assembly cases with the preservation of social order. In *Edwards v. South Carolina*, for example, Justice Clark dissented, arguing that having black students sit at a whites-only lunch counter in the South meant trouble.[73] The state was entitled to remove the students for the protection of society, not because the students were causing a disturbance themselves but because their presence had the potential to create a volatile situation. Similarly, in *Cox v. Louisiana*, involving the picketing of a courthouse, Clark argued that the United States was "dedicated to freedom under law not under mobs, whether they be integrationists or white supremacists. The goal, no matter how laudable, pursued by mobacracy in the end must always lead to further restraints of free expression."[74] Like Justice Clark, Chief Justice Burger saw the preservation of "ordered liberty" as an important function of law. He wrote,

> Civilized people refrain from taking the law into their own hands because of a belief that the government, as their agent, will take care of the problem in an organized, orderly way with as nearly a uniform response as human skills can manage. When we undermine the general belief that the law will give protection against fighting words and profane and abusive language such as the utterances involved as these cases, we take steps to return to the law of the jungle.[75]

On the opposite side of the political thought spectrum stood the classical liberals, such as Douglas, Stewart, Earl Warren, and Black. Douglas, for example, viewed demonstrations on public property as a means of petitioning the government for the redress of grievances, a right protected by the First Amendment. Justice Stewart described peaceful assembly as the exercising of basic constitutional rights in their "most pristine and classic form."[76] Similarly, Chief Justice Warren argued that officials should not be given unfettered discretion to decide whether a demonstration was consistent with the public welfare and safety.[77] It was too dangerous to allow the local authorities to make that decision because they would become censors. Implied in his argument is the notion of the slippery slope that views the state as unable to distinguish valid restrictions on speech from invalid ones.

Justice Black was a more complicated figure than the others, although he was truer to classical liberalism. Some legal scholars have criticized Justice Black's record in reflexive speech cases, arguing he became conservative in his old age. A staunch supporter of speech rights in the political speech cases of the 1950s, Black was often on the dissenting side of reflexive speech cases, holding against the speaker. Although his position in reflexive speech cases seems contrary to his absolutism in Communist cases, it is consistent with his classical liberal notion of property rights. He was conservative to the extent he sought to preserve the values of that philosophy against what he saw as a new social order.

Two of the tenets of classical liberalism are the rule of law and the importance of property. Under classical liberalism, the state's role was limited to the maintenance of order, in the sense of protecting individuals from the actions of other individuals. Because the state's role specifically was to protect individuals from the actions of others, classical liberals did not favor individual self-help. For Black, demonstrators and picketers were going beyond the pale of protected speech into an area that intruded on the rights of other individuals and at the same time engaging in self-help. There was, he argued, no constitutional right to picket on publicly owned streets or on privately owned property. In response to a case involving the picketing of a courthouse, Black in his dissent wrote,

> the streets are not now and never have been the proper place to administer justice.... Experience demonstrates that it is not a far step from what to many seems the earnest, honest, patriotic, kind-spirited multitude of today, to the fanatical, threatening, lawless mob of tomorrow.[78]

Thus, he could hold that the Constitution did not leave states powerless to protect the public from boisterous conduct that disturbed the social order; otherwise streets would cease to be available for the purpose for which they were constructed.[79]

Justice Black's desire to hang onto the past and his distaste for the changing times also came through clearly when he wrote in another reflexive speech case involving the picketing of a mayor's home,

> I believe that the homes of men, sometimes the last citadel of the tired, the weary, and the sick, can be protected by government from the noisy, marching, tramping, threatening picketers and demonstrators bent on filling the minds of men, women, and children with fears of the unknown.[80]

The conservatism of Justice Black can be seen in his approach to symbolic expression. The question in symbolic expression cases is whether the activity is speech, or "speech plus "as it is sometimes called, or conduct. In *Tinker v. Des Moines*, a case involving students wearing black armbands to school to protest the Vietnam War, Justice Black in his dissent argued that there was no constitutional right for individuals to say what they wanted, when they wanted, where they wanted.[81] From his classical liberal position, children had not yet reached the point of sufficient wisdom to exercise freedom of expression. In fact, he argued, students should not be flouting the orders of school officials. Public schools were operated to give students an opportunity to learn, not to talk politics by actual or symbolic speech. "Change has been said to be truly the law of life, but sometimes the old and the tried and true are worth holding," he argued.[82] Black was clearly concerned about the younger generation and what was happening at schools across the United States. He wrote,

> Students all over the land are already running loose, conducting break-ins, sit-ins, lie-ins, and smash-ins. They have picketed schools to force students not to cross their picket lines and have too often violently attacked earnest but frightened students who wanted an education that the pickets did not want them to get.[83]

Interestingly, a conservative outlook did not necessarily mean a justice would find symbolic expression to be conduct. The conservative Justice Powell, who had argued in a reflexive case that one of the hallmarks of a civilized society was the level and quality of its discourse, agreed with Justice White, a conservative pragmatist, that the First Amendment applied to conduct if it had a "substantial communicative intent and impact."[84] Under that test, putting an American flag on the seat on one's pants was communicative, White held, and protected expression. The conservative Justice Powell agreed. But another conservative justice on the bench, Justice Rehnquist, saw only marginal elements of symbolic expression in the case. People could burn objects and deface them to make a statement, but in doing so they infringed on the property interests of others, he argued.

In the two cases involving the American flag, some of the conservative justices considered the communicative intent of the act; others focused on the flag as a national symbol—destroying it implied destruction of the state. For example, Justice Rehnquist argued in *Spence v. Washington* that the right of free speech remained subject to reasonable accommodation to other interests.[85] The state was seeking to protect the flag as an important symbol of nationhood and unity. It was therefore the character, not the cloth, of the flag that was to be protected. Similarly, Justice Fortas argued in *Street v. New York* that burning the flag was action, not speech only.[86] Flags were special property, and protests did not exonerate lawlessness.

The liberal justices were more willing to allow the flag to be used as a symbol of protest. But even they avoided the issue when possible. For example in the *Street* case, the majority held that a New York statute making it unlawful to treat the flag "contemptuously" was void for vagueness. They found that Street had been convicted for his "contemptuous" comments about the flag after he burned it rather than for his actions.[87] The speech was protected, the statute void for vagueness, and the issue of whether burning an American flag amounted to protected speech left for another day.

In the United States, the civil rights demonstrations and Vietnam War protests changed the nature of the claims and the claimants coming before the Supreme Court in this period. Prior to 1963, the majority of political speech cases heard by the Court involved subversive speech—speech that threatened the state—and such dissidents as Communists. From 1963 to 1974, however, reflexive cases—speech that causes the audience to take immediate steps to silence the speaker—became predominant. These cases involved Americans, often students, who sought to bring American reality into line with what they perceived as its ideals. At the same time, the political thought was reemphasizing the dignity of the individual and broadening the values protected by the First Amendment. When combined with justices who exhibited a classical liberal or pragmatic outlook, these factors produced decisions that heavily favored freedom of expression. The majority of justices protected reflexive speech on the basis that individuals should be permitted the freedom to express themselves as they saw fit. The state did not have the right to dictate the form expression was to take. The conservative justices, however, were reluctant to extend protection to speech in reflexive speech cases because they viewed the speech as infringing on the property rights of others and as threatening the social order the state was to maintain.

Canadian Political Speech Cases

There were only two political speech cases that came before the Canadian Supreme Court in this period. Neither case involved subversive or reflexive speech, but they did involve core political speech. The first one concerned the use of union dues to fund a political party;[88] the second one concerned the display of a campaign sign on private property during a federal election.[89]

The Labor Relations Act of British Columbia prohibited a labor union from using membership dues to contribute to a political party. A union challenged the section, arguing it was outside the jurisdiction of the province because it applied to federal elections as well as provincial ones. Preventing the union from funding a political party curtailed a fundamental right of Canadians essential to the proper functioning of a democracy. The majority of the Court, however, disagreed.

Justice Maitland held for the majority that a union, certified as a bargaining agent, was not a voluntary association because membership in the union was a condition of employment. The legislation merely prevented dues paid as a condition of employment from being used to further a political cause with which the individual may not agree. It did not prohibit the union from engaging in political activity; it just could not use its dues to do so.

Justices Abbott and Cartwright disagreed. Justice Cartwright argued that the legislation essentially prohibited the union from any expenditure for political activity because membership dues accounted for virtually all of a union's funds. And the union was prevented from using dues for such purposes even if all members agreed. Justice Abbott, who had been a strong supporter of freedom of expression in the 1950s, went even further. Any attempt to abrogate or suppress the exercise of the right of public debate and discussion was beyond the competence of a provincial legislature, he argued. He wrote,

> The right to join and to support a political party and the right of public debate and discussion fall within that class of rights categorized as *droits publics*. Under our constitution, any person or group of persons in Canada is entitled to promote the advancement of views on public questions by financial as well as by vocal or written means.[90]

At the heart of the case was the protection of the individual versus the social right of public debate on political matters. Here the majority of the Court chose to protect the individual, as the American Court would do when asked to decide the same issue in the 1977 case of *Abood v. Detroit Board of Education*.[91] Although the Canadian and American courts reached the same conclusions, they did so for different reasons. In *Abood*, the majority argued that individuals were free to believe as they wanted and could not be forced into supporting viewpoints with which they disagreed. The majority justices in Canada—Maitland, Taschereau, Fauteux, and Ritchie—took a paternalistic, conservative approach to individuals, seeking to protect them from potential abuses by unions. Unlike the dissenting justices in the case, the majority did not view unions as exercising the same political rights as citizens. Freedom of expression on political matters was a right that belonged to the society as a whole and was exercised on occasion by the individual. Unions were abusing that societal right by depriving the individual of the opportunity to exercise the right. The dissenting justices—Abbott, Cartwright, and Judson—were closer to the political thought of socialized individualism dominant in Canada in the 1930s, in that they saw individuals as belonging to various associations, of which the union was just one. These justices, like the pluralists in the United States, saw these associations as competing for political power.

The difference between the conservative justices in Canada and the socialized individualist justices comes through in the case of *McKay v. The Queen*.[92] McKay, who had displayed an election sign on his front lawn during a federal election, had been convicted under a municipal zoning by-law that prohibited displaying signs on residential premises. Justice Cartwright for the majority held that the right of a voter to attempt to influence the vote of others in an election belonged to the voter as a citizen of Canada. Restriction of that right was outside the jurisdiction of the provinces.

Justice Maitland, however, argued in his dissent that the by-law only incidentally affected political speech. The "pith and substance" of the by-law was the regulation of the use of property, which was validly within the powers of the provinces. He wrote,

> Freedom of discussion is not an unlimited right to urge views, political or other, at any time, in any place, and in any manner. It is freedom subject to law, and, depending on the

nature of the legislation involved, may be subject to certain restrictions, whether federal or provincial.[93]

The quote sounds very much like something Justice Black would have written in the reflexive speech cases. He too argued that freedom of expression did not mean the freedom to speak any time, any where. Justice Black, of course, was referring to demonstrators who were using the property of others and demanding the freedom to do so. Here Justice Maitland was upholding the right of the state to restrict the right of property owners to use the property as they saw fit. Both views are conservative, but Justice Black was seeking to conserve classical liberal values. Justice Maitland was not a classical liberal. He did not fear the state and had no problem with the state enacting laws regulating the use of property in the interest of society as a whole. He was seeking to conserve something closer to idealism.

In the two Canadian cases, then, the justices all viewed the right of political speech as a social right. Individuals exercised the right on behalf of society. The difference among the justices was in their attitude toward the state's role in furthering political speech. The conservative, idealist justices, such as Maitland, were more willing to allow the state to intervene for the protection of individuals and the society as a whole. The justices who were closer to a philosophy of socialized individualism were less willing to permit state intervention, not because of a fear of the state, but because the intervention was restricting public discourse.

SUMMARY OF FINDINGS AND CONCLUSION

The period from 1963 to 1974 pitted change against continuity in the United States and Canada. The civil rights demonstrations, the women's movement, and the anti-war protests in the United States were reactions against the conformity and consensus of the 1950s. Conservatives and members of the new left sought to reestablish the centrality of the individual in political thought after the relativist behavioralism of the immediate postwar era. The conservatives wanted to maintain the traditional American ideals, while the new left advocated change to ensure all Americans enjoyed those ideals. The relativists continued to argue that pluralism was the basis of American democracy.

Canada did not experience the same social instability, but it did undergo changes. The conservatives feared that Canada was being swallowed up by the American mass culture and sought to preserve traditional Canadian values and culture. The left also lamented what it saw as Canada's move toward the materialism of the United States and advocated change to reassert the primacy of the individual in democratic theory. In Quebec, the Quiet Revolution ushered in the modernization of that province, strengthening the identity of the Quebecois and threatening the new found sense of nationhood acquired by the rest of the country in the postwar period.

The focus of the dominant political thought in both countries was on the individual. The political thinkers reacted against the behavioralist concept of the individual as socially constructed and sought to re-emphasize the individual and the notion of self-fulfillment found in the political thought of individualism and idealism. The change in the conception of the individual produced a corresponding change in the conception of the state. The left and conservative thinkers in both countries saw the state as a mechanism to assist the individual in achieving self-fulfillment rather than as an association through which interest groups sought power, as the pluralist liberals saw it.

The emphasis on the individual, found in the political thought, was reflected in the political speech cases in both Canada and the United States. Freedom of expression was seen as furthering the individual right of self-fulfillment as well as the social right of political participation. In the United States, the broadening of the values protected by the First Amendment meant a greater likelihood of success for political speech, especially with the majority of justices being classical liberals or pragmatists. The majority of justices protected reflexive speech on the basis that individuals should be permitted the freedom to express themselves as they saw fit. The state did not have the right to dictate the form expression was to take. The conservative justices, however, were reluctant to extend protection to speech in reflexive speech cases because they either viewed the speech as infringing on the property rights of others or the speaker as engaging in self-help. Both threatened the social order that the state was to maintain. Three conservative justices joined the bench in the early 1970s, but their presence did not shift the majority and the Court continued to provide strong support for freedom of expression. All of the justices were supportive of press rights, viewing the press as a necessary institution for the furthering of democracy.

In Canada, only two political speech cases came before the Court. In these, the justices exhibited an emphasis on the individual although speech continued to be considered a social right. Because the right was seen as belonging to society as a whole and not the individual, the majority of the Court permitted the state to protect the individual from abuses of the social right by interest groups, such as unions.

CHAPTER 6
How do we want to live?: 1975 – 1999

In the period from 1975 to 1999, political thinkers in both Canada and the United States were asking themselves how the individual and society should fit together and what the state's role should be in facilitating that fit. Many intellectuals feared there had been too great an emphasis placed on individualism in the previous two decades to the neglect of communities. The affluence of the 1960s and early 1970s had led to what Canadian political theorist C.B. Macpherson called "possessive individualism," in which self-interest and material well-being were perceived as the highest values.[1] In response, some intellectuals promoted the idea of greater communitarianism. Others sought to restore a sense of morality to politics, arguing that moral individuals would consider the best interest of the community, not just their own self-interest, in decision-making. By the end of the period, there was a sense that a more balanced view of the individual and society was needed. Individuals were feeling out of touch with politics, and the concept of democracy needed to be brought back into the discussion. Individuals were not the autonomous, discrete entities of classical liberalism, but neither was society greater than the sum of its parts as posited by the idealism of Canada at the turn of the century.

POLITICAL THOUGHT FROM 1975 TO 1999

In Canada, the period is marked by the passage in 1982 of the Canadian Charter of Rights and Freedoms (the Charter), the most momentous constitutional event in the country since Confederation in 1867.[2] The constitutional entrenchment of a written bill of rights in Canada represents on its face the acceptance of liberalism as the dominant political thought.[3] It is, of course, not classical liberalism but the modern, pluralistic, rights-based liberalism of twentieth-century America. Ironically, Canada appears to have embraced this modern liberalism at the very time that the United States appears to have lost faith in it.

But the Charter is not a wholesale affirmation of American pluralistic liberalism. It contains some decidedly Canadian features, such as a remnant of parliamentary supremacy in the ability of the legislatures to opt out of the Charter and explicit recognition of some group rights.[4] Despite these features, the Charter is not uniformly accepted in Canada. Before and after its passage, the debate in political thought circles centered on whether a written bill of rights was needed in Canada. The issue was which government branch best protected individual rights—the legislative or the judicial. At the heart of the debate was the concept of the individual, the state, and their relationship. Those promoting the Charter saw the individual as rational and autonomous and needing protection from the state, while those who denied the need for a written bill of rights viewed the individual as an integral component of society and the state as an instrument to further society's interests.

In the United States, the images of harmony and affluence produced by the welfare state were giving way to inflation and unemployment by the mid-1970s.[5] At the same time, Americans continued to reel from the social instability of the 1960s and early 1970s that was produced by the combined effects of the civil rights movement, the protests against the Vietnam War, and Watergate. The blame for the social and economic conditions was placed on liberalism and the liberal tradition in America. As Ronald Dworkin wrote, "The middle-aged blamed liberalism for permissiveness and the young blamed it for rigidity, economic injustice and the war in Vietnam."[6] Government was seen as needing to be "reinvented."[7]

The result was a conservative shift in political thought. There was a call to bring morality and virtue back into politics. Historians revisited the language of classical republicanism in the writings of the founding fathers, arguing that classical republicanism was as influential to the development of the country as was classical liberalism. Classical republicans emphasize the importance of institutional checks and balances to keep individuals in line. Through institutions, individuals develop virtue, defined as active participation in politics.[8] Classical republican theory rests on the notions that the end of politics is the common good and that the greatest threat to a republic is corruption. The state and society are not separate, as in classical liberalism, but work together for the good of all.[9]

Others argued for a renewed emphasis on classical liberalism's notions of limited government and individualism. Classical liberalism assumes the rationality of the individual and a separation of the state from society. As rational beings, individuals are capable of discerning the truth and the good life for themselves. The state's role is restricted to the protection of individuals from the actions of others and to the maintenance of order. The liberalism of the late twentieth century, these scholars argued, had strayed off this path by promoting an active, interventionist government, as opposed to a limited one. A return to classical liberalism's virtues would correct the ills of the modern American society, it was suggested.

Modern liberals, in turn, sought to reestablish ground against the backlash. Theories of justice premised on fairness were put forward to overcome the charges of possessive individualism leveled at modern liberalism. By the end of the period, there was a call for a balancing of all ideologies, an openness to the concepts of classical liberalism and classical republicanism, and a recognition of the diversity of principles that had shaped the country from its inception. Individuals were not to be viewed as abstract entities separate from society. They were still autonomous, but they had a responsibility to their community. Similarly the state could be used to promote communities but not to the detriment of individuals.

American political columnist George Will was one of the conservative thinkers who blamed modern liberalism for the ills of society. In concentrating on productivity and the material world, Americans had neglected the moral world to their peril, he argued in his work *Statecraft as Soulcraft*.[10] The foundation for the rights-based liberalism of the twentieth century was self-interestedness.[11] Liberalism had evolved to a general doctrine of liberation, in which "man should be allowed, even encouraged, to do what he most desires to do (consistent, of course, with other people doing likewise)," he wrote.[12]

The evolution had occurred, according to Will, because the focus of political thought had shifted in the seventeenth century from the ends individuals ought to seek to the individuals themselves and their basic human qualities.[13] Individuals came to be seen as rational, self-interested, and capable of determining the parameters of the "good" life themselves.[14] The state, in turn, was conceptualized in negative terms as a mechanism limited in power to protecting individuals from the actions of others.

According to Will, urbanization and a growing uncertainty about human nature in the nineteenth century led individuals to feel "an increasingly fragile sense of 'self.'"[15] No longer were individuals defined in relation to their association with others in a community.[16] Self-expression became a means of authenticating or validating one's self. Consequently, freedom of expression was measured, not by the quality of what was expressed but by the benefit to the person who did the expressing.[17]

The end result, for Will, was that modern liberalism had separated morality from politics by turning individuals into self-interested creatures with little connection to society. But for Will, politics necessarily involved morality. "Statecraft is soulcraft," he wrote. Although liberals would not admit it, much legislation involved morals, according to Will, because laws conditioned the actions and beliefs of the nation.[18] It was through the "legislation of morality" that social cohesion to shared values was created.[19] Failure on the part of the modern liberals to recognize the importance of morality to social unity and its connection with politics was producing a society devoid of values.

For American political theorist Friedrich Hayek, a lack of morals was not the problem with modern liberals but their emphasis on democracy and their willingness to use the state to further their own ends was.[20] His solution was a return to classical liberalism and its notion of a negative state. For Hayek and the classical liberals, government had to be strictly limited if individuals were to be assured of their freedom. The best government was one that could only restrict others from interfering with an individual's private sphere and that could not interfere with that sphere itself. Checks and balances and a separation of powers were mechanisms used to keep government in line and strictly limited.

Democracy, however, had promoted the belief that government could be controlled by elected majorities. Under democratic theory, traditional limitations on government were not needed because sovereignty rested with the people. But in practice, at least in modern times, elected majorities did not represent the people, Hayek argued. To remain in power, majorities sought the support of interest groups by granting them special benefits. Interest groups in turn could control the majority by threatening to withhold their support unless their demands were met. Interest groups, then, could claim they had the approval of the majority for their measures when in fact they did not. The government, in enforcing the measures, would be using its coercive powers in the service of the interest groups. In such a situation, the state, not other individuals, became the chief threat to individual freedom. Hayek's solution was to restrict the power of legislatures to the enactment of general rules that applied to everyone equally, so that the majority would not be forced to maintain itself by handing out special favors.

The American philosopher John Rawls attempted to salvage what he could of modern liberalism. But even Rawls reflects the conservative shift in political thought. As a pluralist, he began with the assumption that in a normal constitutional democracy individuals would hold a variety of beliefs and doctrines. And like the pluralists before him, Rawls sought to understand how a stable and just society was possible in the face of such diversity.[21] The key for Rawls lay in finding a conception of justice that could "gain the support of an overlapping consensus" of the majority of the people regardless of their beliefs.[22]

Rawls first put forward his theory of justice in 1971.[23] In an effort to explain his theory, he borrowed a technique from the social contract theorists, Thomas Hobbes, John Locke, and Jean-Jacques Rousseau. These theorists imagined humans in a state of nature, or a pre-society world, in an effort to explain how civil society and the state arose in the form in which they did. Rawls argued that if individuals were taken out of society such that they did not know their social position or their abilities in society, they would agree to be governed by certain principles of justice.[24] Essentially, he argued that individuals in a situation in which they did not know whether they would be at the top or bottom of the social scale nor what their own natural capabilities were would advocate a system of distributive justice based on fairness. There were two principles of justice according to Rawls. First, each individual had an equal claim to basic rights and liberties. Second, any social and economic inequality among individuals was permitted but only if there had been equality of opportunity.[25]

His "justice as fairness" theory was based on two assumptions. First, society was viewed as a system of social cooperation between free and equal individuals.[26] Interestingly, Rawls saw society as existing in perpetuity—"it produces and reproduces itself," he wrote[27]—a notion usually associated with classical conservatives and their organic society. A well-ordered democratic society was neither a community nor an association, he continued. It was not an association because it had no ends or aims of its own, and it was not a community because it was not governed by shared religious, philosophical, or moral doctrines.[28]

Second, Rawls assumed that individuals were free by virtue of their powers of reason and their capacity to conceive of justice and the "good." And they were equal to the extent they had these powers to the requisite minimum degree to be fully cooperating members of society.[29] Rawls noted that his definition of equality did not mean everyone was equal in every respect. In a rather conservative vein, Rawls acknowledged that some individuals would have abilities and traits that would naturally lend themselves to positions of civic duty.[30] Rawls, then, like the conservative critics of modern liberalism, was concerned with the notion of possessive individualism and attempted to distance liberalism from that label. His individuals were not self-interested but had an awareness of being situated within and dependent upon society.

Despite these conservative features, however, Rawls continued to argue in the liberal tradition that the state could not determine the one true conception of the good life. One of the reasons for the limited state under liberalism was to ensure that individuals were free to determine their own notions of the good life. The state was prevented from imposing its will on individuals in that regard. Rawls argued that his conception of justice was true to liberalism in that it allowed for a plurality of opposing doctrines each with its own conception of the good life.[31]

In his conception of justice as fairness, Rawls proposed that individuals were equally entitled to basic liberties, which he defined as "freedom of thought and liberty of conscience; the political liberty and freedom of association, as well as the freedoms specified by the liberty and integrity of the person and the rights and liberties covered by the rule of law."[32] These basic liberties were to be given absolute weight against the public good.[33] Therefore, a basic liberty could be limited or denied for the sake of one or more of the other basic liberties but never for reasons of the public good. The basic liberties, then, were not absolute in relation to each other but were essentially to be given a preferred position over the public good.[34]

American political scientist James Kloppenberg also proposed a return to a more conservative kind of liberalism. He noted that liberalism had come under siege in the 1980s and 1990s from the left and the right, both of which were singing the praises of virtue and morality.[35] Contemporary debates in political theory, Kloppenberg argued, focused on liberalism and individual rights versus classical republicanism and social responsibility.[36] But, Kloppenberg argued, the best approach was to abandon the debates between liberalism and classical republicanism and turn instead to the idea of deliberative democracy.[37]

For Kloppenberg, deliberative democracy involved a recognition of America's multiculturalism. The central issue for democracy was accommodating differences, but Americans had a tendency to reduce every issue to an either/or question.[38] Such dichotomies left no room for compromise.[39] Instead, Kloppenberg wanted to encourage greater accommodation through the fostering of a democratic self. A democratic self would have, according to Kloppenberg, an awareness of one's membership in a particular community and in society as a whole. Essentially, Kloppenberg was arguing that individuals ought to take into account not only their own interests, but also those of the larger society.[40]

Kloppenberg's desire to balance competing ideologies through a renewed emphasis on democracy is also seen in the Canadian political thinkers of the 1990s. As in the United States, the major political discussion in Canada in the 1970s and 1980s concerned liberalism versus communitarianism. The debate centered on whether Canada needed an entrenched bill of rights to protect individuals from the government.

Until World War II, Canadians looked for the most part to Great Britain for their legal and political traditions. The British North America Act, Canada's organizational document, was an ordinary act of the British parliament and contained no mention of individual rights. The Supreme Court of Canada was not even the highest court in the land until 1949. But after World War II, Britain's weakened status on the world scene, the dominance of the United States as a world leader, and the influence of the American mass media all combined to shift the focus of Canadian thought from its historically British roots to its neighbor to the South.[41] The result was an increased emphasis on liberalism and individual rights. At the same time, as one group of Canadian political thinkers noted, the founding of the United Nations in 1945 and the proclamation of the Universal Declaration of Rights in 1948 "fostered the view that democracy depends, above all, on achieving a binding consensus on liberal democratic values."[42]

The combined American and international influences culminated in passage of the Canadian Charter of Rights and Freedoms in 1982. The Charter, of course, is not a completely American-style document. It contains both individual and group rights and retains ties to the traditional notion of parliamentary supremacy.[43] But it significantly shifted the role of the Supreme Court from that of a constitutional arbitrator between the federal and provincial governments to that of an active participant in determining social policy along the lines of the U. S. Supreme Court. That shift in role also meant the discussion of rights shifted from the political realm to the legal.

Such a major constitutional change not surprisingly became the focus of the Canadian political thought. Some intellectuals continued to lament the movement toward the rights-based liberalism of the United States as they had in the 1960s and early 1970s. Others, taking a cue from their American counterparts, looked to the history of Canadian political thought to find liberal and classical republican traditions, eschewing the standard conservative, tory influence. By the end of the 1990s, at least one of the political thinkers, like the American Kloppenberg, was trying to move away from ideologies and toward participatory or discursive democracy.

Political scientist David Bell sought to conceptualize power, influence, and authority to gain a greater understanding of politics.[44] Bell defined politics as talk. "To the extent that talk *affects* others (and most talk does), it has by definition assumed political overtones," he wrote. And politics ultimately had to be concerned with how people affected each other.⁴⁵ Bell noted that traditionally the state was defined in terms of the legitimate use of coercion and violence. But such a definition was not viable in modern societies, where violence signified a breakdown of authority, not its legitimate use.⁴⁶ Thus Bell's goal was to work toward a redefinition of the state through the conceptualization of the terms power, influence, and authority.

Bell defined power as a communication that involved threats or rewards. For example, "if you do X, I will do Y," was a situation of power, not authority.⁴⁷ According to Bell, successful use of power presupposed control over some resource that might be used as a sanction, either as a threat or a reward.⁴⁸ Influence was similar to power but lacked the sanctions. It involved a kind of prediction in the form of advice, encouragement, or warning—"If you do X, Y will happen."⁴⁹ A person's ability to influence others did not depend on resources, but on the ability of the person to change people's perceptions of contingencies.⁵⁰

But authority, according to Bell, was a relationship between a superior and subordinates in which the superior communicated orders and the subordinates obeyed them.⁵¹ The commands of the superior were accepted because the command itself was viewed as legitimate.⁵² Two kinds of legitimacy existed historically, he argued—substantive and procedural. In substantive legitimacy, the validity of the superior's actions depends on the substance of those actions. If the actions further personal interests as opposed to the public's interest, the actions are not legitimate.⁵³ Under procedural legitimacy, the validity of the superior's actions depends on the procedure used. So long as agreed upon procedure is used, the actions are legitimate regardless of the motive or the interests furthered.⁵⁴

But in either type of legitimacy, so long as the language of authority worked and the authority did not have to resort to power or influence, the authority was legitimate.⁵⁵ This notion that legitimate authority was authority people accepted is also found in Leslie Armour's work, *The Crisis of Community*. For Armour, a Canadian political scientist, "the law works because, by and large, people accept it."⁵⁶ The same sentiment is not found in the American thinkers. In the United States, there is a tendency to see the law and authority in terms of coercive powers.⁵⁷

Armour's main argument was that the idea of an organic society was deeply embedded in Canadian history and its roots were still present.⁵⁸ Armour defined an organic society as one in which the parts worked together to form an intelligible whole but each part had a unique place. Thus for Armour, an organic society could also be pluralistic, for the whole was organized to permit a variety of cultures within it.⁵⁹ Societies were not just aggregates of individuals, but networks within which individuality could appear.⁶⁰

Armour argued that the early Canadian political philosophers were highly influenced by the Hegelian and Thomist traditions.⁶¹ The result was a Canadian worldview emphasizing community, reason, and a collective relation to nature.⁶² Such a worldview required a different view of knowledge, Armour noted, from the individualist worldview of the United States. In the individualist view, knowledge was relative to the individual and was concerned with improving the individual's well-being. In the Canadian worldview, knowledge was a property of the community and was transmitted by shared traditions and institutions.⁶³ For Armour, the Canadian worldview and view of knowledge explained why Canadians had never taken their politicians and their political system very seriously. "If the community is a reality, it need not be brought into being and sustained by exceptional individuals. The common response to events, rather, is the one to be trusted," he wrote.⁶⁴

The Canadian view, however, came under challenge after World War I, when individuals lost faith in the organic society, Armour observed.⁶⁵ The result was a movement toward the individualist view of knowledge with its corresponding reliance on science and empirical data. But Armour questioned the concept of scientific knowledge, arguing that science too was a product of its community.⁶⁶ Similarly, he argued that bills of rights should be regarded with suspicion because they tended to entrench existing knowledge, class biases, and interests.⁶⁷

Indeed, entrenched bills of rights had not usually done what was expected of them because they tended to give special advantage to certain groups. Just protecting "freedom of speech" per se, without explaining what was meant by it, gave an advantage to those who could afford to control a medium of communication, such as a newspaper or broadcasting station, he argued.[68]

Armour proposed a different way of looking at rights based on the assumption of an organic society. He put duties first, arguing that from individuals' duties and obligations as citizens of the community they derive their rights.[69] "It is because I have an obligation as a citizen that I have a right to be heard, a right to know, a right not to be hassled in a way which will keep me from doing my duty," he wrote.[70] Armour went on to outline his understanding of the organic society. The "nation" was a principle reflected in the shared experiences of the collective and expressed through moral convictions.[71] It involved the common outlook and strategy of the society.[72] Within the nation, communities were what legitimated and gave shape to the various institutions—economic, legal, educational, and political. The state, or the political institution, he argued, coordinated the other institutions. Each of the institutions had its own goals, except for the state, which had no goal of its own. The common good and the ideal of justice, for example, were goals of the legal institution, not the political. The state's function was to deal with the problems arising from outside forces or from conflicts among the other institutions, and its guiding principles for coordinating the various institutions were the basic values of the culture itself.[73] The ultimate limit on the state's powers was that it could not wipe out whole cultures or compel them to take on new forms.[74] And the most important individual right was the right to move from one group to another.[75]

Like Armour, political philosopher Charles Taylor was concerned with the status of political life and community in Canada. After having lived with the individualist American rhetoric for several decades, he saw Canadians turning toward conservative Canadian thinkers, who spoke from an older and different tradition.[76] Intrigued by the shift, he sought to explore modern conservatism in Canada. What he found was a non-ideological tradition that had few guiding principles other than history, a belief in an organic society, allegiance to that society, and the promotion of diversity.

Present in Taylor's work, and in the Canadian thinkers he discusses, as well as in Bell and Armour, is the notion of allegiance. The suggestion is that Canadians obey the government and its laws because they believe in its institutions. A society based on allegiance allows diversity in a way a society based on social contract, as in the United States, does not, Taylor argued.[77] Quoting the Canadian historian W.L. Morton, Taylor noted that with the economic hardships, the dependency of the early Canadians on England, and the country's pluralist culture, only the objective reality of a monarchy and monarchical institutions could have formed the basis for Canadian unity.[78] The result was an emphasis on community and the mutual obligation of individuals, themes central to the conservative tradition in Canada.[79] The notion of mutual obligation meant a different concept of freedom. Taylor quoted Canadian political thinker Stephen Leacock to illustrate the point, "True liberty . . . implies a sacrifice for each one of us of some of his rights in order that other people may have their rights too."[80]

Although Canadian conservatism traced its heritage to the tories of pre-capitalistic England, it had made its own significant alterations to that tradition along the way, according to Taylor, thus the title of his work, *Radical Tories*.[81] They were "conservatives with a conscience" because although they respected the traditional order, they were also concerned with social justice and were willing to use public power to curtail private greed, he wrote.[82] In other words, order for these conservatives meant not just law and order, but also social order.[83] Taylor concluded that contemporary conservatism in Canada was a conservative-radical mix, "based on a sense of community and order, a feeling for the land, a respect for human diversity and human rights, a concern for social justice, and a non-ideological approach to the problems of political and economic organization."[84]

Taking a cue from the renewed emphasis on classical republicanism in the United States, liberal Canadian political thinkers took a look back at the writings of the country's founding fathers in an effort to downplay the importance of the conservative, tory influence on the country's origins. Interestingly, while American conservatives sought out a classical republican tradition to counter liberalism, Canadian liberals turned to classical republicanism to counter conservativism.

In *Canada's Origins: Liberal, Tory, or Republican*, the editors, Janet Ajzenstat and Peter Smith, noted that the traditional view of Canadian political history held liberalism to be the dominant influence in the nineteenth century, modified by a strain of tory conservatism.[85] They argued that liberalism faced a challenge from "a republican ideology on the political left, rather than toryism on the right."[86] "The formative influence in Canada's past was not solely liberal, or the combination of liberal and tory conservatism, but a lively opposition between liberalism and civic republicanism with a progressive agenda," they wrote.[87]

According to Ajzenstat and Smith, classical republicanism emphasized community and democracy in opposition to liberalism's emphasis on the individual and economic development.[88] For Ajzenstat and Smith, classical republicanism, with its roots in the writings of Jean-Jacques Rousseau, supposed that those representing the community in institutions of government would articulate a sense of the common good and an idea of civic virtue to which all members of the polity would adhere.[89] As Smith went on to explain, however, virtue was always liable to corruption, which led to tyranny. Thus, classical republicans put their faith in political and social institutions to guard against corruption and to inculcate the values of civic virtue.[90] These features of classical republicanism were found in the Loyalists, Smith argued. They believed institutions were essential for the ultimate happiness and freedom of individuals.[91] Ajzenstat and Smith concluded then that Canada was the product of a combined tradition of liberalism and classical republicanism, not tory conservatism.

Canadian constitutional law scholar Allan Hutchinson, like his American contemporary, James Kloppenberg, argued that such historical wranglings were not solving anything. In his book *Waiting for Coraf: A Critique of Law and Rights*, he argued in favor of discursive democracy and away from the ideologies of liberalism, especially the rights-based liberalism of modern America, and classical republicanism.[92]

Rights-talk, as Hutchinson called rights-based liberalism, depicted individuals as separate and egoistic and held individual values as the only values of importance.[93] "It imagines a world consisting of independent, self-sufficient, and equal persons who confidently draw up and robustly pursue their own life plans," he wrote.[94] But such a depiction of the human condition was false because it did not describe the actual situation of humans in society.[95] Rights-talk ignored the fact that people were constrained by the social context in which they lived and defined by their relations with others.[96] Rights-talk also managed to treat all individuals the same while claiming to celebrate their diversity.[97] For Hutchinson, the central paradox of such liberalism was that individuals seeking maximum freedom to pursue their own self-interest could only do so by curbing another's freedom to do the same.[98]

In contrast to liberals, classical republicans emphasized civic virtue over universal rights and citizens over abstract individuals.[99] But, Hutchinson argued, classical republicanism, especially when pushed to the extreme of communitarianism, focused on the substance of community values without sufficient regard for individuals within that community. The answer had to be in a theory that recognized that individuals were neither absolutely opposed to community nor completely determined by community.[100] For Hutchinson, that theory was dialogic democracy.

Democracy was not a system of governing, nor a set of political institutions. It was, however, a society in which power was held by citizens.[101] Attention needed to be shifted from individuals and the personal end of self-expression to the dialogic interactions of communication, Hutchinson argued.[102] To achieve this democratic conversation, the traditional liberal public/private distinction would have to be done away with and the state be seen as an instrument of the citizens, not as an opponent as it was in liberalism.[103] According to Hutchinson, liberalism erred in making government coterminous with the state. Government was only one part of the state. Although distrust of the government was not entirely groundless, it blinded liberals to the threat of unchecked private power in modern society and the role government could play as the promoter of liberty, he wrote.[104]

Maintaining the dichotomy between public or state action, where the state and the government were synonomous, and private action meant that increasingly powerful corporations could affect decisions of governmental agencies without impunity.[105] Under Hutchinson's theory, the state consisted of much more than the government. For Hutchinson, "The state is all the institutions, processes, values, and truths that gel to deprive individual citizens of control over their own identity and destiny."[106]

The result of viewing the state in this way would be an on-going public debate about the meaning of the good life in which individuals had the right to hear, to be heard, and to be answered.[107] It would also mean that in exercising those rights, individuals would have to take their responsibility to others into account, according to Hutchinson.[108] Although he does not explicitly state it, his notion of rights, like Armour's, is tied to the concept of duty. Citizens have rights because they have duties to the community. Rights, under Hutchinson's dialogic democracy, were not to further self-fulfillment, but to ensure the democratic process.

Hutchinson acknowledged that the most difficult tasks of the democratic state were to balance personal autonomy with social solidarity and to accommodate diversity and plurality without destroying the unity of the nation.[109] A democratic state needed to be based on the premise that "the fate of each of us is unavoidably tied to the fate of all of us and that the self and the collectivity are not antagonistic entities, but complementary components of a political community."[110] Thus, the resolution of freedom of speech issues, for example, was not, according to Hutchinson, a matter of legal principle, but an ideological struggle over the kind of society people wanted to have and the kind of individuals they wanted to be.[111] And it was only through dialogue that the good life could be achieved.[112]

In the final quarter of the twentieth century, then, political thought in the United States took a conservative shift away from what had come to be seen as possessive individualism. Some intellectuals, such as George Will, argued that a lack of morality and a relativist philosophy had produced self-interested individuals who had no regard for society. Morals and values had to be reconnected to politics for social unity. Others, like Friedrich Hayek, saw the rise of the positive state as the problem. The state had to be redefined in negative terms if freedom were to be achieved. And still others sought a greater sense of justice and a more participatory democracy.

The same issues were being grappled with by the Canadian political thinkers in this period. But while the Americans were taking a conservative shift, Canadians were taking a liberal one. Passage of the Canadian Charter of Rights and Freedoms in 1982 was both heralded and criticized as a movement by Canada toward American rights-based liberalism. At the same time, however, there continued to be an emphasis on rights and duties as opposed to rights alone. And running throughout the Canadian political thought in this period are threads of community and allegiance.

At the heart of the debates in both countries were the issues of how the individual and society were to fit together and what role the state should play in facilitating that fit. The political thought of both was seeking a workable balance between personal autonomy and social solidarity. Although such political thinkers as the American James Kloppenberg and the Canadian Allan Hutchinson strike the balance in very similar ways, the differences on this issue between Canadians and Americans at a deep-rooted level come through clearly in the case law of the period.

POLITICAL SPEECH CASES

While the majority of the political speech cases in the first three-quarters of the century involved threats to either democracy or social stability, especially in the United States, the cases in the period from 1975 to 1999 dealt with almost mundane issues in comparison—campaign financing, corporate speech, the right of public employees to participate in politics. But at the same time, these issues are at the core of the right of freedom of expression in a democracy. Perhaps because these cases are central to the democratic political process and because there were no extraneous factors such as war or great social instability affecting judicial decision-making, they point out more clearly than do the cases in any of the earlier periods the deep-rooted differences between the United States and Canada in terms of how the individual, the state, and their relationship are conceptualized.

American Political Speech Cases

Corresponding perhaps to the conservative shift in society, the number of political speech cases before the U.S. Supreme Court from 1975 to 1999 was less than half of what it had been in the period from 1963 to 1974. There were twenty-four political speech cases in this period compared with sixty-three in the previous period. What is more interesting is that the percentage of wins for freedom of expression dropped from approximately eight-six percent in the previous period to approximately sixty-seven percent, with the majority of the losses coming between 1981 and 1986. For example, in the nine political speech cases prior to 1981, speech lost in only one.[113] But between 1981 and 1986 freedom of expression lost five out of six.[114] Justice Sandra Day O'Connor was appointed in 1981, but she does not appear to have been a swing vote, although her presence bolstered the conservative majority. In 1986, however, Justice Antonin Scalia was appointed, and his presence does seem to have tipped the balance back in the direction of protecting speech. The more recent appointments of

Justices Anthony M. Kennedy, David H. Souter, Clarence Thomas, Stephen G. Breyer, and Ruth Bader Ginsberg have produced a Court with a conservative reputation but one that is relatively balanced in terms of the justices' political philosophies.

Unlike earlier periods, there is no dominant philosophy on the bench. Justices exhibit the characteristics of classical liberals, modern pluralist liberals, classical republicans, and conservatives. Classical liberal justices exhibit a distrust of the state, and by extension democracy, and are wary of any intervention by the state into the lives of individuals. Restrictions on speech will chill individuals, inhibiting the search for the truth. Thus, classical liberal judges place an emphasis on the quantity of speech rather than on its quality. Justices Warren E. Burger, Potter Stewart, Scalia, and Kennedy all exhibit characteristics of classical liberalism.

Like the classical liberals, modern pluralist liberals have a distrust of democracy. However, they are willing to use the state to equalize individuals. They argue that one cannot have freedom without a certain minimum standard of living. Therefore, while classical liberals emphasize freedom over equality, modern liberals emphasize equality over freedom. In the period from 1975 to 1999, Justices William J. Brennan, Thurgood Marshall, and John P. Stevens reflect the modern liberal position.

Against classical and modern liberalism stands the political philosophy of classical republicanism. Classical republican justices are concerned with the prevention of corruption and the maintenance of institutions. Justices William H. Rehnquist, Lewis F. Powell, Jr., and Byron R. White in this period exhibit the characteristics of classical republicans. Although none of the justices in this period can be considered a classical conservative, Justices Harry A. Blackmun and O'Connor do reveal conservative tendencies. Conservative justices tend to look toward tradition and history as guiding principles and are concerned with the maintenance of social order.[115]

The result of the presence of these various philosophies is that while for the most part justices with the same political philosophy vote the same way in the same case, the classical liberals and modern liberals are not always on the same side and the classical liberals and classical republicans are not always against each other. The alliance among the philosophies depends upon the nature of the case and the claimant, making broad conclusions and generalizations difficult. Having said that, however, it is clear that the justices' decisions are consistent with their political philosophy in terms of how they conceptualize the individual, the state, and their relationship.

Adding to the complexity of the justices' positions is the nature of the cases coming before the bench. Canadian legal scholar Alan Hutchinson wrote in 1999, "Contrary to popular impression, the twentieth century has not been the century of the individual. Nor has it been the century of the government. . . . It is the century of the corporation."[116] His statement may or may not apply to the century, but it does aptly describe the last quarter of it, judging from the political speech cases before the Court. Cases in the early part of the twentieth century involved, for the most part, subversive speech—speech of Communists and Socialists aimed at subverting the American democratic system. By the 1960s, subversive speech had taken a back seat to reflexive speech. Reflexive speech involved Americans, many of them students, who protested the Vietnam war and civil rights abuses. In turn, reflexive speech has been replaced in this period to a great extent by corporate speech and the issue of election financing.

The question in these cases is not simply whether the state can infringe on an individual's freedom of expression as was the case in the subversive and reflexive political speech cases. Here, the issues range from whether a corporation is entitled to First Amendment rights to whose First Amendment rights should be protected when they conflict. And many of these cases involve what the Court called "core political speech"—speech directed to the election process itself. For the purposes of organization, the cases will be discussed under four general categories because each raises different issues: reflexive speech, finance and the electoral process, access to property, and the political participation of public employees.

Reflexive speech issues had been relatively settled in the 1960s and early 1970s. Reflexive speech is speech that causes the audience to take immediate steps to silence the speaker. At issue in these cases is the state's right to maintain order versus the right to speak and peacefully assemble. It includes for the purposes of this discussion symbolic speech because the issue remains the same. The fear on the part of the state was not that the audience would agree with the argument of the speaker or the sentiment of the symbolic expression, but that the audience would become hostile and violence erupt. Of the six reflexive speech cases in this period, three involved symbolic speech,[117] two picketing,[118] and one peaceful assembly.[119] In only one of the cases did speech lose.[120]

Classical republican and conservative justices, with their emphasis on order, have a tendency to see reflexive speech as a disruption of society. Classical liberals are usually willing to support reflexive speech when it involves speakers engaged in the act of speaking but are less sympathetic when the speech involves symbolic expression. Modern liberals, on the other hand, are more willing to extend First Amendment protection to symbolic expression.

The most important of the reflexive speech cases in the period were the two flag-burning cases. Flag burning had arisen in an earlier case, but the Court had dodged the issue of whether the act was symbolic expression and therefore constitutionally protected, deciding the case instead on the defendant's spoken words at the time.[121] But in *Texas v. Johnson*, there was no escaping.[122] In upholding Johnson's right to burn the American flag to express his contempt of the Reagan administration, the Court split along political philosophy lines.[123] The majority was made up of classical liberals and modern liberals who were willing to allow the expression, while the dissenters tended to be classical republicans and conservatives.

Writing for the majority, Justice Brennan argued that while the flag served as a symbol of the country, the state could not foster its own view of the flag by prohibiting individuals from using it to express ideas. "Johnson was not, we add, prosecuted for the expression of just any idea; he was prosecuted for his dissatisfaction with the policies of this country, expression situated at the core of our First Amendment values," he wrote.[124] The notion that the state cannot prohibit expression because society finds the idea disagreeable or offensive is of course at the heart of classical liberalism. Brennan's faith in individuals to do the right thing is clear when he wrote:

> We are tempted to say, in fact, that the flag's deservedly cherished place in our community will be strengthened, not weakened, by our holding today. Our decision is a reaffirmation of the principles of freedom and inclusiveness that the flag best reflects, and of the conviction that our toleration of criticism such as Johnson's is a sign and source of our strength.[125]

For classical liberals, who believe that a universal truth will arise from the marketplace of ideas, the answer to individuals who criticize the government is more speech. And Brennan clearly has faith in the individual's ability to reason. He suggested that individuals should counter flag burning with their own conduct such as displaying the flag, saluting it, and giving it a proper burial. Through such behavior, individuals would persuade flag burners they were wrong, he held.

For the classical republican justices, Rehnquist and White, however, Johnson did not have the right to burn the American flag. The flag was a unique symbol. Johnson was free to say anything about the flag that he wanted, but he was not free to destroy the symbol, Chief Justice Rehnquist held. It was Johnson's use of the symbol, not the idea he expressed, that was being punished. For Rehnquist, Johnson's actions had no expressive content, they were the equivalent of "a grunt or roar." "Surely one of the high purposes of a democratic society is to legislate against conduct that is regarded as evil and profoundly offensive to the majority of people," he wrote.[126] Such a sentiment would never be expressed by a classical liberal. In fact, Justice Kennedy, in his concurring opinion, wrote that the Constitution compelled the Court to protect Johnson's right to burn the flag even though he personally found the act offensive and recognized that the majority of Americans did as well.

Classical liberals and classical republicans were not always at odds in symbolic expression cases, however, as is made clear in the case of *Clark v. Community for Creative Non-Violence*.[127] The classical republican Justice White, for the majority, upheld a National Park Service rule prohibiting overnight sleeping in the park as a valid time, place, and manner restriction. The government had a substantial interest in preserving park property, he held. Concurring in the decision, Chief Justice Burger, a classical liberal, argued that the actions of the campers were not speech but conduct that interfered with the rights of others. Therefore, the state was permitted to restrict the activity.

Two of the modern liberals, Justices Marshall and Brennan, disagreed with the majority's argument. The action of the campers was symbolic speech, they held. The majority in its decision "denatured" the right of the campers in failing to recognize that public officials have strong incentives to over-regulate. What separates these modern liberals, with their distrust of the state, from the classical liberals of the majority, is their willingness to extend First Amendment protection to symbolic expression.

While reflexive speech cases pit individuals against the state, the cases involving elections and financing are more complex. The issues range from whether corporations have the right to freedom of expression to whether an individual's right to expression outweighs a group's right. There were nine cases dealing with the election process and financing in this period.

Classical liberals were more willing to allow corporate speech than the others on the bench. Traditionally classical liberals favor a government policy of laissez-faire, and that approach comes through clearly in these cases. In *Buckley v. Valeo*, for example, Chief Justice Burger held that requiring a political candidate to disclose the names of contributors and the amounts they contributed to the candidate's campaign was unconstitutional.[128] Candidates of minority parties especially would suffer because they were most in need of anonymous support. The disclosure requirement would essentially function to chill contributors, he argued. In contrast to Burger's classical liberalism and his focus on the individual is Justice Marshall's modern liberalism and his emphasis on equality. The limits on expenditures for political candidates were valid, according to Marshall, because of the public's interest in "promoting the reality and appearance of equal access to the political arena."[129]

The classical republican Justice White also agreed that the limits were valid, but his interest was in preventing corruption. He accepted the premise that Congress had the power to protect the electoral process against "the two great natural and historical enemies of all republics, open violence and insidious corruption."[130] And he held, "expenditure ceilings reinforce the contribution limits and help eradicate the hazard of corruption."[131] On the other hand, Justice Rehnquist, also a classical republican, actually saw the limits as promoting the possibility of corruption by enshrining the "Republican and Democratic Parties in a permanently preferred position."[132] Just because no third party had posed a credible threat to the two major parties since 1860 did not mean that Congress could take legal steps to ensure no party would again, he argued.

The same concern about corruption can be found in the *Buckley v. American Constitutional Law Foundation* case, which involved the constitutionality of conditions Colorado put on ballot-initiatives. Justice Rehnquist, in his dissent, held that the state could require petition circulators to be registered voters. To preserve order, he argued, certain rules and guidelines had to be set by the state and followed by the individual in society's best interest. The purpose of the conditions, according to Rehnquist, was to prevent fraud in the circulation of petitions and to ensure that the issues were decided by local voters, rather than by out-of-state interests. Justice Thomas, in a concurring opinion, on the other hand, held that the practical effect of requiring the petitioners to be registered voters would be a reduction "in the voices available to convey political messages," a liberal notion.[133]

The issue of whether corporations were entitled to the right of freedom of expression points out clearly the differences between the modern liberals, classical liberals, and classical republicans in terms of how they view the individual and the state. In *Austin v. Michigan Chamber of Commerce*, for example, a majority of the Court, made up of modern liberals and classical republicans, held that a Michigan law prohibiting corporations from contributing to political campaigns from their general treasury fund was valid.[134] Justice Marshall, a modern liberal, upheld the law on the basis that its purpose was to prevent the corrosive effects of amassed wealth, thanks to the corporate form. Justice Brennan, also a modern liberal, concurred, adding that the purpose of the act was to protect small businessmen who needed the services of the Chamber of Commerce but who might not agree with the Chamber's political activities. Thus, the modern liberals sought to protect individuals from what they perceived as the all-encompassing power of corporations. Presumably, the classical republican justices were on the side of the majority because of the potentially corruptive nature of corporate power in elections.

But the classical liberals had no fear of corporations nor of their influence on individuals. In his dissent, Justice Scalia argued that denying corporations the right to use treasury funds for political activity denied the corporation the right to speak. He compared a corporation to a wealthy individual. Nobody would suggest that an individual could be denied the right to speak simply because he or she was a billionaire, he argued. For Scalia, the majority's premise that allowing corporations to use general treasury funds for political campaigns coerced shareholders and members of the corporation into supporting speech they did not agree with was not valid. If people did not like the speech, they could sell their shares, he wrote. Fairness was not part of the First Amendment. In fact, he continued, "the premise of our system is that there is no such thing as too much speech—that the people are not foolish but intelligent and will separate the wheat from the chaff."[135]

Justice Kennedy, another classical liberal, agreed with Justice Scalia that the act discriminated on the basis of the speaker. He noted there was no reason to conclude "independent speech by a corporation is any more likely to dominate the political arena than speech by the wealthy individual."[136] He also agreed that the government could not restrict the quantity of speech. "The suggestion that the government has an interest in shaping the political debate by insulating the electorate from too much exposure to certain views is incompatible with the First Amendment," he wrote.[137]

The dissenting opinions of Justices Scalia and Kennedy reveal two tenets of classical liberalism. First, that people are rational, and second, that to arrive at a universal truth, all information must be presented. Thus there is an emphasis in classical liberalism on the quantity rather than the quality of speech. The final arbiter of the quality of speech must be individuals themselves, not the state.

The classical liberals and classical republicans took the same position in *First National Bank of Boston v. Bellotti*, a case involving the right of corporations to use general treasury funds to speak on political issues not directly affecting them.[138] Justice Burger, a classical liberal, had no difficulty with the idea of corporate speech, holding that "the First Amendment does not 'belong' to any definable category of persons or entities: It belongs to all who exercise its freedoms."[139]

But the classical republican justices were not convinced. Freedom of expression was an individual right, not a corporate right, Justice White wrote in his dissent. Individuals needed the right of freedom of speech for self-expression. Corporations, on the other hand, were only interested in profits. Like the classical liberals, White was interested in protecting the free exchange of ideas but prohibiting corporate speech would not affect that, he concluded. Justice Rehnquist agreed with White. The right of individuals to speak would not be affected if corporations were denied speech, nor would the free flow of information be diminished. Shareholders and CEOs of the corporation could still speak, he held.

Although Rehnquist and White were both classical republican and usually on the same side in cases,[140] they were on opposite sides in the case of *F.E.C. v. National Conservative Political Action Committee.*[141] Writing for the majority, Justice Rehnquist held that the only reason to restrict funding for political campaigns was to avoid corruption, which he defined as subversion of the political process. He found no evidence of corruption in this case. He wrote,

> The fact that candidates and elected officials may alter or reaffirm their own positions on issues in response to political messages paid for by the PACs can hardly be called corruption, for one of the essential features of democracy is the presentation to the electorate of varying points of view.[142]

Justice White, on the other hand, held that there was an important government interest in preventing apparent as well as real corruption. He was willing to defer to the legislature because, he concluded, elected representatives were in the best position to know if large-scale expenditures were a significant threat to the integrity of the election process. The majority was simply protecting the right of contributors to make contributions to a P.A.C., not their right to speak. "The First Amendment protects the right to speak, not the right to spend," he wrote, "and limitations on the amount of money that can be spent are not the same as restrictions on speaking."[143]

At issue in the cases involving access to property was whether individuals had a right to the use of government property for speech purposes. How the justices decided the issue depended on whether they took the position of the government, the one seeking access, or the audience. Classical liberals, with their emphasis on property rights, and classical republicans, with their emphasis on institutions, were more willing to uphold the government's position. The modern liberals, who emphasize equality and information flow, had a tendency to side with the individual seeking access or with the audience. In the case of *U.S. Postal Service v. Greenburgh Civic Association*, for example, Justice Rehnquist for the majority wrote that a mailbox was not a public forum, although it was government property.[144] Groups, such as the Greenburgh Civic Association, were not at liberty to put flyers into home mailboxes without paying postage. For Rehnquist, the issue was not speech, but the rights that went along with property, and individuals had no automatic right to the use of government property. The postal service, an American institution, was not to have its efforts to efficiently distribute mail subverted by individuals using mailboxes for free.

But the modern liberals, Justices Marshall and Stevens, dissented. The issue was not property rights, but speech rights, they argued. And the postal service should surely be considered a public forum. Both Marshall and Stevens were troubled by the majority's classification of privately owned mailboxes as government property. Marshall argued that the civic association's First Amendment rights were being denied because it was prevented from hand-delivering flyers to private mailboxes. Stevens, on the other hand, argued that the case should be looked at from the point of view of the owner of the mailbox rather than from the point of view of either the government or the civic association. The Court had, in effect, upheld a statute "that interferes with the owner's receipt of information that he may want to receive. . . . The nationwide criminal statute at issue here deprives millions of homeowners of the legal right to make a simple decision affecting their ability to receive communication from others."[145]

Justice Stevens took a similar position in the case of *Arkansas Educational Television Commission v. Forbes.* At issue was whether the AETC, a public television station, had to invite all political candidates to a debate it was airing. Stevens argued that the broadcasters used no objective criteria to reject Ralph Forbes, an independent candidate, from the debate. The AETC was not an ordinary broadcaster, but an employee of the government and as such it could not arbitrarily deny Forbes the right to participate in the debate. Justice Kennedy, for the majority, however, upheld the right of public broadcasters to exercise editorial discretion in deciding who could participate in a political debate. The classical liberal Kennedy was more concerned with preserving the quantity of speech overall than he was in preserving the right of one individual to speak. He feared that forcing broadcasters to allow every candidate in to speak would lead them not to broadcast the debate at all. Thus, he viewed the case from the standpoint of the audience, not that of the speaker. As a classical liberal, he also sought to protect the radio station as a business entity from outside control by individuals.

The same split between the modern liberals and the classical liberals and classical republicans can be seen in the cases involving public employees. For example, the case of *Elrod v. Burns* involved deputy sheriffs who were fired from their positions when a new sheriff was elected.[146] The issue was whether public employees who were discharged because of their partisan political affiliation could claim their First Amendment rights were violated. The deputy sheriffs complained that they were being coerced into supporting the party in power simply to maintain their jobs. Justice Brennan, writing for the majority, acknowledged that patronage had a long history in the United States, but he held, the right of the individual took precedence over political parties. The source to which the Court had to turn for guidance in deciding the case was the system of government the First Amendment protected, he wrote,

> a democratic system whose proper functioning is indispensably dependent on the unfettered judgment of each citizen on matters of public concern. Our decision in obedience to the guidance of that source does not outlaw political parties or political campaigning and management. Parties are free to exist and their concomitant activities are free to continue. We require only that the rights of every citizen to believe as he will and to act and associate according to his beliefs be free to continue as well.[147]

The classical liberals and classical republicans on the bench disagreed. Justice Powell wrote in his dissent that "patronage hiring practices have contributed to American democracy by stimulating political activity and by strengthening parties, thereby helping to make government accountable."[148] And patronage hiring practices enabled party organizations to function at the local level, he held. Revealing his classical republican views, he wrote that individuals did not take part in political activities because of some "academic interest in 'democracy,'" but because of the hope of some reward.[149] It was a case in which the Court ought to defer to the legislature.

The same split, although with a reversed outcome, is found in *Connick v. Myers*.[150] Myers, a district attorney, had refused to accept a transfer and had conducted a survey of her colleagues regarding office morale. Justice White, for the majority, acknowledged that the First Amendment was fashioned to ensure the unfettered interchange of ideas and that speech concerning public affairs was the essence of self-government. But he concluded, "when employee expression cannot be fairly considered as relating to any matter of political, social, or other concern to the community, government officials should enjoy wide latitude in managing their offices, without intrusive oversight by the judiciary in the name of the First Amendment."[151] And here, White argued, Myers was speaking not as a citizen, but as an employee on a matter of personal interest.

Justice Brennan dissented. He argued that one of the central purposes of the First Amendment was to protect the dissemination of information on which individuals may make reasoned decisions about government. He argued that the majority had used a narrow conception of public concern. The First Amendment protected dissemination so that people and not the courts could decide what were matters of public concern, he argued.

The American cases in this period, then, reveal a Court that has no dominant political philosophy. The competing philosophies of classical liberalism, modern liberalism, and classical republicanism find alliances with each other depending on the issues involved. The

How do we want to live?: 1975–1999 191

classical liberals, with their faith in the rationality of individuals and distrust of the state, are strong protectors of freedom of expression, but they are against individuals taking the law into their own hands. Classical liberal justices are in favor of corporate speech and side with business interests and property rights. The classical republicans, who see individuals as being ruled by their passions, put their faith in institutions. Classical republican justices view reflexive speech as disruptive of the social order. They are also willing to defer to the legislatures on matters involving the electoral process because of their concern with the threat of corruption. Like the classical liberals, they support property rights. And finally the modern liberals have a tendency to emphasize equality rights and seek to remedy what they see as the inequality that results from the classical liberal doctrine of laissez-faire. Therefore, modern liberal justices are willing to extend protection to symbolic expression. They also seek to protect the individual against corporate influence.

Canadian Political Speech Cases

During this period, seventeen political speech cases were heard by the Canadian Supreme Court. As in the American cases of the period, these cases involved core political speech. Unlike previous eras in which the speech in question was seen as a threat against society and democracy, these cases involved speakers who were not trying to change the system, but who wanted to exercise their right to speak out on political issues. There were four pre-Charter cases[152] and thirteen post-Charter cases[153] in the period.

All of the justices exhibit a combination of pragmatic, classical republican, and idealist thought. Like the pragmatists, they advocate balancing individual and societal rights and, in the post-Charter cases, require empirical evidence to support allegations of infringement of rights. Also like the pragmatists, there is no belief in an absolute truth. In fact, in comparison to the American cases, the concept of truth-seeking plays a very insignificant role in the Canadian political speech cases. There is, however, an emphasis on institutions, the rule of law, and social order. But unlike the classical republicans, there is no discussion of corruption, suggesting that these justices have a more positive view of the individual than do the American classical republican justices.

Despite the presence of features of pragmatism and classical republicanism, the attitude of the justices toward the individual, the state, and their relationship reveal the continued strength of idealism in Canada. Under idealism, the individual is a component part of society that has no existence separate from the whole. The needs of the individual are subordinated to the needs of the society, and once society has enunciated its needs, the individual is to obey. Individuals have a duty under idealism to seek a higher, moral life through identification with the good of the society. These tenets of idealism can be seen in the Canadian justices' willingness to hold individuals responsible for their actions, a characteristic that comes out clearly in the libel cases of the period and in the way they discuss the state as part of society, not separate from it. Not surprisingly, there is greater willingness to defer to the legislatures than is found on the American Court.

The pre-Charter cases involved issues of reflexive speech,[154] libel,[155] and the right of public employees to political speech,[156] and speech lost in each one. The common feature among these cases was the emphasis on order and the rule of law. In the two public employee cases, a unanimous Court maintained that public employees generally have the right of freedom of speech but just not in the particular circumstances of these two cases.[157]

The case of *Fraser v. Public Service Staff Relations Board*,[158] for example, involved a federal public servant who had been fired for criticizing the party in power on issues unrelated to his job or even the agency for which he worked. Justice David Dickson, writing for the majority, sounded a theme common in the Canadian pre- and post-Charter cases. He said that the issue was to find the balance between the right of the individual as a member of the Canadian democratic community to speak on public issues and the duty of the individual as a federal civil servant to fulfill the functions of his job. Dickson acknowledged that some speech by public servants was permitted. In fact, "[a]n absolute rule prohibiting all public participation and discussion by all public servants would prohibit activities which [sic] no sensible person in a democratic society would want to prohibit," he wrote.[159] He also acknowledged that the employee's speech in this case was unrelated to his employment. But, he continued, federal service positions had two dimensions. The first was the ability of the individual to do the job, and the second was the perception of the job held by the public. Public employees had to have "knowledge, fairness, integrity," and loyalty to the Canadian government, not to a political party, he wrote. The public had an interest in both the actual and the apparent impartiality of the public service.

Dickson acknowledged that Fraser had been impartial in performing his duties but held that it was not unreasonable to conclude that the public would not have perceived him as impartial because he had engaged in "sustained and highly visible attacks on major Government policies."[160] For Dickson, maintaining the public's confidence in the institution was more important than the individual's right to speak, a classical republican notion. Employees of the government could not jeopardize the institution of government during the tenure of their employment.

The same reasoning was applied in a case involving Ontario public servants who complained they were prevented from participating in political activities at both the provincial and federal levels.[161] They acknowledged they could be prevented from doing so at the provincial level but challenged the ability of the provincial government to prevent them from participating in federal elections. Justice Beetz agreed with Dickson's decision in *Fraser*, holding that the impartiality of the public service was an essential prerequisite of responsible government. Dickson himself in this case said that freedom of speech was important but that no single value could bear the full burden of upholding a democratic system of government and that the impartiality of the public service was important to the democratic structure.[162]

This idea that freedom of speech is not given a preferred position in Canada is also found in *A.G. and Dupond v. Montreal*.[163] The case arose after the city of Montreal banned all assemblies, parades, or gatherings on public property for a thirty-day period in November of 1969 on the grounds that public gatherings would cause "tumult, endanger safety, peace or the public order."[164] Justice Beetz, for the majority, held that no freedom was so enshrined as to be above competent legislation and that the city was within its power to take preventive measures to avoid "conditions conducive to breaches of the peace."[165] The ordinance did not interfere with freedom of speech, according to Beetz, because it prohibited all gatherings irrespective of ideology or political view. And further, Beetz argued, freedom of speech was distinct from and independent of the holding of demonstrations and assemblies. Demonstrations were not a form of speech, but of collective behavior. "They are of the nature of a display of force rather than of that of an appeal to reason; their inarticulateness prevents them from becoming part of language and from reaching the level of discourse," he wrote, a statement with which classical liberals would agree.[166]

Justice Bora Laskin, on the other hand, saw the ordinance as a mini-criminal code and therefore outside the constitutional powers of the city. Only the federal government could legislate in the area of criminal law. But even if it had been a federal law, Laskin would have been concerned with the nature of the ordinance because it barred people from gathering even for innocent purposes,

> not because of any problem as to whether certain public areas should be open at certain times or on certain days or occasions ... but because of a desire to forestall the violent or the likely violent. This is the invocation of a doctrine which should alarm free citizens even if it were invoked and applied under the authority of the Parliament of Canada.[167]

It can be seen from these pre-Charter cases that Canadian judges favored the rule of law and society over the rights of individuals to speak freely. Although some justices, such as Dickson and Laskin, wrote about the importance of freedom of expression in a democracy, the Court overall was willing to restrict the individual's right to expression in favor of societal rights. The Court's emphasis on society over the individual caused some Canadians to herald the passage of the Charter as a beacon of hope for individual rights. Others, of course, feared the Charter's enactment signaled the end of the community in Canada and the entrenchment of American rights-based individualism in the Canadian political landscape.

From a strictly legal perspective, the Court's role changed because it now has the power to declare acts of Parliament unconstitutional because they infringe on an entrenched right under the Charter. Before the Charter was passed, the Court was limited to declaring whether the act came within the legislature's enumerated powers under the British North America Act.[168] Questions of legislative motive or intention were supposed to be irrelevant to the Court's decision-making. Despite the fear among some intellectuals that the Charter would also produce a doctrinal change in the Court, the justices themselves are remarkably consistent in their beliefs and attitudes toward freedom of expression in the pre- and post-Charter cases. The post-Charter cases involved a variety of speech issues, and speech won in two.

The first political speech case in which the Court applied the Charter involved protesters in front of a courthouse in British Columbia.[169] The protesters were members of the British Columbia public servants union, and they were protesting wages and working conditions. The chief justice of the British Columbia Supreme Court on his own initiative issued an injunction prohibiting the picketers from picketing the courthouse. The picketers appealed the injunction claiming it violated their right of freedom of expression under section 2(b) of the Charter.[170]

Justice Dickson in upholding the injunction argued that the case involved the fundamental right of Canadians to have access to the courts. Unimpeded access to courts was fundamental to the preservation of every legal right and freedom, he wrote. Rights and freedoms would have no value if people were denied access to the courts to vindicate them. Dickson acknowledged that picketing was a form of expression and that freedom of expression was a highly valued right, but, he argued, a balance had to be made between individual values and societal values. In this case, without the public's right to access to the courts, the individual right to freedom of expression would be meaningless. Dickson's views are similar to those of the American conservative pragmatist Justice Felix Frankfurter who argued in the 1941 criminal contempt case of *Bridges v. California* that justice was the highest right in an organized society and the very foundation of orderly government.[171]

A second judge in the Canadian case, Justice McIntyre, agreed with Dickson, arguing that free access to courts was essential for the rule of law. He too acknowledged that picketing involved some element of expression, but he held that the action in this case was calculated to infringe on the Charter rights of those seeking access to the courts. The issue for McIntyre was whether any group could have a Charter right to interfere with the Charter rights of others; a question he answered in the negative. Interestingly, the justices viewed the case as one of individuals infringing on the rights of other individuals, not as the state infringing on the rights of individuals, suggesting that the state was not seen as an entity separate from society.

The individual right to freedom of expression did not always lose to societal rights, however. For example, the Court did uphold the right of individuals to distribute political flyers in a public airport.[172] At issue was access to government property again but also the validity of time, place, and manner restrictions. The justices all concurred in the outcome but disagreed on the means to get there.

Justice Lamer, for example, argued that the government administered property for the benefit of its citizens as a whole, and therefore citizens had an interest in seeing the property administered in a manner consistent with the intended purpose. Section 2(b) of the

Charter could not be interpreted, Lamer argued, by considering only the interest of the person communicating. The interests of the government and other citizens also had to be taken into account. Freedom to communicate depended on whether the form of expression was compatible with the property's purpose. Sounding very much like an idealist, he wrote that one's rights were always circumscribed by the rights of others. Having said that, however, he held that distributing leaflets in the public thoroughfares of an airport was not incompatible with the function of the airport.[173]

Justice Claire L'Heureux-Dube, on the other hand, argued that political speech enhanced personal growth and self-realization. She noted that free debate was often seen as necessary to the discovery of truth, especially by classical liberals. But for her, as for pragmatists, there was no political truth. It was the idea expressed in the statement that was to be encouraged during a political debate not the truth of the statement itself. For L'Heureux-Dube, the justification for political speech was not some abstract search for truth, but the tangible goal of preserving democracy. Rather than applying formulaic tests in freedom of expression cases, she argued the Canadian Court ought to look at the cases in their context and to balance the individual's right versus the government's objective and means under section 1 of the Charter.

Section 1 of the Charter provides that the rights and freedoms set out in the Charter are subject to "such reasonable limits prescribed by law as can be demonstrably justified in a free and democratic society." It is in the context of section 1 that the judicial balancing of interests proposed by L'Heureux-Dube is to occur.[174] Essentially, L'Heureux-Dube was advocating ad hoc balancing, an approach to speech cases that was adopted by pragmatists in the United States but later rejected by the U.S. Supreme Court in favor of preferred position balancing. L'Heureux-Dube further argued that the Charter's basic purpose in protecting freedom of expression was to promote the free exchange of ideas, the open debate of public affairs, the effective working of democratic institutions, and the pursuit of knowledge and truth.

L'Heureux-Dube went on to discuss the doctrines of vagueness and overbreadth, which are not traditionally part of the jurisprudence of Canada. Sounding similar to the classical liberals with their notion of the chilling effect, she wrote that with a vague law most people would "shy from exercising their freedoms rather than facing potential punishment."[175] Although L'Heureux-Dube seems to be moving toward an American approach in her discussion of vagueness, she diverges from the American path when it comes to the question of the law being narrowly tailored. In American jurisprudence, a law must be narrowly tailored to meet a substantial government interest. In Canada, the Court uses the term "minimal impairment" instead of "narrowly tailored," such that to be valid a law must only minimally impair an individual's right of expression. But L'Heureux-Dube rejected a strict application of the minimal impairment standard in cases where the law only indirectly affected speech. If the government's purposes were legitimate and the measure was reasonable in the circumstances, then the standard of minimal impairment need not be applied, she held. To hold otherwise, she said, would mean the government would never be able to legislate in areas that indirectly affected speech. Unlike the American justices, then, L'Heureux-Dube takes a practical approach to government, suggesting that the Court is willing to defer to the legislature when the law appears not to have been aimed directly at speech.

The same sentiment was expressed by Justice Beverly McLachlin. She too said the minimal impairment rule should not be applied strictly. A law should not be struck down simply because the Court could think of a way to make it less restrictive, she held. The Court had to take into account legislators' difficulty in drafting generally applicable laws. For McLachlin, the purpose of freedom of expression under the Charter was to permit members of society to communicate their ideas and values to others. Expression going beyond this purpose should not be protected. To hold otherwise, she argued, would oblige the state "to defend in the courts its restriction of expression which [sic] does not raise the values and interests traditionally associated with the free speech guarantee. Indeed, a failure to invest s. 2(b) with meaningful content . . . threatens to trivialize the Charter guarantee of free expression."[176] The statement reveals McLachlin's idealism in her deference to the state.

When the Canadian justices were faced with virtually identical facts to an American case, their view of the individual and the state put them in direct opposition to the American Supreme Court's decision. In *Lavigne v. O.P.S.E.U.*, the issue was whether a non-member's dues could be used by a union for activities other than collective bargaining purposes.[177] In support of his position that the activities of the union violated his rights of association and freedom of expression, Lavigne relied on the American case of *Abood v. Detroit Board of Education*.[178]

The U.S. Supreme Court in *Abood* viewed the payment of union dues as compelled expression of political views and recognized a right not to associate. Justice Bertha Wilson in Canada, however, argued that the right of association protected by section 2(d) of the Charter was restricted to positive association rights.[179] The purpose of freedom of association was to recognize the social nature of humans and to protect individuals from state-enforced isolation, she held. Freedom of association protected the collective pursuit of common goals. To hold otherwise would trivialize the right, she wrote. Wilson acknowledged that financial support was a form of expression as was refusing to provide financial support. But compelled financial support did not necessarily violate freedom of expression. Lavigne was free to speak his mind on any issue, she argued. He had in fact deliberately chosen not to join the union and in so doing had forfeited his rights to complain about how the union was spending his dues.

While agreeing with the outcome, Justice LaForest, joined by Justices John Sopinka and Gonthier, said that the freedom to associate necessarily included within it the freedom not to associate. The essence of the right of association was the protection of the individual's interest in self-actualization and fulfillment that could only be realized through combining with others. Although meant to protect collectivity, freedom of association ultimately furthered individual goals, he held, because at the core of the guarantee of association was the individual's freedom to choose the path to self-actualization. It was an aspect of an individual's autonomy, and forced association would stifle an individual's potential for self-fulfillment and realization as surely as voluntary association would develop it, he argued. Having said that, however, LaForest made clear freedom of association was not a right of isolation. He said he did not wish to suggest that individuals could opt out of the necessary and inevitable associations of a democratic society, such as the family, the workplace, and citizenship. In the case at hand, he noted, the compelled association was tempered by the fact that the union was organized on democratic principles.

Justice McLachlin also believed that freedom of association protected the right of individuals to realize their full potential by acting in association with others. But for her, it was social self-actualization that lay at the heart of the freedom. Humans, she argued, were social animals and could fully actualize themselves only in interaction with others. Like LaForest, she was willing to accept a right not to associate but held that its purpose was to protect individuals against enforced ideological conformity, and that was not the case here.

Although the facts in *Lavigne* are in all important respects identical to those in *Abood*, the Canadian and American courts came to different conclusions. The Canadian justices themselves accounted for the difference on the basis that in the United States there is no explicit right of association found in the Bill of Rights. The American Court has developed the right as a derivative of the right of freedom of expression. Therefore, the justices in *Abood* framed the issue in terms of compelled speech. In Canada, on the other hand, the right of association is specifically protected in section 2(d) of the Charter. Freedom of association, in Canada, therefore, exists separate from the right of freedom of expression. Presumably, the Canadian Court was arguing that because the right of association in the United States is tied to freedom of expression and freedom of expression is given a preferred position by the Court, the American Court had no choice but to find against the union. But since freedom of expression is not given a preferred position in Canada anyway, it is not clear why the Court felt obliged to go to such lengths to point out the differences between the rights in the two countries.

A more compelling justification for the difference in the outcomes is the different attitudes toward democracy. In *Abood*, Justice Lewis Powell Jr., for example, argued that a union was not democratic because unlike governments that are representative of the people, a union is representative of only one segment of the population. The key to the case for all of the Canadian justices, on the other hand, was that the union was organized on democratic principles. Lavigne could have had a voice in the union if he had chosen to become a member. Because he did not take advantage of that option, he could not complain when the union supported issues with which he did not agree. In Canada, in the Court's view, it is the individual who must be responsible enough to take action and participate in society. The same sentiment can be found in a case involving the Native Women's Association of Canada (NWAC).

The NWAC argued that its freedom of expression was being infringed because the government of Canada chose to fund four native groups but not the NWAC. The groups were being funded to consider the issue of aboriginal self-government in Canada and to attend constitutional debates. The NWAC claimed the four groups were male-dominated, against equality for women, and did not speak on behalf of native women. At issue was whether the government of Canada had a positive duty to fund freedom of expression.

Writing for the majority, Justice Sopinka held that the evidence did not support the NWAC's position and that the government did not have to automatically consult groups of the opposite perspective just because it consulted one group. Section 2(b) of the Charter did not guarantee any particular means of expression or place a positive obligation upon the government to consult anyone. Again, there is idealism's deference to the state, implying faith in the state and the unity of state and society.

Justice L'Heureux-Dube in her concurring opinion agreed that the government had no positive obligation to the NWAC in this case but did not rule out the possibility that the government might bear such an obligation in the future. Traditionally, freedom of expression had been discussed in terms of "freedom from" government interference, she noted. But a philosophy of non-interference may not in all circumstances guarantee the optimal functioning of the marketplace of ideas. She could envision situations in which speakers were being effectively denied their right of freedom of expression and needed the help of the government to exercise their right. In such a situation, the government would then be required to facilitate expression in a manner consistent with the Charter.

On the flip-side of the money and politics issue was the case of *Libman v. Quebec (A.G.)*.[180] The question was whether provincial limits on expenses incurred during referendums infringed a group's freedom of expression. A unanimous Court held that the limits furthered political expression by ensuring equal dissemination of information. The object of the act was to guarantee the democratic nature of referendums by promoting equality among the options submitted by the government and free and informed voting. It was designed, the Court held, to promote electoral fairness and flowed from the principle of the political equality of citizens. Limits on spending were to ensure a right of equal participation in democratic government and furthered the ability to make informed choices, an objective underlying freedom of expression.

In commenting on the Court's role in constitutional cases, the Court said it would give great deference to the legislature in cases where the legislature had to reconcile competing interests. Where, however, government played the role of the singular antagonist to the individual, the Court would judge the legislature more harshly. The latter situations arose primarily in criminal law, the Court noted, and courts were specialists in protecting liberty and interpreting legislation but not in policymaking. In the case at hand, the legislature had to strike a balance between freedom of individual expression and equality among different expression for the benefit of all.

Despite the Court's desire to encourage informed decision-making, it was not unanimous in deciding whether restrictions on the reporting of polls prior to elections was constitutional. Under the Federal Elections Act, polls could not be reported on within the seventy-two hours preceding an election. In his dissent, Justice Gonthier, joined by Justices Lamer and L'Heureux-Dube, argued that some voters used polls to make decisions even though those polls could be inaccurate, misrepresented, and misunderstood. Voters needed time to discuss and scrutinize information, but the closer to the election day, the less time there was to assess, scrutinize, and correct polls. The purpose of the act, then, was to improve information to the public during election campaigns. Gonthier disliked the idea that the Charter was being made to, in his eyes, further substantial commercial interests in publishing opinion poll results by defeating a reasonable attempt by Parliament to allay potential distortion of voter choice. The legislators, not the courts, were in the best position to decide the effect of polls. Everyone was vulnerable to misinformation that could not be verified, and the democratic process cared about each voter, he argued.

Justice Bastarache, on behalf of the majority, on the other hand, reveals a more rights-based philosophy. He argued that the dissenters treated Canadian voters as naive. He argued that there could be some Canadian voters who relied on inaccurate polling to base their voting decision, but he preferred to assume that Canadians had a certain degree of maturity and intelligence and that they would not be so naive as to forget issues. In previous cases in which the Court protected certain groups of Canadians, Bastarache noted, it did so on the belief that Canadians widely accepted as facts that certain expression was harmful. Thus, the Court felt it could protect historically disadvantaged groups, such as blacks and women, from the effects of hate speech and pornography, for example, although there was no scientific basis establishing harm, because Canadians commonly believed such expression to cause harm. But Canadian voters were not historically disadvantaged, Bastarache held.

The two cases in this period that clearly point out the differences between the American and Canadian view of the individual involved civil and criminal libel. In the civil libel case of *Hill v. Church of Scientology*,[181] the Court refused to follow the U.S. Supreme Court's decision in *New York Times v. Sullivan*[182] and constitutionalize libel law, and it refused to adopt the American actual malice standard as the common law standard, even though Hill would have been considered a public official in the United States.

At the time the defamatory statements were made, Hill was a crown attorney, the equivalent of a district attorney, investigating criminal charges against the Church of Scientology. At a press conference, the Church's attorney made defamatory statements about Hill that were not true. Before the Court, the Church argued that the proper standard to be applied in the case was the actual malice standard. In rejecting this approach, Justice Peter Cory, speaking for the Court, noted that an individual's reputation could not be divided into two parts, one related to personal life and the other related to employment. "Reputation is an integral and fundamentally important aspect of every individual. It exists for everyone quite apart from employment," Cory wrote.[183] The Church had impugned "the character, competence, and integrity" of Hill himself, not the government.

Justice Cory noted that little had been written about the value of reputation but insisted that reputation was the most cherished value of all. A good reputation was related to the innate worthiness and dignity of the individual, he wrote. Democracy had always recognized and cherished the fundamental importance of the individual and that importance had to be based on the individual's good reputation. Libel was an invasion of privacy and an affront to individual dignity. It was not expecting too much of people, Cory continued, to expect they would ascertain the truth of their statements. The laws of civil libel simply demanded a reasonable level of responsibility. Cory's statements reveal his idealist roots. Under idealism, the individual is defined in terms of the society. Therefore, the society's views about the individual affects that individual's ability to achieve self-fulfillment through society. The emphasis on society is also reflected in Cory's desire to hold individuals accountable for their speech. The individual has a right to speak but has a duty to do so in a way that does not harm society. The same sentiments were expressed by the Court in a criminal libel case. The Criminal Code of Canada provides:

> 298.(1) A defamatory libel is matter published, without lawful justification or excuse, that is likely to injure the reputation of any person by exposing him to hatred, contempt or ridicule, or that is designed to insult the person of or concerning whom it is published.
> (2) A defamatory libel may be expressed directly or by insinuation or irony
> (a) in words legibly marked on any substance; or
> (b) by any object signifying a defamatory libel otherwise than by words.
> 299. A person publishes a libel when he
> (a) exhibits it in public;
> (b) causes it to be read or seen; or
> (c) shows or delivers it, or causes it to be shown or delivered, with intent that it should be read or seen by the person whom it defames or by any other person.
> 300. Every one who publishes a defamatory libel that he knows is false is guilty of an indictable offence and liable to imprisonment for a term not exceeding five years.[184]

In *R. v. Lucas*, Lucas and his wife were convicted of criminal libel for demonstrating in front of a police station with placards accusing a police officer of failing to investigate a child sexual abuse case.[185] The placards also suggested that the officer himself had engaged in sexual abuse of children. None of the allegations was true. In upholding the constitutionality of the criminal libel sections,[186] Justice Cory again revealed his idealist roots, saying that protection of an individual's reputation for willful and false attack recognized both the innate dignity of the individual and the integral link between reputation and meaningful participation of the individual in Canadian society.

For Cory, the existence of criminal, as well as civil, libel showed that Parliament believed individuals who willfully and knowingly published lies about others deserved to be punished. He thus reinforced the notion of rights and duties. The principal object of criminal law was the recognition of society's abhorrence of a criminal act. Criminal law treated all offenses as offenses against society. It was important, Cory said, that society discourage the intentional publication of lies targeted to expose another individual to hatred and contempt. The criminal sanctions against libel were justified because the harm it caused was so grievous. Justice Cory noted that individuals such as police officers and social workers who were particularly vulnerable to defamatory statements especially needed the protection of the criminal law because often those libeling them did not have the funds to satisfy a civil judgment. Therefore, such individuals would be left without recourse if the criminal section were found to be unconstitutional. Giving protection to defamatory libel, Justice Cory held, would trivialize and demean freedom of expression.

It can be seen from an examination of the pre- and post-Charter cases in this period that at least in the area of political speech, the Canadian justices exhibit a consistency in their conception of the individual, the state, and their relationship. Individuals are seen as accountable for their actions and responsible to others for the effect of those actions. At the same time, there is virtually no evidence of distrust of the state, as is found in the American cases. The state is seen as a mechanism or instrument to further society by ensuring individuals are held accountable to others. The state is also seen as part of society in the sense that the Court recognized it is made up of individuals whom the Court assumed are doing the best they can. Although there is a classical republican emphasis on institutions and the maintenance of faith in those institutions, the purpose of the institutions does not seem to be the prevention of corruption as it is in traditional classical republican thought. The case law in this period lends support to Leslie Armour's argument that idealism is deep-rooted in the Canadian psyche. It also reflects the emphasis on community, diversity, and the state found in both Armour's work and that of the conservative Charles Taylor.

SUMMARY OF FINDINGS AND CONCLUSION

At issue in the last quarter of the twentieth century for the political thinkers in both Canada and the United States was how best to balance the interests of the individual and society and what role the state should play in achieving that balance. There was a reaction against the individualism of the 1960s and early 1970s in which self-interest and material well-being were perceived as the highest values.

In the United States, the response came in a conservative shift. Some intellectuals argued that morals and values had to be reconnected to politics for social unity. Others sought to redefine the state in negative terms if freedom were to be achieved. And still others sought a greater sense of justice and a more participatory democracy. Canadian political thinkers were grappling with the same issues in this period. Passage of the Canadian Charter of Rights and Freedoms in 1982 was both heralded and criticized as a movement by Canada toward American rights-based liberalism. At the same time, however, Canadian political thought continued to emphasize community and society.

While the majority of the political speech cases in the first three-quarters of the century involved threats to either democracy or social stability, especially in the United States, the cases in the period from 1975 to 1999 dealt with issues of core political speech. And the cases point out more clearly than do the cases in any of the earlier periods the deep-rooted differences between the United States and Canada in terms of how the individual, the state, and their relationship are conceptualized.

The American cases in this period reflect the conservative shift of the political thinkers but, at the same time, reveal a Court that has no dominant political philosophy. The competing philosophies of classical liberalism, modern liberalism, and classical republicanism combine with each other depending on the issues involved. Overall, however, the Court seems to conceptualize individuals as autonomous. Even the classical republicans who favor community do not put society ahead of the individual in the way that the Canadian judges do. Despite the relative faith in individuals and their ability to reason, the Court exhibits a distrust of the state and by extension individuals. Again, even the classical republicans who generally are more democratic than classical liberals are concerned with the prevention of corruption.

In comparison, the Canadian Court appears to have more faith in society and the state. It is remarkably consistent in attitude toward the individual and the state in the pre-and post-Charter cases. The justices exhibit characteristics of pragmatist and classical republican thought, but those characteristics are heavily tempered by idealism. Individuals are seen as accountable for their actions and responsible to others for the effect of those actions. At the same time, there is virtually no evidence of distrust of the state, as is found in the American cases. The state is seen as a mechanism or instrument to further society by ensuring individuals are held accountable to others. The state is also seen as part of society in the sense that the Court viewed government as consisting of individuals. Although there is a classical republican emphasis on institutions and the maintenance of faith in those institutions, the purpose of the institutions does not seem to be the prevention of corruption as it is in the traditional republican thought.

CHAPTER 7
Conclusion

In working democracies, a tension exists between liberty—the desire of individuals to freely express themselves without fear of government interference—and authority—the desire of the state to restrict expression to protect public safety and welfare. Legal scholar Pnina Lahav has described this tension as the key to understanding the law of freedom of expression in democracies. Focusing on freedom of the press, Lahav has theorized that the press law of a country is determined by the political philosophy of that country. In other words, how the tension between liberty and authority is resolved in a democracy depends on how the political thought of the country conceptualizes the individual, the state, and their relationship.

MAJOR TRENDS IN POLITICAL THOUGHT IN THE UNITED STATES AND CANADA

In the United States, the major trend in political thought in the last half of the nineteenth century was individualism. Individuals were seen as discrete, rational beings. Society was composed of autonomous individuals who had contracted together for their own protection. The role of the state was restricted to the protection of individuals from the actions of others and the maintenance of order.

But during the progressive era from 1900 to 1920, the political thought of the United States underwent a shift toward more government intervention and away from strict individualism. The dominant political thought was pragmatism. Pragmatists continued to see individuals as autonomous but recognized that individuals existed in a community and that their actions affected others. The role of the state was to assist in promoting the betterment of society through the implementation of workable solutions to what were now seen as social problems.

Following World War I, the focus of American thought shifted back to the individual, but no one political philosophy was dominant. Individuals were no longer considered rational although they were seen as capable of reason. There was a tendency in the political thought to view democracy less idyllically than in the past. The democratic state was seen as maintaining power through coercion and emotion, rather than by reason.

The diversity among individuals that troubled the political thinkers following World War I was seen as the strength of American society after World War II. The dominant political thought was pluralism, grounded in relativism. For pluralists, the basis of democracy in the United States was competitive minority interest groups. Underlying American democracy was a culture that valued diversity and openness and that was held together by a foundation of homogeneity. There was a heavy emphasis on shared values and beliefs. Like the pragmatists before them, the pluralists saw the state as a mechanism to promote and further equality. They also continued the pragmatic elitist approach to individuals, believing them to be malleable and susceptible to social engineering.

By the mid-1960s, however, the political thinkers were reacting against the behavioralist concept of the individual as socially constructed. These intellectuals sought to re-emphasize the individual and the notion of self-fulfillment found in the political thought of individualism. The change in the conception of the individual produced a corresponding change in the conception of the state. The state was seen as a mechanism to assist the individual in achieving self-fulfillment rather than as an association through which interest groups sought power, as the pluralist liberals saw it. By the last quarter of the twentieth century, the political thought took a conservative shift. Some intellectuals argued that morals and values had to be reconnected to politics for social unity. Others sought to redefine the state in negative terms if freedom were to be achieved. And still others sought a greater sense of justice and a more participatory democracy.

In Canada, in the last half of the nineteenth century, the dominant political thought was idealism, which viewed society as an organic whole. Individuals were part of that whole but had no identity separate from their existence in society. It was through their self-identification with society that individuals could realize themselves and achieve a higher moral life. Individuals were autonomous to the extent they had a duty to themselves and society to seek a higher moral life.

Although there was a movement toward reform and government intervention from 1900 to 1920, the dominant political thought remained idealism in Canada until near the end of World War I. The political thinkers became disillusioned with idealism and its reification of the state during the War. They sought then to reconceptualize the state and give greater autonomy to individuals. The answer was socialized individualism. Under socialized individualism, the state was a corporation that operated within society as an agent of society to maintain its unity and cohesiveness. But the unity of society depended ultimately on the individual, who by nature was both autonomous and a seeker of harmony.

After World War II, Canadians were increasingly influenced by the United States, resulting in a focus on civil liberties. Conservative political thinkers lamented the movement toward the mass society and away from the idealist sense of community. Left-wing intellectuals put greater emphasis on individual rights and saw the state as a mechanism to promote the well-being of the individual. The focus on individual rights culminated in passage of the Canadian Charter of Rights and Freedoms in 1982. The Charter was both heralded and criticized as a movement by Canada toward American rights-based liberalism. At the same time, however, Canadian political thought continued to emphasize community and society, as it had from the days of idealism.

The most striking differences between the Canadian and American political thought in this period are evident in the themes that stretch the entire century. In the United States, individuals and their autonomy have always been the focus. Although it was acknowledged at the turn of the century that individuals could not be discrete and that their actions did affect others, individuals continue to be seen as autonomous, and society to be seen for the most part as a means to allow individuals to fulfill themselves. The state's role, whether limited or interventionist, changes according to how the American political thinkers believe individuals can best achieve self-actualization. In Canada, on the other hand, community and society take precedence over the individual. The individual is seen as achieving self-actualization only through society. The individual owes a duty to society to seek self-fulfillment. Perhaps because of the emphasis on society, the state is seen as more benevolent than it is in the United States. In Canada, the state is a mechanism whose purpose is to further society and ensure its smooth operation. In the United States, the state's role is to ensure individuals have the freedom to achieve their own version of the good life.

Despite their differences, the political thought of the two countries does share some similarities. The thinkers in both countries are attempting to find ways to promote the good life. Both moved from extreme positions, individualism and idealism, toward a balancing of the interests of the individual and society. Although they appeared initially to be getting closer together because they were moving toward a balance, they now appear to be on parallel tracks. They have each struck the balance between the individual and society in a way that is compatible with their initial starting points. That is, the American political thought weights the scale slightly in favor of the individual and the Canadian political thought weights the scale slightly in favor of society. To use language from First Amendment theory, one gives the individual a preferred position, the other gives a preferred position to society.

Perhaps not surprisingly given their geographic proximity and their similar legal and political traditions, the two countries have influenced each other in terms of political thought. Much of the Canadian political thought is a reaction against what the thinkers perceived as happening in the United States. Conservatives such as George Grant, for example, lamented the movement of Canada toward American rights-based liberalism. Other political thinkers took a cue from the American political thought and pushed for individual rights. Passage of the Charter of Rights and Freedoms in 1982 is evidence of the American influence in that regard. A reciprocal influence is not found in the American political thought although American thinkers did react to the 1960s writings of Canadian C.B. Macpherson who criticized the United States for its possessive individualism.

THE CORRELATION BETWEEN POLITICAL THOUGHT AND FREEDOM OF EXPRESSION LAW

The American cases in the period 1900 to 1920 reflect a conservatism on the part of the justices and a reliance on late eighteenth-early nineteenth century political thought. The justices favored the rule of law and sought to preserve government institutions against the threats of individuals. In contrast, the dissenting justices at the beginning of the period used individualism and the doctrine of natural rights to uphold freedom of expression. By the end of the period, pragmatism could be found in the dissenting opinions. These justices called for a balancing of the interests of the individual and society and questioned the notion of an absolute truth. They saw freedom of expression as a social right necessary to further the betterment of society.

The Canadian cases also reflected nineteenth century thought in the first two decades of the twentieth century, specifically idealism. Idealism was used to restrict the individual's right to freedom of expression on the basis that the restriction was required by society. At the same time, early in the period, the courts described freedom of expression as an individual right, reflecting the influence of the British constitutional, liberal tradition on Canadian thought. By the end of the period, some of the judges reflected the progressive thought in Canada, which called for a balancing of individual and societal interests, and upheld freedom of expression on the grounds that not every statement against society warranted restriction.

In the 1920s and early 1930s, the majority of political speech cases pitted the disenchanted, such as Communists and the unemployed, against governments that sought to preserve the status quo. The American justices in the period revealed a conservative, classical republican political philosophy dating from the previous century. At the same time in Canada, the judges in the lower courts reflected the traditional idealism of that country.

From the early 1930s on, the American justices revealed a pragmatic political philosophy. The lone Supreme Court case in Canada suggested that the Canadian justices were perhaps moving by 1938 toward the then contemporary notion of socialized individualism. Both high courts saw freedom of expression as a social right that was essential to the democratic process.

The Canadian justices tended not to reflect the relativist/absolutist debate of the 1940s and 1950s in their opinions, but the American justices did. Many of the American justices in the period could be clearly identified as relativist or absolutist. The importance of the debate to freedom of expression is that relativism supported the use of a balancing approach to First Amendment cases, meaning less protection for speech. While the majority of the justices in the period held a liberal political philosophy, either classical liberal, pragmatic, or relativist, only the classical liberals, with their fear of the state and their faith in individuals, were consistently in favor of freedom of expression. Pragmatists, with their questioning of absolute truths, had been supportive of freedom of expression in the 1920s and 1930s. But their belief in balancing interests, along with the addition of pragmatists and relativists who had conservative outlooks, led to less support for freedom of expression in this period. The more conservative justices

Conclusion

were willing to defer to Congress when it came to subversive speech or speech that threatened the overthrow of the government.

The emphasis on the individual found in the political thought in the 1960s was reflected in the political speech cases in both Canada and the United States. Freedom of expression was seen as furthering the individual right of self-fulfillment as well as the social right of political participation. In the United States, the majority of judges were classical liberals or pragmatists.

In Canada, only two political speech cases came before the Court in the 1960s and early 1970s. In these, the justices exhibited an emphasis on the individual although speech continued to be considered a social right. Because the right was seen as belonging to society as a whole and not the individual, the majority of the Court permitted the state to protect the individual from abuses of the social right by interest groups, such as unions.

While the majority of the political speech cases in the first three-quarters of the century involved threats to either democracy or social stability, especially in the United States, the cases in the period from 1975 to 1999 dealt with issues of core political speech. And the cases point out more clearly than do the cases in any of the earlier periods the deep-rooted differences between the United States and Canada in terms of how the individual, the state, and their relationship are conceptualized.

The American cases in this period reflect the conservative shift of the political thinkers but, at the same time, reveal a Court that has no dominant political philosophy. The competing philosophies of classical liberalism, modern liberalism, and republicanism combine with each other depending on the issues involved. Overall, however, the Court seems to conceptualize individuals as autonomous and exhibits a distrust of the state.

The Canadian Court is remarkably consistent in attitude toward the individual and the state in the pre-and post-Charter cases. Individuals are seen as accountable for their actions and responsible to others for the effect of those actions. The state is viewed as a mechanism or instrument to further society by ensuring individuals are held accountable to others. The state is also seen as part of society in the sense that the court viewed government as consisting of individuals.

It is possible to conclude from this study that there is a correlation between political thought and freedom of expression law. Political thought was implicitly, and on occasion explicitly, reflected in the political speech cases in both countries, but there were greater shifts in the political thought than there were in judicial decision-making. The political thinkers in each period reacted to events, such as wars and civil unrest, by attempting to reconceptualize the individual, the state, and/or their relationship. While the justices certainly reacted to those events as well, they appeared to be more consistent in their political philosophy.

For example, the civil unrest of the 1960s affected Justice Hugo L. Black. He reacted negatively to the protesters and demonstrators and sought to restrict their freedom of expression. But in doing so he remained true to his classical liberal political philosophy. The facts of the cases coming before him do not appear to have made him rethink how he viewed the individual. Rather, he drew on different aspects of his political philosophy to justify his position. In the subversive cases, he permitted the speech by emphasizing his faith in the American people that they would not adopt the ideas advocated. In the reflexive cases, he upheld restrictions on the speech by emphasizing the rule of law and by declaring the actions of the speaker to be conduct.

Although the shifts in concepts were greater in the political thought, the philosophy of the courts in both countries did follow the pattern of the political thought, usually lagging behind it by a decade or two. For example, pragmatism developed in the United States in the period 1900 to 1920, and from 1937 to 1945 the majority of Supreme Court justices were pragmatists. In Canada, the Court followed the political thought, exhibiting characteristics of first idealism and then socialized individualism.

There were justices in each period whose political philosophy was very close to the contemporary political thought. Usually these justices were found on the dissent until new justices were appointed.

Conclusion 217

For example, Justice Rand on the Canadian Court exhibited characteristics of socialized individualism on an otherwise idealist bench. His dissenting opinion in *Boucher v. The King* was later accepted as the majority opinion when more justices were appointed who shared his political thought.[1] Similarly, Justice Brandeis with his pragmatic views found himself on the dissenting side in freedom of expression cases until more pragmatists were appointed. Between 1945 and the mid-1950s, the U.S. Supreme Court was actually ahead of the political thought in discussing American society in terms of a consensus and referring to the "genius" of the Constitution. From this study it cannot be determined whether the Court influenced the political thought in this regard because the political thinkers do not refer to the Court as a source for their ideas.

Differences in the political thought of American and Canadian justices has resulted in differences in freedom of expression law in areas such as freedom of the press and libel law. It has also resulted in different arguments being relied on by the justices to justify their decisions and a difference in the way the concepts of rights and truth are discussed. Different political philosophies on the part of justices on the same court can also account for differing opinions in individual cases.

At the heart of the different philosophies is the conceptualization of the individual and the state. The strongest supporters of freedom of expression are those justices who have faith in the ability of individuals to reason, view the individual as autonomous, and have a distrust of the state.[2] Correspondingly, those justices who do not have faith in the ability of individuals to reason, see individuals in terms of society, and do not distrust the state support an individual's right to freedom of expression the least.[3] Between these two, fall the majority of justices, varying in the degree of faith they have in the individual and in the state and in the degree of autonomy they grant the individual. Overall, the American Court had greater faith in the individual and a distrust of the state than did the Canadian Court, which tended to defer to the state to promote society.

The difference in the attitude toward the state and the individual can be seen, for example, in the cases dealing with freedom of the press and with libel. In the United States, the media were seen as fulfilling a vital function in the working of a democracy. Because of their distrust of the state, the justices had a tendency to protect the media when they sought to criticize the government and get information to the people. The Canadian cases reflect the opposite result. The Canadian Supreme Court was less supportive of press rights, at least in libel cases, than it was of speech rights. Criticism of politicians threatened the democratic process because it would keep the best individuals from seeking office, essentially a conservative position that reflected the Court's idealist roots.

The Canadian Court refused to adopt the American actual malice standard in libel cases in part because of the importance of the individual's reputation. Individuals are defined in relation to society; therefore, society's view of an individual affects that individual's ability to seek fulfillment. Individuals have the right to speak, but they are to be held accountable for what they say to harm another's reputation. This notion that rights have corresponding duties has a long tradition in Canada and fits with the concept of the individual as a component part of society. Individuals have rights, but they have a duty to exercise those rights in a way that will not harm society.

The concept of duty is not found in the American cases. Freedom of expression cases are framed in terms of the individual versus the state as opposed to the individual versus society. In libel cases involving public officials, for example, the American Court places no emphasis on the individual speaker's accountability. The Court is more concerned with information flow regarding the actions of public officials than with an individual's reputation. Because the state must be constantly watched for abuses of power, getting information about the state to the public, even information that later turns out to be incorrect, is vitally important.

This distrust of the state and the emphasis on information flow can be seen in the traditional American justifications for freedom of expression—the marketplace of ideas, the "slippery slope" argument, and the chilling effect. The notion of the marketplace of ideas depends on information getting out to the public. It is also tied to the concept of individuals as autonomous, rational beings in that individuals need this information to make reasoned decisions about how they want to live. Similarly, the "slippery slope" argument is tied to a distrust of the state. The argument is that once the state makes an incursion into the area of protected speech, it will make ever greater incursions. And once the state does infringe on freedom of expression, individuals will be chilled from speaking for fear of reprisals. Therefore, the state must be strictly limited at the outset to prevent future abridgement of speech rights and to ensure individuals are able to exercise their rights without fear.

None of these three justifications for freedom of expression are found in the Canadian cases. The state is not considered separate from society as it is in the United States, and therefore there is no fear that the state cannot be controlled and no need for the slippery slope argument. Neither is there a need for a marketplace of ideas concept because the individual seeks self-fulfillment through society. Individuals need information to determine what is best for the democracy as a whole, not what is best for them. Individuals are not seen as searching for "the truth," which is a central component of the marketplace of ideas. Although in the post-Charter cases, the Canadian Court referred to the attainment of truth as one of the justifications for protecting speech, the emphasis has never been on truth in the Canadian cases.

The American cases, on the other hand, do focus on truth. The marketplace of ideas is based on the notion that if all the information is presented, the truth will reveal itself. It was premised originally on the concept that an absolute truth was determinable. The concept of truth has gone through changes in American political thought. Within the time frame of this study, it was first seen as absolute, then for the pragmatists as a process of verification, and finally as relative. How the American justices conceptualized truth affected in part the level of protection they were willing to grant freedom of expression. It was the pragmatic notion of truth as process that provided Justices Louis Brandeis and Oliver Wendell Holmes Jr., for example, with the basis for their dissents in the early political speech cases. Brandeis and Holmes were unwilling to restrict the speakers' right to freedom of expression because their ideas could later turn out to be the truth. The justices who believed in an absolute truth, on the other hand, were satisfied that the speech was not true and therefore upheld its restriction.

Despite the differences between the political thought of the two countries overall, there were times when the justices shared similar political philosophies, producing similar results and when they held different philosophies but reached similar decisions using similar justifications. For example, in the 1920s and early 1930s, the justices in the United States revealed a conservative, classical republican political philosophy. At the same time in Canada, the judges in the lower courts reflected idealism. Under both philosophies, the maintenance of social order was paramount. For American justices, social order was necessary to preserve the status quo, while for Canadian judges, social order was the basic foundation of civil society. Implicit in both positions is an assumption that without organized society there would be anarchy.

From the 1930s until 1945, the American justices revealed a pragmatic political philosophy. The lone Supreme Court case in Canada suggested the justices were moving toward socialized individualism. Both high courts saw freedom of expression as a social right that was essential to the democratic process. Implicit in both positions is faith in individuals and their ability to reason. Thus despite the difference in their political philosophies—pragmatism versus socialized individualism—the justices reached similar results using similar justifications.

There was no evidence of Canadian influence on the American Court. The Canadian Court did look at American cases, but not until after passage of the Charter in 1982 and only then for guidance. The Canadian Court made clear its intention to keep a "made-in-Canada" approach. It chose to incorporate only those features of the American law that fit within the Court's political philosophy.

THE RESOLUTION OF THE TENSION BETWEEN LIBERTY AND AUTHORITY

From 1900 to 1920, then, the tension between liberty—the desire of individuals to freely express themselves without fear of government interference—and authority—the desire of the state to restrict expression to protect public safety and welfare—was resolved in favor of authority in both countries. The reliance on late eighteenth-early nineteenth century political thought on the part of the American judges and idealism on the part of the Canadian judges meant that speech critical of government institutions was suppressed because it threatened the peace, security, and order of society. Under these philosophies, the individual was subordinated to the right of government to protect society and other individuals.

From 1921 to 1945, however, the tension was resolved increasingly in favor of liberty in both countries. Underlying the movement toward liberty was a fundamental faith in the individual and in reason. Accordingly, as the justices moved from conservative, classical republicanism to pragmatism in the United States and from idealism to socialized individualism in Canada, the greater the protection for political speech grew.

But from 1946 to 1962, the tension was resolved in the United States in favor of authority. The primary reasons were the balancing approach used by the Court and the fear of communism. The positive aspects of the period, however, were the establishment by the classical liberals of such justifications for freedom of expression as the "slippery slope" and the chilling effect arguments. In Canada, the cases were split, and it cannot be said that the tension was resolved in favor of either liberty or authority. But the Court established strong precedents for the protection of freedom of expression in the future. Underlying the positive features in both countries was a fundamental faith in the individual. From 1963 to 1974, the tension was once again resolved for the most part in favor of liberty. And it was the emphasis on the dignity of the individual that permitted the tension to be resolved in that way.

In conclusion, how the tension between liberty—the desire of individuals to freely express themselves without fear of government interference—and authority—the desire of the state to restrict expression to protect public safety and welfare—is resolved depends in part on how the political thought of a country conceptualizes the individual, the state, and their relationship. The more faith placed in individuals and their autonomy and the more distrust of the state, the greater the protection for freedom of expression. The more individuals are seen as part of society and the more the state is trusted, the greater the restriction on expression for the protection of public safety and welfare.

Endnotes

CHAPTER 1

[1] Robert H. Bork, *Neutral Principles and Some First Amendment Problems*, 47 IND. L.J. 23 (1971).

[2] Pnina Lahav, Press Law in Modern Democracies 350 (1985).

[3] THOMAS I. EMERSON, TOWARD A GENERAL THEORY OF THE FIRST AMENDMENT 3 (1966).

[4] Ruth Walden, *A Government Action Approach to First Amendment Analysis*," 69 JOURNALISM Q. 66 note 5 (1992) (citing R.I. CORD, J.A. MEDEIROS, W.S. JONES, POLITICAL SCIENCE: AN INTRODUCTION 119 (1974)).

[5] "Public law principally pertains to the institutions of government—their operations and interactions with private citizens. Constitutional, administrative, and criminal law are major areas of public law. Private law, on the other hand, centers on relationships among private citizens such as commercial contracts and family disputes." HERBERT JACOB, LAW AND POLITICS IN THE UNITED STATES 34 (1986).

[6] LAHAV, *supra* note 2.

[7] *Id.* at 347.

[8] SEYMOUR MARTIN LIPSET, CONTINENTAL DIVIDE: THE VALUES AND INSTITUTIONS OF THE UNITED STATES AND CANADA xiii (1990).

[9] *See, e.g.*, Lewis R. Katz, *Reflections on Search and Seizure and Illegally Seized Evidence in Canada and the United States*, 3 CAN.-U.S. L.J. 103 (1980); Roger Gibbons, *The Impact of the American Constitution on Contemporary Canadian Constitutional Politics"* in THE CANADIAN AND

AMERICAN CONSTITUTIONS IN COMPARATIVE PERSPECTIVE 131 (Marian C. McKenna ed. 1993).

[10] KENT GREENAWALT, FIGHTING WORDS: INDIVIDUALS, COMMUNITIES, AND LIBERTIES OF SPEECH, 11 (1995).

[11] This definition of political speech is taken from Bork, *supra* note 1, and Lillian R. BeVier, *The First Amendment and Political Speech: An Inquiry Into the Substance and Limits of Principle*, 30 STANFORD L.R. 300 (1978). Unlike Bork and BeVier, however, this definition includes advocacy to violence because as Harry Kalven noted, "If a man is seriously enough at odds with the society to advocate violent overthrow, his speech has utility not because advocating violence is useful but because the premises underlying his call to action should be heard." HARRY KALVEN JR., A WORTHY TRADITION 120 (1988). Bork and BeVier exclude such speech on the grounds that it is inherently anti-democratic. In determining whether a case involves political speech, the intention of the speaker is considered. Therefore cases involving Jehovah's Witnesses, although important for establishing the boundaries of political speech, are excluded because the Witnesses were making statements on religious grounds, not political ones. Similarly, cases involving conscientious objectors are excluded.

[12] *See, e.g.*, EMERSON, *supra* note 3, ALEXANDER MEIKLEJOHN, FREE SPEECH AND ITS RELATION TO SELF-GOVERNMENT (1948).

[13] A Lexis/Nexis search of freedom of speech, freedom of expression, and freedom of the press from 1931 to 1949 revealed no Privy Council cases, although the Supreme Court of Canada dealt with the issue of press freedom at least three times in the same time period.

[14] For the purposes of this study, "individual right" refers to constitutional rights that protect individual interests from the government. It is used instead of "civil rights" or "civil liberties" because these terms have different meanings in Canada. In Canada, "civil rights" has been used traditionally to refer to private law, such as contract and tort law, while "civil liberties" or "human rights" are used to refer to constitutional rights. Robert A. Sedler, *Constitutional Protection of Individual Rights in Canada: The Impact of the New Canadian Charter of Rights and Freedoms*, 59 NOTRE DAME L. REV. 1207 at note 57 (1984).

[15] LIPSET, *supra* note 8, at xiv. *See also*, SEYMOUR MARTIN LIPSET, THE FIRST NEW NATION: THE UNITED STATES IN HISTORICAL AND COMPARATIVE

PERSPECTIVE (1963); SEYMOUR MARTIN LIPSET, REVOLUTION AND COUNTERREVOLUTION: CHANGE AND PERSISTENCE IN SOCIAL STRUCTURES (rev. ed. 1988).

[16] *Id.* at xiii. Although people living in either Canada or the United States may properly be called "Americans," for the purposes of this book, people living in the United States will be called Americans and people in Canada will be called Canadians.

[17] *Id.* at 2.

[18] *Id.* at 2-3. Katz, *supra* note 9, at 104.

[19] Ellis Katz & G. Alan Tarr, *Introduction, in* FEDERALISM AND RIGHTS x (Ellis Katz and G. Alan Tarr eds., 1996).

[20] The first constitutional document was the Royal Proclamation Act of 1763, which established British law in Quebec and created a General Assembly. The most recent is the Constitution Act, 1982.

[21] Douglas A. Alderson, *The Constitutionalization of Defamation: American and Canadian Approaches to the Constitutional Regulation of Speech*, 15 ADVOC. Q. 396 (1993).

[22] *Id.* at 397.

[23] Richard A. Preston, *Introduction, in* PERSPECTIVES ON REVOLUTION AND EVOLUTION 7 (Richard A. Preston ed., 1979).

[24] Seymour Martin Lipset, *Revolution and Counterrevolution—Some Comments at a Conference Analyzing the Bicentennial of a Celebrated North American Divorce, in* PERSPECTIVES ON REVOLUTION, *supra* note 23, at 22, 29, 31.

[25] LIPSET, *supra* note 8, at 8, 14.

[26] *Id.* at xiii. The British North America Act, 30 & 31 Vict., c. 3 (1867) (U.K.). The British North America Act is now officially known as the Constitution Act, 1867. For historical accuracy and to avoid confusion with the Constitution Act, 1982, it will be referred to in the text as the BNA Act.

[27] Jennifer Reid, *"A Society Made by History": The Mythic Sources of Identity in Canada*, 27 CAN. REV. AM. STUD. 4 (1997).

[28] In 1774, the Quebec Act replaced the General Assembly with an appointive council on which Catholics might serve and guaranteed the continuation of the French civil law in Quebec. Calvin R. Massey, *The Locus of Sovereignty: Judicial Review, Legislative Supremacy, and*

Federalism in the Constitutional Traditions of Canada and the United States, 1990 DUKE L. J. 1256-1257.

[29] Reid, *supra* note 27, at 5.

[30] *Id.* at 4.

[31] Katz, *supra* note 9, at 104. In this study, the U.S. "Constitution" will be capitalized because it refers to a specific document. The Canadian "constitution" will not be capitalized because it includes a collection of documents and an unwritten constitution.

[32] Jennifer Smith, *Canadian Confederation and the Influence of American Federalism, in* THE CANADIAN AND AMERICAN Constitutions, *supra* note 9, at 65. *See also,* Massey, *supra* note 28, at 1238; William Eaton, *Canadian Judicial Review and the Federal Distribution of Power,* 7 AM. J. COMP. L. 48 (1958); William R. McKercher, *The United States Bill of Rights: Implications for Canada, in* THE U.S. BILL OF RIGHTS AND THE CANADIAN CHARTER OF RIGHTS AND FREEDOMS 7, 11 (William McKercher ed., 1983).

[33] Smith, *supra,* at 66.

[34] *Id.* at 72; Eaton, *supra* note 32, at 48. Canadian historian Robert C. Vipond argued that the Canadians actually favored a federalism close to that expressed by James Madison and that they were attempting to avoid John Calhoun's states rights view of federalism. Robert C. Vipond, *1787 and 1867: The Federal Principle and Canadian Confederation Reconsidered,* 22 CAN. J. POL. SCI. 5 (1989).

[35] Marian C. McKenna, *Introduction, in* THE CANADIAN AND AMERICAN CONSTITUTIONS, *supra* note 9, at xvi.

[36] LIPSET, *supra* note 8, at 43.

[37] Massey, *supra* note 28, at 1258.

[38] DOUGLAS V. VERNEY, THREE CIVILIZATIONS, TWO CULTURES, ONE STATE: CANADA'S POLITICAL TRADITION 20 (1986).

[39] Eaton, *supra* note 32, at 48. Can. Statutes 28 Vict., c. 11.

[40] *Id.* at 47.

[41] *Id.* at 51-52.

[42] *Id.* at 52.

[43] *Id.* at 55-56. Massey argued that the Privy Council's decisions produced a shift in the baseline presumption. Rather than starting from the presumption that section 91 vests a general legislative power in the federal

Endnote 227

government and then determining what remains of provincial authority, the process is reversed. An equivalent but opposite shift has occurred in American constitutional law. American courts proceed from the presumption that the states may legislate in only those domains the national government leaves untouched. Massey concluded that "the courts of the two nations act as if they were interpreting their neighbor's constitution." Massey, *supra* note 28, at 1265.

[44] Kenneth M. Holland, *Federalism in a North American Context: The Contribution of the Supreme Courts of Canada, the United States and Mexico*, in THE CANADIAN AND AMERICAN CONSTITUTION, *supra* note 9, at 87, 88.

[45] Massey, *supra* note 28, at 1265.

[46] *Id.* at 1230.

[47] Holland, *supra* note 44, at 91. *See also* Massey, *supra*, at 1230.

[48] *See, e.g.*, LIPSET, *supra* note 8; Katz, *supra* note 9; Alan F. Westin, The *United States Bill of Rights and the Canadian Charter: A Socio-Political Analysis*, in THE U.S. BILL OF RIGHTS, *supra* note 31, at 27; F.L. Morton, *The Politics of Rights: What Canadians Should Know About the American Bill of Rights*, in THE CANADIAN AND AMERICAN CONSTITUTION, *supra* note 9, at 107.

[49] Peter Brett, *Reflections on the Canadian Bill of Rights*, 7 ALTA. L. REV. 302 (1969).

[50] Westin, *supra* note 48, at 34.

[51] Katz, *supra* note 9, at 104.

[52] *Id.* at 104-105; Westin, *supra* note 48, at 38, LIPSET, *supra* note 8, at xiii.

[53] Westin, *supra*, at 38; Katz, *supra* note 9, at 105.

[54] Massey, *supra* note 28, at 1301.

[55] McKercher, *supra* note 32, at 9. According to Westin, "This negative orientation toward government illustrates the kind of political ideology that is fundamental to understanding the American civil liberties experience." Westin, *supra* note 48, at 31.

[56] Leonard H. Leigh, *Civil Liberties and the Canadian Constitution*, 1 ALTA. L. REV. 305 (1958).

[57] *Id.* at 304.

[58] LIPSET, *supra* note 8, at 14.

[59] *Id.*

[60] *Id.* at 93

[61] *Id.* These models were developed by Professor Herb Packer, *The Courts, The Police and the Rest of Us*, 57 J. CRIM. L. COMP. & POL. SCI. 238 (1966) and are also referred to in Katz, *supra* note 9, at 108.

[62] LIPSET, *supra* note 8, at 92.

[63] Douglas A. Schmeiser, *The Role of the Court in Shaping the Relationship of the Individual to the State, the Canadian Supreme Court*, 3 CAN.-U.S. L.J. 67 (1980).

[64] *Id.* at 68. The BNA Act did not contain limitations on the exercise of power within each level of government, except to the extent that the Act divided powers between the two levels of government; therefore, it provided courts with no legal basis for overriding otherwise valid government action that interfered with individual rights. In practice, however, the Canadian courts were able to protect individual rights by holding that the legislature was legislating in an area outside the scope of its powers. Sedler, *supra* note 14, at 1193, 1203.

[65] Schmeiser, *supra* note 63, at 67.

[66] *Id.* Holland accounted for the shift in the Canadian court's perspective during the 1970s as a move to appease the province of Quebec. During the period 1960 to 1975, the provinces, led by Quebec, began to agitate for decentralization. Quebec demanded the constitutional room that would allow a positive role for the provincial government in secularizing and modernizing its society. The court responded favorably in the early seventies although it remained centrist with respect to the rest of the provinces. Holland, *supra* note 44, at 93.

[67] *See also*, Madame Justice Claire L'Heureux-Dubé, Two Supreme Courts: A Study in Contrasts, *in* THE CANADIAN AND AMERICAN CONSTITUTION, *supra* note 9, at 149, 150.

[68] The Can. Bill of Rights, 1960, (Can.) c. 44, R.S.C. 1985, App. III. Section 1 of the Canadian Bill of Rights provided:

It is hereby recognized and declared that in Canada there have existed and shall continue to exist without discrimination by reason of race, national origin, colour, religion, or sex, the following human rights and fundamental freedoms, namely,

(d) freedom of speech,

(e) freedom of assembly and association, and
(f) freedom of the press.

[69] The BNA Act served as the principal constitutional document of Canada from 1867 until 1982 when the Canada Act, 1982 was passed by the U.K. Parliament. Until the Canada Act, ownership of the Canadian constitution remained with Great Britain and could only be amended there. The Constitution Act, 1982 removed all of the British Parliament's authority over Canada and repatriated the Canadian constitution. The Constitution Act, 1982, contains 60 sections, of which the first 34 constitute the Charter of Rights and Freedoms, which protects individual rights. The Charter is Part I of the Constitution Act, 1982, enacted as Sched. B to the Canada Act, 1982 (U.K.), c. 11. The Charter came into force on April 17, 1982.

[70] Christopher Manfredi, *The Use of United States Decisions by the Supreme Court of Canada Under the Charter of Rights and Freedoms*, 23 CAN. J. POL. SCI. 499 (1990).

[71] *Id.* at 500. In 1959, Edward McWhinney warned against the use of American precedents by Canadian courts. He wrote, "The fact that Canadian federalism is pluralistic in character means that the judicial decisions of essentially monistic federal societies like the United States, while making interesting reading in view of the clarity and directness of their reasoning and the freedom with which policy issues are discussed, must be received with some caution and certainly not treated as automatically conclusive in regard to questions of ultimate value choice. Edward McWhinney, *The Supreme Court and the Bill of Rights—The Lessons of Comparative Jurisprudence*, 37 CAN. B. REV. 39 (1959).

[72] McKercher, *supra* note 32, at 18.

[73] *Id.*

[74] Sedler, *supra* note 14, at 1212. *See also*, Greenawalt, *supra* note 10, at 11.

[75] *Id.*

[76] Manfredi, *supra* note 70, at 500.

[77] Christopher P. Manfredi, *The Canadian Supreme Court and American Judicial Review: United States Constitutional Jurisprudence and the Canadian Charter of Rights and Freedoms*, 40 AM. J. COMP. L. 224 (1992). *See also* Alderson, *supra* note 21, at 407.

[78] Secondary picketing occurs when strikers picket, for example, a store that sells their employer's goods to put pressure on the employer instead of or in addition to picketing the employer.

[79] Manfredi, *supra* note 77, at 225. Alderson explained that "'expression' under s. 2(b) of the Charter embraces all content irrespective of meaning or message to be conveyed" and includes conduct as long as the conduct "conveys or attempts to convey a meaning." The court can take a liberal approach to the definition of expression because of the s. 1 balancing provision. Section 1 means that a law can violate a Charter right and still not violate the charter. Alderson, *supra* note 21, at 408, 410.

[80] Section 33 of the Canadian Charter of Rights and Freedoms provides:
Parliament or the legislature of a province may expressly declare in an Act of Parliament or of the legislature, as the case may be, that the Act or a provision thereof shall operate notwithstanding a provision included in section 2 to 15 of this Charter.

[81] Steven Simpson, Cultural Crossroads: A Comparative Analysis of the Constitutional Protection for Freedom of Expression in Canada and the United States Following Passage of the Canadian Charter of Rights and Freedoms in 1982 5 (1993) (unpublished Ph.D. dissertation, University of Washington).

[82] McKercher, *supra* note 32, 12.

[83] C. Beckton, *Freedom of Expression — Access to the Courts*, 61 CAN. B. REV. 103 (1983).

[84] Massey, *supra* note 28, at 1266.

[85] *Id.* at 1299.

[86] Manfredi, *supra* note 70, at 518.

[87] *Id.*

[88] Beckton, *supra* note 83, at 102. *See also*, René Nunez, *Calibrating the Scales of Justice: Balancing Fundamental Freedoms in the United States and Canada*, 14 ARIZ. J. INT'L & COMP. L. 569 (1997).

[89] McKercher, *supra* note 32, at 18.

[90] *Id.*

[91] *Id.* at 23-24.

[92] Sedler, *supra* note 14, at 1228.

[93] *Id.* at 1230 note 128.

[94] Manfredi, *supra* note 70, at 507. Sedler argued that although the Canadian Court regularly cited and discussed U.S. cases, there was no evidence that those cases were treated as authoritative or especially persuasive. Robert Sedler, *The Constitutional Protection of Freedom of Religion, Expression, and Association in Canada and the United States: A Comparative Analysis*, 20 CASE W. RES. J. INT'L L. 618 (1988).

[95] Holland, *supra* note 44, at 94.

[96] *Id.*

[97] Morton, *supra* note 48, at 115-116.

[98] *Id.* at 117.

[99] Gibbons, *supra* note 9, at 136.

[100] *Id.* at 135.

[101] *Id.* at 136.

[102] *Id.*

[103] *Id.* at 136-137.

[104] *Id.* at 141.

[105] Christopher Manfredi, *Adjudication, Policy-Making and The Supreme Court of Canada: Lessons from the Experience of the United States*, 22 CAN. J. POL. SCI. 313 (1989).

[106] Morton, *supra* note 48, 114.

[107] *Id.*

[108] *See e.g.*, Michael R. Doody, *Freedom of the Press, the Canadian Charter of Rights and Freedoms, and a New Category of Qualified Privilege*, 61 CAN. B. REV. 124 (1983); Nunez, *supra* note 87; Amy R. Stein, *Libel Law and the Canadian Charter of Rights and Freedoms: Towards a Broader Protection for Media Defendants*, 10 FORDHAM INT'L L.J. 750 (1987).

[109] *See, e.g.*, Doody, *supra*; Stein, *supra*.

[110] *See, e.g.*, Alderson, *supra* note 21; Thomas A. Hughes, *The Actual Malice Rule: Why Canada Rejected the American Approach to Libel*, 3 COMM. L. & POL'Y 55 (1998); Sedler, *supra* note 93; Karla K. Gower, *The Homolka Press Ban: A Comparative Analysis of Canadian and American Approaches to the Fair Trial/Free Press Issue*, 10 SW. MASS COMM. J. 47 (1995).

[111] Nunez, *supra* note 88.

[112] Greenawalt, *supra* note 10, at 8.

[113] W.F. Bowker, *Basic Rights and Freedoms: What are they?*, 37 CAN. B. REV. 43 (1959). Bowker quoted Justice Stuart in *R. v. Trainor*, [1917] 1 W.W.R. 415 (Alta.): "Courts should not, unless in cases of gravity and danger, be asked to spend their time scrutinizing with undue particularity the foolish talk in bar rooms."

[114] *Id.* at 45. *R. v. Russell*, [1920] 1 W.W.R. 624 (Man.).

[115] Criminal Code, R.S.C. 1927, c. 36, s. 98; repealed Stats. of Can. 1936, c. 29, s. 1; Bowker, *supra* note 113, at 45.

[116] Bowker, *supra* note 113, at 45. Alien Registration Act of 1940, 54 Statutes at Large 670–671 (1940); currently in 18 U.S. Code sec. 2385. Commonly called the Smith Act, the Act while still in effect is seldom used.

[117] Bowker, *supra*, at 46. *R. v. Boucher*, [1951] S.C.R. 265, [1951] 2 D.L.R. 369.

[118] GREENAWALT, *supra* note 10, at 13. *See also* Kent Greenawalt, *Free Speech in the United States and Canada*, 55 L. & CONTEMP. PROBS. 5 (1992).

[119] Westin, *supra* note 48, at 28.

[120] *Id.* at 29.

[121] *Id.* at 30.

[122] LAWRENCE BEER, FREEDOM OF EXPRESSION IN JAPAN: A STUDY IN COMPARATIVE LAW, POLITICS, AND SOCIETY (1984).

[123] Westin, *supra* note 48, at 29.

[124] *Id.* at 30.

[125] *Id.* at 38.

[126] Sedler, *supra* note 94, at 621.

[127] LAHAV, *supra* note 2, at 348.

[128] *Id.* at 349.

[129] *Id.* at 350.

[130] The Pentagon Papers case would be an example of the state's attempt to hold onto the authoritarian/instrumental conception of press law. *New York Times Co. v. United States*, 403 U.S. 713, 91 S.Ct. 2140, 29 L. Ed. 2d 822, 1 Media L. Rep. (BNA) 1031 (1971).

[131] LAHAV, *supra* note 2, at 347.

[132] *Id.*

[133] Alderson, *supra* note 21.

[134] James M. Buchanan, The Limits of Liberty: Between Anarchy and Leviathan (1975).

CHAPTER 2

[1] Arnold Haultain, *A Search for an Ideal*, 22 CAN. MAG. 427–8 (1904).

[2] The study focuses on the dominant political thought in the two countries. This is not to suggest that this was the only thought at the time. The political thought in both countries was always varied. The nineteenth century thought is important to this study because all political thought "weaves the past into the present." Pnina Lahav, *Holmes and Brandeis: Libertarian and Republican Justifications for Free Speech*, 4 J.L. & POL. 451 (1987).

[3] *See* text accompanying notes 7-20.

[4] *See* text accompanying notes 23-36.

[5] Implicit in the different conceptions of the individual and society is a difference in an understanding of the word "freedom." Philosopher Mortimer Adler has identified two senses of the word that come into play here: freedom as self-realization, in which individuals ought to be allowed to do what they desire; and freedom as self-perfection, in which liberty occurs when individuals do what they ought to do. Political thought that stresses rights rather than duties tends to define freedom as self-realization. The American mechanistic or instrumental view of society in the last half of the nineteenth century reflected this notion of freedom. Freedom occurred when individuals were at liberty to realize themselves. The organic concept of society found in Canadian political thought of the same period defined freedom as self-perfection. Freedom occurred when individuals' baser instincts were subordinated to the higher, rational aspects of their personality through self- identification with society. MORTIMER J. ADLER, THE IDEA OF FREEDOM: A DIALECTICAL EXAMINATION OF THE CONTROVERSIES ABOUT FREEDOM (Vol. 11, 1961).

[6] A.J. BEITZINGER, A HISTORY OF AMERICAN POLITICAL THOUGHT 398 (1972). *See also*, RICHARD HOFSTADTER, SOCIAL DARWINISM IN AMERICAN THOUGHT 5 (1955).

[7] HERBERT SPENCER, FIRST PRINCIPLES 311-342, 359 (1880).

[8] *Id.* at 245, 342. Spencer saw individuals as discrete and self-made. MULFORD Q. SIBLEY, POLITICAL IDEAS AND IDEOLOGIES: A HISTORY OF POLITICAL THOUGHT 498 (1970).

[9] SPENCER, *supra* note 7, at 506. *See also* BEITZINGER, *supra* note 6, at 399.

[10] SPENCER, *supra* note 7, at 506.

[11] HOFSTADTER, *supra* note 6, at 51.

[12] WILLIAM GRAHAM SUMNER, WHAT SOCIAL CLASSES OWE TO EACH OTHER (1885).

[13] BEITZINGER, *supra* note 6, at 405.

[14] SUMNER, *supra* note 12, at 17-18. "Certain ills," he argued, " belong to the hardships of human life. They are natural. They are part of the struggle with Nature for existence."

[15] *Id.* at 19.

[16] BEITZINGER, *supra* note 6, at 405.

[17] SUMNER, *supra* note 12, at 39.

[18] *Id.* at 34.

[19] *Id.* at 120.

[20] *Id.* at 101. Therefore, government must not impinge upon individuals, except to provide for neutral conditions of security. *Id.* at 35. If left alone, individuals would have only natural ills to worry about, and he wrote, "Those we will endure or combat as we can." *Id.* at 121.

[21] S.E.D. SHORTT, THE SEARCH FOR AN IDEAL: SIX CANADIAN INTELLECTUALS AND THEIR CONVICTIONS IN AN AGE OF TRANSITION, 1890-1930 34 (1976). For Macphail, legislation could not make individuals equal. In fact, Macphail argued that Americans followed an "incorrect theory of society" based on the fallacy of equality. For Macphail, egalitarianism was rooted in a desire to escape work by stealing from society's most industrious members. A political philosophy grounded on the equality of individuals undermined society's goal of securing liberty and order. *Id.* at 33.

[22] *Id.* at 25.

[23] Georg Wilhelm Friedrich Hegel (1770-1831) was a philosophic idealist. He argued that individuals were constituted by their social relations. Individuals could achieve self-realization only by organic union with society. CHARLES HIRSCHFELD, CLASSICS OF WESTERN THOUGHT: THE MODERN WORLD 326 (1964).

[24] SHORTT, *supra* note 21, at 20.

[25] DOUG OWRAM, THE GOVERNMENT GENERATION: CANADIAN INTELLECTUALS AND THE STATE, 1900–1945 6 (1986).
[26] *Id.* at 7.
[27] JOHN WATSON, COMTE, MILL, AND SPENCER: AMERICAN OUTLINES OF PHILOSOPHY v (1895).
[28] *Id.* at 167.
[29] *Id.* at 169-170.
[30] STEPHEN LEACOCK, ELEMENTS OF POLITICAL SCIENCE 77 (rev. ed. 1921).
[31] WATSON, *supra* note 27, at 148. It was the idea of a good higher than merely an individual good that held individuals together in a society, Watson argued. Because the higher good was partially realized in social laws and institutions, individuals felt constrained by their reason to submit to that higher good. *Id.* at 229.
[32] *Id.* at 256.
[33] *Id.* at 280.
[34] *Id.*
[35] *Id.* at 268. "Each individual is a member in an organism and realizes himself only as he makes the common good his end," wrote Watson. *Id.* at 270.
[36] *Id.* at 270. When individual rights were interfered with, the perpetrator was subject to punishment. The object of such punishment was to maintain the social unity against the whims of individuals and to awaken in individuals the consciousness that they were all members of one body. The ideal society was not one in which each surrendered all to the society, but rather one in which individuals attempted to secure the moral perfection of all, by acting from the point of view of a universal good in conformity with the unchangeable nature of God. *Id.* at 272.
[37] Spencer's view was that society's evolution had to be left alone, free of all human intervention. HOFSTADTER, *supra* note 6, at 123.
[38] In this regard, the pragmatists reflected Enlightenment thought, which believed that the state had no monopoly over the truth and the free speech was crucial for the process of discovering the truth. *See generally*, Lahav, *supra* note 2.
[39] Laissez-faire capitalism was at the height of its power at the beginning of the twentieth century. DOLBEARE, *supra* note 11, at 381. *See also*, HOFSTADTER, *supra* note 6, at 120.

[40] BEITZINGER, *supra* note 6, at 461-2.

[41] PAUL L. MURPHY, THE SHAPING OF THE FIRST AMENDMENT: 1791 TO THE PRESENT 82 (1992).

[42] DOLBEARE, *supra* note 11, at 9.

[43] WILLIAM JAMES, PRAGMATISM 28 (1975).

[44] *Id.* at 28, 30.

[45] *Id.* at 23. Empiricism is the doctrine that all knowledge is derived from experience. For idealists, the only thing that exists with certainty is the mind. Spencer was an empiricist and Watson was an idealist.

[46] JAMES, *supra* note 43, at xxviii. "What we call truth, guiding us to successful action and the consequent maintenance of life, is simply the accurate correspondence of subjective and objective relations." SPENCER, *supra* note 7, at 96-97.

[47] *Id.* at 97.

[48] *Id.* at 107.

[49] By 1897-1898, Dewey had stopped using Hegel's system of categorization and was on his own. JOHN DEWEY, PHILOSOPHY, PSYCHOLOGY AND SOCIAL PRACTICE 9 (Joseph Ratner ed., 1963).

[50] *Id.* at iii.

[51] BEITZINGER, *supra* note 6, at 472.

[52] DEWEY, *supra* note 49, at 17.

[53] *Id.*

[54] *Id.* at 60. See also, BEITZINGER, *supra* note 6, at 473.

[55] MARK GRABER, TRANSFORMING FREE SPEECH: THE AMBIGUOUS LEGACY OF CIVIL LIBERTARIANISM 66 (1991).

[56] *Id.* at 66.

[57] *Id.* at 67.

[58] DEWEY, *supra* note 49, at 72. Although Dewey rejected the determinism of Spencer, he owed his notion of nature and society as processes of becoming to social Darwinism and evolutionary theory.

[59] GRABER, *supra* note 55, at 66. Thinkers who dominated in prewar years, such as Roscoe Pound and John Dewey, were advocates of sociological jurisprudence and pragmatism. MURPHY, *supra* note 41, at 85. See also, BEITZINGER, supra note 6, at 474.

[60] HERBERT CROLY, PROGRESSIVE DEMOCRACY 195 (1914) [hereinafter CROLY, PROGRESSIVE DEMOCRACY].

[61] *Id.* at 198.

[62] *Id.* at 199.

[63] HERBERT CROLY, THE PROMISE OF AMERICAN LIFE 6 (1911).

[64] *Id.* at 9-10.

[65] *Id.* at 12. At the same time, the system of American government as set up was based "at bottom on a profound suspicion of human nature." CROLY, PROGRESSIVE DEMOCRACY, *supra* note 60, at 40.

[66] CROLY, *supra* note 63, at 12.

[67] *Id.* at 18.

[68] *Id.* at 20.

[69] *Id.*

[70] *Id.* at 25.

[71] Croly is referring to the utilitarian justification for democracy. For a discussion of the modern liberal tradition and utilitarianism, *see* SIBLEY, *supra* note 8, at 489-498.

[72] CROLY, *supra* note 63, at 149.

[73] *Id.* at 152. Kenneth Dolbeare has argued that Croly's work marks the shift in liberalism from an emphasis on laissez-faire to one on interventionist government. At the same time, the work contains elements of conservatism. DOLBEARE, *supra* note 11, at 440.

[74] WILLIAM LYON MACKENZIE KING, INDUSTRY AND HUMANITY: A STUDY IN THE PRINCIPLES UNDERLYING INDUSTRIAL RECONSTRUCTION viii (intro. David Jay Bercuson, 1973).

[75] OWRAM, *supra* note 25, at 37. King was aided in his pursuit of government intervention by the recession of 1912 to 1913. Although it was not Canada's first recession, it felt new because more of the population were now employees. Reformers called for government intervention to aid those in need. In response, the Province of Ontario appointed a commission to study the problem of unemployment in the recession. The commission reported that unemployment during a recession was not the fault of the individual. The conclusion was important because it meant that the government could no longer place the blame on the personal attributes of the unemployed. Unemployment was now a social problem, not an individual one, and required a society-wide solution. The commission failed to adopt a mandatory system of unemployment insurance, however. The notion of individuals controlling their own destiny was still strong enough

to forbid that step. The principle of laissez-faire was decaying in the face of industrialization and urbanization, but voluntarism remained strong. *Id.* at 73-77.

[76] *Id.* at 38.
[77] *Id.* at 17.
[78] *Id.*
[79] *Id.* at 22-23.
[80] *Id.* at 25.
[81] *Id.*
[82] *Id.* at 30.
[83] An "ideology of service" developed in which everyone worked for the war effort. And as in the United States, Germany was soon given the face of evil. *Id.* at 80-83.
[84] Section 6 of the War Measures Act, 1914 (5 Geo. V.) provides:

The Governor in Council shall have power to do and authorize such acts and things, and to make from time to time such orders and regulations, as he may by reason of the existence of real or apprehended war, invasion or insurrection deem necessary or advisable for the security, defence, peace, order and welfare of Canada; and for greater certainty, but not so as to restrict the generality of the foregoing terms, it is hereby declared that the powers of the Governor in Council shall extend to all matters coming within the classes of subjects hereinafter enumerated, that is to say:—

(a) censorship and the control and suppression of publications, writings, maps, plans, photographs, communications and means of communication.

[85] OWRAM, *supra* note 25, at 90.
[86] O.D. Skelton, *Current Events*, 26 QUEEN'S QUARTERLY 128 (1918).
[87] OWRAM, *supra* note 25, at 100.
[88] *Id.* at 103.
[89] *Id.* at 104.
[90] *Id.* at 106.
[91] *Id.* at 32. Leacock had been educated in political economy at the University of Chicago beginning in 1899. His professors were already modifying social Darwinism to stress the collective nature of society as opposed to individual survival. Returning to Canada, Leacock took a post

teaching at McGill University in Montreal. He became increasingly concerned about what he perceived as the materialism and alienation of modern society. STEPHEN LEACOCK, SOCIAL CRITICISM: THE UNSOLVED RIDDLE OF SOCIAL JUSTICE AND OTHER ESSAYS xii (Alan Bowker ed., 1996).

[92] LEACOCK, *supra* note 91, at xxxiii.

[93] *Id.* at 6.

[94] *Id.* at xxxix.

[95] LEACOCK, *supra* note 30, at 76.

[96] *Id.* at 76. Spencer and Sumner saw the state as mechanistic. *See supra* text accompanying notes 7-20.

[97] Watson is an example of a philosopher who followed the organic or idealist theory of society. *See supra* text accompanying notes 27-36.

[98] LEACOCK, *supra* note 30, at 84.

[99] *Id.* at 355.

[100] *Id.* at 357.

[101] LEACOCK, *supra* note 91, at 74. The series of articles were published a year later in book form.

[102] *Id.* at 75.

[103] *Id.* at 127.

[104] *Id.* at 134. Leacock's attitude toward individuals here is an example of conservatism.

[105] *Id.*

[106] *Id.* at xxxiv.

[107] *Id.* at 135.

[108] *Id.* at 136.

[109] *Id.* at 142.

[110] PAUL MURPHY, WORLD WAR I AND THE ORIGINS OF CIVIL LIBERTIES IN THE UNITED STATES 46-48 (1979) [hereinafter MURPHY, WORLD WAR I]. Previously, informal social controls were imposed by the private sector. But with urbanization and industrialization the ability of society to control deviance decreased. *See also*, MURPHY, *supra* note 41, at 88.

[111] GRABER, *supra* note 55, at 76.

[112] CROLY, *supra* note 63, at 4. *See also*, MURPHY, WORLD WAR I, *supra* note 110, at 45 ("When courts in Progressive era were called on to protect or deny civil liberties, they had to decide whether the individual seeking those

liberties was sufficiently committed to American values to ensure that extension of civil liberties to him would not basically threaten society.").

[113] GRABER, *supra* note 55, at 77 (1991).

[114] ZECHARIAH CHAFEE, JR., FREEDOM OF SPEECH 24 (1920). Mark Graber argued that Chafee's book was the first constitutional defense of free speech that thoroughly broke with tradition. For Graber, the traditional approach was to treat free speech as an individual right and a natural right. Chafee turned it into a societal right, necessary for a free democracy. GRABER, *supra* note 55, at 138-143.

[115] CHAFEE, *supra* note 114, at 36.

[116] *Id.* at 34.

[117] *Id.* at 34-35.

[118] *Id.* at 38.

[119] LEACOCK, *supra* note 91, at 118.

[120] *Id.*

[121] *Id.*

[122] Mulford Sibley has argued that by World War I, Americans had moved away from extreme individualism toward a form of thought influenced to some degree by Hegelian organicism, which supports the argument that Canadian and American thought was closer by 1920 than it had been in 1900. SIBLEY, *supra* note 8, at 489.

[123] In *Turner v. Williams*, 194 U.S. 279 (1904), the attorney for the appellant referred the Court to Spencer for the general principle of liberty in his argument before the Court. And in *Schaefer v. U.S.*, 251 U.S. 466 (1920), Justice Brandeis in dissent referred to Chafee.

[124] The social Darwinism of Spencer and Sumner did find reflection in the economic and property rights cases of the same time period. Social Darwinists put an emphasis on property rights and the accumulation of wealth. The result was that the majority of the Court promoted the notion of liberty of contract and broadly extended due process to include a substantive component in property rights cases. At the same time, the Court narrowly construed civil liberties, such as freedom of speech and of the press, on the basis of eighteenth century political thought. BEITZINGER, *supra* note 6, at 422.

[125] MARGARET A. BLANCHARD, REVOLUTIONARY SPARKS: FREEDOM OF EXPRESSION IN MODERN AMERICA x (1992). Blanchard refers to the Supreme

Endnote 241

Court's interpretation of the First Amendment as a mid-twentieth-century phenomenon.

[126] MURPHY, WORLD WAR I, *supra* note 110, at 48. *See also*, MURPHY, *supra* note 41, at 46.

[127] MURPHY, *supra* note 41, at 66-67.

[128] Extract from sec. 3 of Title I of the Espionage Act enacted on June 15, 1917, provides:

Whoever, when the United States is at war, shall willfully make or convey false reports or false statements with intent to interfere with the operation or success of the military or naval forces of the United States or to promote the success of its enemies and whoever, when the United States is at war, shall willfully cause or attempt to cause insubordination, disloyalty, mutiny, or refusal of duty, in the military or naval forces of the United States, or shall willfully obstruct the recruiting or enlistment service of the United States, to the injury of the service or of the United States, shall be punished by a fine of not more than $10,000 or imprisonment for not more than twenty years, or both.

Act of June 15, 1917, c. 30, Title I, §3.

[129] The 1918 amendments to the Espionage Act added the following to sec. 3 of the earlier Act:

Whoever, when the United States is at war, shall willfully utter, print, or publish, any disloyal, profane, scurrilous, or abusive language about the form of government of the Untied States, or the Constitution of the United States . . . shall be punished by a fine of not more that $10,000 or imprisonment for not more than twenty years, or both.

Act of May 16, 1918, c. 75, §1, U.S. Comp. Stat., 1918, § 10212c.

[130] U.S. ex rel. Turner v. Williams, 194 U.S. 279 (1904); Patterson v. Colorado, 205 U.S. 454 (1907); Fox v. Washington, 236 U.S. 273 (1915); Goldman v. U.S., 245 U.S. 474 (1918); Toledo Newspaper Co. v. U.S., 247 U.S. 402 (1918).

[131] SIBLEY, *supra* note 8, at 511.

[132] BEITZINGER, *supra* note 6, at 316.

[133] *Id.* at 419.

[134] *Id.* Thomas Jefferson believed that the basic harmony among men could best be promoted with minimal legal restraints. Others saw the law as an instrument for regulating human behavior in the name of both social harmony and individual freedom. SIBLEY, *supra* note 8, at 586.

[135] 205 U.S. 454 (1907).

[136] The traditional view of freedom of speech at the time of the drafting of the American Constitution, as described by British legal commentator Blackstone, was that speech was to be free from prior restraint by government but subject to prosecution if false, malicious, or having a bad tendency. Truth was not a defense. BEITZINGER, *supra* note 6, at 260.

[137] 205 U.S. at 463. Justice Holmes delivered the opinion.

[138] 247 U.S. 402 (1918).

[139] 247 U.S. at 419.

[140] Social contract theories viewed the state as a contractual agreement among individuals. The American Declaration of Independence is a practical expression of John Locke's social contract theory. SIBLEY, *supra* note 8, at 292-3, 386.

[141] 194 U.S. 279 (1904).

[142] 194 U.S. at 286.

[143] 194 U.S. at 292.

[144] The King v. Hoaglin, 12 C.C.C. 226 (N.W. Terr. S.C. 1907); R. v. Felton, 25 C.C.C. 207 (Alta. S.C. 1915); R. v. Cohen, 28 D.L.R. 74 (Alta. S.C. 1916); R. v. Trainor, 33 D.L.R. 658 (Alta. S.C. 1916); R. v. Giesinger, 32 D.L.R. 325 (Sask. S.C. 1916); R. v. Manshrick, 32 D.L.R. 584 (Man. C.A. 1916); R. v. Bainbridge, 28 C.C.C. 444 (Ont. S.C. 1917); The King v. Barron, 44 D.L.R. 332 (Sask. C.A. 1918); The King v. Russell, 51 D.L.R. 1 (Man. C.A. 1920).

[145] Section 134 of the Criminal Code provides that any one who speaks seditious words is guilty of an indictable offence, and Section 132 declares that "seditious words are words expressive of a seditious intention." Seditious intention is not defined in the Criminal Code. The courts have defined it as intention "to bring into hatred or contempt, or to excite disaffection against, the person of His Majesty or the government and constitution of the country, to excite people to attempt otherwise than by lawful means the alteration of any matter in the state by law established, to raise discontent and disaffection among His Majesty's subjects, or to

promote feelings of ill-will and hostility between different classes of His Majesty's subjects." R. v. Trainor (1916), 33 D.L.R. 658 at 664.

[146] 12 C.C.C. at 228. Section 136 of the Revised Code of 1906 provided that:

> Every one is guilty of an indictable offence and liable to one year's imprisonment who wilfully and knowingly publishes any false news or tale whereby injury or mischief is or is likely to be occasioned to any public interest.

The section is based on an ancient British statute that codified the common law regarding false statements that would cause discord between the King and his people. The decision in *Hoaglin* was the first reported decision in Canada under the section. *Note: Spreading false news—Revised Cr. Code sec. 136*, 12 C.C.C. 229.

[147] 28 C.C.C. 444, 445 (S.C. Ont., 1917).

[148] 205 U.S. 454.

[149] 205 U.S. at 465.

[150] 249 U.S. 47 (1919).

[151] *See* GRABER, *supra* note 55, at 106 ("*Schenck* was the first major decision on the constitutional meaning of free speech.").

[152] 249 U.S. at 52.

[153] 249 U.S. 204 (1919).

[154] Frohwerk v. U.S., 249 U.S. 204 (1919); Debs v. U.S., 249 U.S. 211 (1919); and Abrams v. U.S., 250 U.S. 616 (1919).

[155] Abrams v. U.S., 250 U.S. at 621.

[156] *See e.g.* Rex v. Felton, 25 C.C.C. 207 at 211. "It does seem quite clear, however, that on the principle that a man is presumed to intend the natural consequences of his act, it would always be open to a Judge or a jury to infer the intent from the words and the circumstances under which they are spoken."

[157] R. v. Trainor (1916), 33 D.L.R. 658 at 667.

[158] 33 D.L.R. 658 at 664.

[159] R. v. Trainor (1916), 33 D.L.R. 658 at 667.

[160] *See e.g.*, MURPHY, *supra* note 41; Harry Kalven, Jr., *Professor Ernst Freund and Debs v. United States*, 40 U. CHI. L. REV. 235 (1973); Douglas Ginsburg, *Afterward to Ernst Freund and the First Amendment Tradition*, 40 U. CHI. L. REV. 243 (1973); Gerald Gunther, *Learned Hand and the Origins of*

the Modern First Amendment Doctrine: Some Fragments of History, 27 STAN. L. REV. 719 (1975); David Rabban, *The Emergence of Modern First Amendment Doctrine*, 50 U. CHI. L. REV. 1205; Fred D. Ragan, *Justice Oliver Wendell Holmes, Jr., Zechariah Chafee, Jr., and the Clear and Present Danger Test for Free Speech: The First Year, 1919*, 58 J. OF AM. HIST. 24 (1971). But *see* GRABER, *supra* note 55, at 108 (Holmes never unambiguously supported a free speech claim).

[161] 250 U.S. at 627. ("I never have seen any reason to doubt that the questions of law that alone were before this Court in the cases of *Schenck, Frohwerk* and *Debs*, 249 U.S. 47, 204, 211, were rightly decided.").

[162] 250 U.S. at 630.

[163] *See* text accompanying notes 46-48.

[164] *See* text accompanying notes 52-59.

[165] Pierce v. U.S., 252 U.S. 239 at 247 (1920).

[166] 252 U.S. at 251.

[167] 252 U.S. at 267 (American School of Magnetic Healing v. McAnnulty, 187 U.S. 94, 104).

[168] 252 U.S. at 269.

[169] 251 U.S. 466 at 475 (1920).

[170] 251 U.S. at 482.

[171] 251 U.S. at 486. Brandeis is expressing here his distrust in the ability of the masses to use their reason in times of high emotion. Such sentiments reflect American classical republicanism on the part of Brandeis.

[172] Roscoe Pound was the leading advocate in the progressive era of what became known as sociological jurisprudence. Pound believed that judges, instead of merely applying abstract principles of law, should balance the individual and social interests in the cases before them. Roscoe Pound, *The Scope and Purpose of Sociological Jurisprudence*, 24 HARV. L. REV. 591 (1911).

[173] 252 U.S. at 269.

[174] GRABER, *supra* note 55, at 74.

[175] Concepts important to eighteenth century Enlightenment thought were reason, the law of nature, natural rights, and social contract. BEITZINGER, *supra* note 6, at 100.

CHAPTER 3

[1] Stephen Brooks, Canadian Democracy: An Introduction 27 (1996).

[2] Nativism is the favoring of those native to a country over those foreign born. Nativists in the United States during World War I exhibited, as historian Stanley Coben described it, "hostility toward certain minority groups, especially radicals and recent immigrants, fanatical patriotism, and a belief that internal enemies seriously threaten[ed] national security." Stanley Coben, *A Study in Nativism: The American Red Scare of 1919-20*, 79 Pol. Sci. Q. 52,53 (1964).

[3] DOUG OWRAM, THE GOVERNMENT GENERATION: CANADIAN INTELLECTUALS AND THE STATE, 1900-1945 111 (1986). Canada entered the war two years before the United States did and was never considered strategically important by either Great Britain or Germany. Both countries engaged in extensive propaganda campaigns in the United States that fueled the nativism, a fear of anything not native to the United States or "un-American."

[4] The post-war period required a major intellectual reorientation between the relationship of the state and the individual. *Id.* at 114.

[5] The Winnipeg General Strike of 1919 began with a walkout by metal and building trades workers in the City of Winnipeg, Manitoba, but soon became a violent clash between organized labor and government. "The strike lasted for almost six weeks, and during this time all business, industry, and transportation stopped. Communication to and from the city was forbidden by the strike leaders, and the newspapers were suspended. The strikers organized a system of espionage, intimidation and terrorism, and drove the police from the streets. Riots were common; many persons were injured and there was extensive property damage." D. A. SCHMEISER, CIVIL LIBERTIES IN CANADA 207 (1964). *See also*, D. C. MASTERS, THE WINNIPEG GENERAL STRIKE (1950); ROBERT BOTHWELL, IAN DRUMMOND & JOHN ENGLISH, CANADA: 1900 TO 1945 164-167 (1987); DAVID JAY BERCUSON, CONFRONTATION AT WINNIPEG (1990). One of the strike leaders, a Communist, was found guilty of sedition and sentenced to two years' imprisonment. R. v. Russell (1920), 1 W.W.R. 624, 33 C.C.C. 1 (Man. C.A.). The concept of "one big union" had been used in the United States, Great Britain, and Australia for several years before it was adopted by

laborers in Western Canada. It was to be an all-embracing union for all laborers. In Canada, the labor unions and farmers' unions came together under the One Big Union that had a hand in instigating the Winnipeg General Strike. OWRAM, *supra* note 2, at 107. *See also*, BERCUSON, *supra*, at 98-99. The Western farmers seemed to represent a greater challenge to the Canadian government than the labor unions did. BOTHWELL, *supra*, at 135-136.

[6] OWRAM, *supra* note 2, at 102.
[7] *Id.* at 116.
[8] *Id.*
[9] *Id.* at 118.
[10] R. M. MACIVER, THE MODERN STATE 20 (1926). MacIver had been born in Scotland and educated at the University of Edinburgh and Oxford. He began teaching at the University of Toronto in 1915. OWRAM, *supra* note 2, 117.
[11] *Id.*
[12] *Id.* at 480.
[13] *Id.* at 153.
[14] *Id.* at 157.
[15] The state was also permitted to regulate expression related to libelous or defamatory opinion. Libel was the expression of opinion with malicious intent to injure the person. According to MacIver, the issue was not whether the libel was true or false, but rather the intention of the person expressing the opinion. *Id.* at 152.
[16] *Id.* at 150.
[17] *Id.* at 151.
[18] *Id.* at 22, 183.
[19] *Id.* at 185.
[20] *Id.* at 149.
[21] *Id.* at 459.
[22] *Id.* at 474.
[23] *Id.* at 481.
[24] *Id.* at 482.
[25] WALTER LIPPMANN, PUBLIC OPINION (1922).
[26] *See generally*, MICHAEL L. SANDERS & PHILIP M. TAYLOR, BRITISH PROPAGANDA DURING THE FIRST WORLD WAR, 1914–18 (1982); David Wayne

Hirst, German Propaganda in the United States, 1914–1917 (1962) (unpublished Ph.D. dissertation, Northwestern University); and STEPHEN VAUGHN, HOLDING FAST THE INNER LINES: DEMOCRACY, NATIONALISM AND THE COMMITTEE ON PUBLIC INFORMATION (1980).

[27] LIPPMANN, *supra* note 25.
[28] The pragmatists such as John Dewey and William James saw knowledge in the same way. *See* Chap. Two, text accompanying notes 46-59.
[29] LIPPMANN, *supra* note 25, at 270.
[30] *Id.* at 275.
[31] *Id.* at 278.
[32] *Id.* at 75.
[33] *Id.* at 378.
[34] Lippmann was not alone in his elitism. Harold Lasswell, in his study of propaganda techniques in World War I, noted that "familiarity with the ruling public had bred contempt." Democrats had deceived themselves, he wrote, when they believed that the "public would reign with benignity and restraint. The good life is not in the mighty rushing wind of public sentiment. It is no organic secretion of the horde, but the tedious achievement of the few." HAROLD D. LASSWELL, PROPAGANDA TECHNIQUE IN THE WORLD WAR 4 (1927).

Canadian conservative political thinkers also took an elitist approach to individuals. The conservative R.B. Bennett, for example, wrote, "It is almost incomprehensible that the vital issues of death to nations, peace or war, bankruptcy or solvency, should be determined by the counting of heads and knowing as we do that the majority under modern conditions . . . are untrained and unskilled in dealing with the problems which they have to determine." R. B. Bennett, *Democracy on Trial*, CANADIAN PROBLEMS AS SEEN BY TWENTY OUTSTANDING MEN OF CANADA 13 (n.d.). In tracing the history of democracy, Bennett noted that the franchise kept broadening regardless of ability. Finally women were added to the electorate and "without previous training in respect of the problems with which they had to deal. And so democracy became in the ultimate analysis a struggle on the part of those who govern to obtain the greatest number of heads of the men and women over 21 regardless of any other condition." *Id.* at 14.

[35] REINHOLD NEIBUHR, MORAL MAN AND IMMORAL SOCIETY: A STUDY IN ETHICS AND POLITICS (1932).

[36] *Id.* at xi.

[37] *Id.* at xv, xvi.

[38] *Id.* at xx.

[39] *Id.* at xx, xxiii.

[40] *Id.* at 4, 19.

[41] *Id.* at 33.

[42] *Id.* at 88.

[43] *Id.*

[44] *Id.* at 91.

[45] *Id.* at 214.

[46] *Id.* at 272-273.

[47] T. V. SMITH, THE AMERICAN PHILOSOPHY OF EQUALITY (1927).

[48] *Id.* at 151.

[49] *Id.* at 190.

[50] *Id.* at 250.

[51] *Id.* at 271.

[52] *Id.* at 276.

[53] *Id.* at 305, 316.

[54] The collapse of the Canadian economy began in the fall of 1929. OWRAM, *supra* note 2, at 136.

[55] *Id.* at 171.

[56] H. M. Cassidy, *An Unemployment Policy: Some Proposals*, CAN. PROBLEMS AS SEEN BY TWENTY OUTSTANDING MEN OF CANADA 49, 51 (n.d.).

[57] *Id.* at 55.

[58] The test for state intervention under utilitarianism is the greatest happiness of the greatest number. It examines every custom in the light of immediate utility. RUSSELL KIRK, THE CONSERVATIVE MIND 35 (1953).

[59] Alexander Brady, *Parliamentary Democracy in* CANADA AFTER THE WAR: STUDIES IN POLITICAL, SOCIAL AND ECONOMIC POLICIES FOR POST-WAR CANADA 31, 39 (Alexander Brady & F.R. Scott eds., 1944).

[60] William Price, *Political Changes by Force and Violence in* CANADIAN PROBLEMS AS SEEN BY TWENTY OUTSTANDING MEN OF CANADA 307, 310 (n.d.).

[61] *Id.* at 312.

[62] LEAGUE FOR SOCIAL RECONSTRUCTION, SOCIAL PLANNING FOR CANADA (Univ. of Toronto Press, 1975) (1935).

[63] *Id.* at vii.

[64] *Id.* at 34.

[65] *Id.* at 225.

[66] *Id.*

[67] Charlotte Whitton, The Reconstruction of the Social Services in CANADA AFTER THE WAR: STUDIES IN POLITICAL, SOCIAL AND ECONOMIC POLICIES FOR POST-WAR CANADA 88, 88 (Alexander Brady & F.R. Scott eds., 1944).

[68] *Id.* at 120.

[69] DENIS MONIERE, IDEOLOGIES IN QUEBEC: THE HISTORICAL DEVELOPMENT 214 (Richard Howard trans., 1981).

[70] *Id.* at 216.

[71] J. B. Desrosiers, *Principles et Description de L'Organisation Corporative in* L'ACTION NATIONALE 145-147 (1938), *quoted in Id.* at 217.

[72] MONIERE, *supra* note 69, at 136.

[73] As Bishop Lafleche stated, "The faith will be the cement of the nation." *Id.,* at 137. Lafleche challenged the separation of church and state by arguing that since the authority of the state came from God, it could not be neutral in religion; it had to be Catholic. Another of the Quebec political thinkers in the late 1800s, Bishop Bourget, rejected the principles of popular sovereignty, freedom of opinion, and the separation of church and state. He proclaimed, instead, uncritical obedience to the church and the established government. *Id.* at 136-139.

[74] *Id.* at 218.

[75] *Id.* at 223.

[76] By the end of the 1930s, powerful and unorthodox politicians had risen to power in two provinces. William Aberhart's populist Social Credit government was elected in 1935. The Union Nationale party of Maurice Duplessis had gained power in Quebec. Duplessis' party was a right-wing populist party that many intellectuals considered bordered on fascism. OWRAM, *supra* note 2, at 221.

[77] MONIERE, *supra* note 69, at 223.

[78] THURMAN ARNOLD, THE FOLKLORE OF CAPITALISM 10 (1937).

[79] *Id.*

[80] *Id.* at 14-15, 20.
[81] *Id.* at 20.
[82] *Id.* at 21.
[83] *Id.* at 44.
[84] *Id.* at 23.
[85] *Id.*
[86] *Id.* at 24.
[87] *Id.* at 349.
[88] *Id.* at 393.
[89] ERICH FROMM, ESCAPE FROM FREEDOM viii (1941).
[90] *Id.* at vii.
[91] *Id.* at 241.
[92] *Id.* at 257.
[93] *Id.* at 265.
[94] MULFORD Q. SIBLEY, POLITICAL IDEAS AND IDEOLOGIES: A HISTORY OF POLITICAL THOUGHT 511 (1970).
[95] A.J. BEITZINGER, A HISTORY OF AMERICAN POLITICAL THOUGHT 316 (1972).
[96] 255 U.S. 407.
[97] *Id.* at 414.
[98] Justice Sutherland expressed the same sentiment in *Herndon v. Georgia*, 295 U.S. 441 (1935). Again the notion was that the state could defend itself against even the mere possibility of attack. Sutherland, an individualist and an advocate of the doctrine of laissez-faire when it came to economic liberty, saw the state's primary duty as maintaining the status quo and order. No doubt, Sutherland saw individuals such as Herndon, who was convicted of attempting to incite in insurrection in Georgia, as interfering with the natural evolution of society by threatening the status quo. And the state was entitled even under the doctrine of laissez-faire to protect individuals from the actions of others that threatened each individual's right to struggle to survive.
[99] 268 U.S. 652, 667 (1925).
[100] *Id.*
[101] *Id.* at 668.
[102] The Declaration of Independence provides:

Endnote

> That whenever any Form of Government becomes destructive of these ends, it is the Right of the People to alter or to abolish it, and to institute a new Government, laying its foundation on such principles and organizing its powers in such form, as to them shall seem most likely to effect their Safety and Happiness.

Abraham Lincoln repeated that sentiment in his inaugural address seventy years later:

> This country, with its institutions, belongs to the people who inhabit it. Whenever they shall grow weary of the existing government, they can exercise their constitutional right of amending it, or their revolutionary right to dismember or overthrow it.

CARL SANDBURG, ABRAHAM LINCOLN, THE WAR YEARS 133 (1939).

[103] 301 U.S. 242 (1937) (McReynolds, Sutherland, Butler concurring).

[104] *Id.* at 275.

[105] *Id.* at 276.

[106] Whitney v. California, 274 U.S. 357, 375 (1927).

[107] *Id.*

[108] *Id.* at 375, 376.

[109] Gitlow v. New York, 268 U.S. 652 (1925).

[110] Some scholars credit President Roosevelt's 1937 "court packing plan" with being the catalyst that caused the Supreme Court to shift its perspective away from economic liberty. *See e.g.*, DAVID M. O'BRIEN, CONSTITUTIONAL LAW AND POLITICS: STRUGGLES FOR POWER AND GOVERNMENTAL ACCOUNTABILITY Vol. I 118 (1995). While that may be true with respect to the cases on economic liberty, it is clear that the appointment of Justices Roberts and Hughes in 1930 changed the dynamic of the Court for the purposes of freedom of expression. There is also evidence that their appointments began the shift away from economic liberty as well.

[111] De Jonge v. Oregon, 299 U.S. 353, 365 (1937). In *Stromberg v. California*, 283 U.S. 359, 369 (1931), Hughes wrote: "The maintenance of the opportunity for free political discussion to the end that government may be responsive to the will of the people and that changes may be obtained by lawful means, an opportunity essential to the security of the Republic, is a fundamental principle of our constitutional system."

[112] Near v. Minnesota, 283 U.S. 697, 708 (1931).

[113] Hague v. C.I.O., 307 U.S. 496, 513 (1939).
[114] *Id.* at 516.
[115] Herndon v. Lowry, 301 U.S. 242, 258 (1937).
[116] Thomas v. Collins, 323 U.S. 516, 545 (1945).
[117] *Id.*
[118] *Id.*
[119] *Id.* at 531.
[120] 314 U.S. 252 (1941).
[121] *Id.* at 268.
[122] *Id.* at 271.
[123] *Id.* at 279.
[124] *Id.* at 281.
[125] *Id.* at 282.
[126] *Id.* at 293.
[127] The speaker lost in: Milwaukee Publishing Co. v. Burleson, 255 U.S. 407 (1921); Gitlow v. N.Y., 268 U.S. 652 (1925); Vajtauer v. Comm'r of Immigration, 273 U.S. 103 (1927); Whitney v. California, 274 U.S. 357 (1927). The speaker won in: Fiske v. Kansas, 274 U.S. 380 (1927).

[128] The speaker won in: Stromberg v. California, 283 U.S. 359 (1931); Near v. Minnesota, 283 U.S. 697 (1931); DeJonge v. Oregon, 299 U.S. 353 (1937); Herndon v. Lowry, 301 U.S. 242 (1937); Kessler v. Strecker, 307 U.S. 22 (1939); Hague v. C.I.O., 307 U.S. 496 (1939); Bridges v. California, 314 U.S. 252 (1941); Schneiderman v. U.S., 320 U.S. 118 (1943); Baumgartner v. United States, 322 U.S. 665 (1944); Hartzel v. United States, 322 U.S. 680 (1944); Thomas v. Collins, 323 U.S. 516 (1945); Bridges v. Wixon, 326 U.S. 135 (1945); Keegan v. United States, 325 U.S. 478 (1945). The speaker lost in: Herndon v. Georgia, 295 U.S. 441 (1935).

[129] References are made pursuant to s. 55 of the Supreme Court Act, R.S.C. 1927, c. 35.

[130] William Aberhart's populist Social Credit party had been elected in 1935. OWRAM, *supra* note 2, at 221.

[131] Re Alberta Legislation, [1938] 2 D.L.R. 84, 116 (S.C.C.).
[132] *Id.* at 107.
[133] *Id.*

Endnote 253

[134] *Id.* at 119. Justices Kerwin, with whom Justice Crocket concurred, and Hudson struck the Press Bill on the grounds that it was part of the overall legislative scheme of banking and taxation, which was *ultra vires* (outside the jurisdiction of) the provincial government. They refrained from expressing any views on the constitutional question of freedom of expression.

CHAPTER 4

[1] For a discussion of relativism and its relation to democratic theory, see EDWARD A. PURCELL, JR., THE CRISIS OF DEMOCRATIC THEORY: SCIENTIFIC NATURALISM AND THE PROBLEM OF VALUE (1973).

[2] *Id.* at 211.

[3] KENNETH DOLBEARE, AMERICAN POLITICAL THOUGHT 475 (4th ed. 1998).

[4] Scientific naturalism was a belief that absolute truths did not explain the universe. No *a priori* truths existed. Only concrete, scientific investigation could yield true knowledge. Knowledge was empirical, particular, and experimentally verifiable. PURCELL, *supra* note 1, at 3.

[5] Positivism was essentially scientific naturalism. Positivism maintained that metaphysical concepts were meaningless. Only propositions that could be experimentally and observationally verified were true. "Since there was no scientific way to verify the ethical judgment of good or bad, the judgment itself could have no cognitive meaning." *Id.* at 48.

[6] A.J. BEITZINGER, A HISTORY OF AMERICAN POLITICAL THOUGHT 539 (1972).

[7] *Id.* at 538.

[8] Joseph R. McCarthy, a Republican senator from Wisconsin, began his crusade against Communists in February 1950. Although the anti-Communist hysteria had begun prior to McCarthy's entrance on the national scene as a red baiter, McCarthyism is used to describe "the blind, mindless persecution of essentially innocent individuals for their political beliefs" of the post-World War II era. MARGARET A. BLANCHARD, REVOLUTIONARY SPARKS: FREEDOM OF EXPRESSION IN MODERN AMERICA 245 (1992).

[9] KENNETH M. DOLBEARE, AMERICAN POLITICAL THOUGHT 520 (3rd ed. 1996).

[10] DOLBEARE, *supra* note 3, at 475.

[11] DANIEL J. BOORSTIN, THE GENIUS OF AMERICAN POLITICS 8 (1953).

[12] *Id.* at 11.

[13] *Id.* at 16.

[14] *Id.* at 132.

[15] *Id.* at 25.

[16] *Id.* at 137-138.

[17] *Id.* at 157.

[18] *Id.* at 14.

[19] *Id.* at 168.

[20] Hartz argued that because the United States did not have a feudal tradition, it also has not had a Socialist tradition. Socialism, according to Hartz, arose out of the revolutionary liberal revolt against the principles of class. Those conditions did not exist in the United States. LOUIS HARTZ, THE LIBERAL TRADITION IN AMERICA 6 (1955).

[21] *Id.* at 55.

[22] *Id.* at 58.

[23] *Id.* at 11, 56.

[24] *Id.* at 97.

[25] Historian Edward Purcell has argued that relativism has a central ambiguity. One of the problems with relativism, according to both Hartz and Purcell, was that it led to conformity while preaching diversity. Relativism was both descriptive and prescriptive in that it described what the political thinkers assumed was American society and prescribed that society as what ought to be. In a sense, relativists were absolute in their relativism. Diversity was cherished, but it was a diversity within strictly prescribed limits. Un-Americanism, Purcell argued, was a product of relativism, not of absolutism. It was this aspect of relativism that Hartz and Purcell criticized, but which the relativists themselves were unable to see. PURCELL, *supra* note 1.

[26] DANIEL BELL, THE END OF IDEOLOGY 373 (1960).

[27] *Id.* at 374.

[28] *Id.* at 371.

[29] *Id.* at 269.

[30] PURCELL, *supra* note 1, at 260.
[31] ROBERT A. DAHL, A PREFACE TO DEMOCRATIC THEORY 146 (1956).
[32] PURCELL, *supra* note 1, at 260.
[33] This definition of classical conservative has been taken from KENNETH M. DOLBEARE & LINDA J. MEDCALF, AMERICAN IDEOLOGIES TODAY: SHAPING THE NEW POLITICS OF THE 1990s 222-223 (2nd ed. 1993).
[34] *Id.* at 223. Liberals, in the twentieth century, are the pragmatists and pluralists or relativists, those who seek a positive state to further the betterment of society.
[35] RUSSELL KIRK, THE CONSERVATIVE MIND 9 (1953).
[36] *Id.* at 401.
[37] *Id.*
[38] *Id.* at 424.
[39] *Id.* at 428.
[40] PETER VIERECK, CONSERVATISM REVISITED ix (1949).
[41] *Id.* at 86.
[42] *Id.* at 105.
[43] The Smith Act of 1940 made it a crime to knowingly advocate the overthrow of the government by force or violence; or to help organize a society that engaged in such advocacy; or to knowingly become a member of it; or to conspire with other to these things. In the first 17 years after its passage, the federal government had obtained 145 indictments and 89 convictions under the Act. J.A. CORRY & HENRY J. ABRAHAM, ELEMENTS OF DEMOCRATIC GOVERNMENT 254, 256 (4th ed. 1964). The Internal Security (McCarran) Act of 1950 required all Communist-action and Communist front groups to register with the government, to provide lists of their membership and financial records, and to label all mail as "Communist." *Id.* at 256.
[44] VIERECK, *supra* note 39, at 113.
[45] The Fifth Amendment provides:
No person shall be held to answer for a capital, or otherwise infamous crime, unless on a presentment or indictment of a Grand Jury, except in cases arising in the land or naval forces, or in the Militia, when in actual service in time of War or public danger; nor shall any person be subject for the same offence to be twice put in jeopardy of life or limb; nor shall be compelled in any criminal case to be a witness

against himself, nor be deprived of life, liberty, or property, without due process of law; nor shall private property be taken for public use, without just compensation.

[46] ALEXANDER MEIKLEJOHN, FREE SPEECH AND ITS RELATION TO SELF-GOVERNMENT 27 (1948).

[47] *Id.* at 24, 25.

[48] *Id.* at 46.

[49] *Id.* at 48.

[50] C. WRIGHT MILLS, THE POWER ELITE 12 (1956).

[51] *Id.* at 242.

[52] *Id.*

[53] *Id.* at 246.

[54] *Id.* at 266.

[55] *Id.* at 293.

[56] *Id.* at 300.

[57] *Id.* at 298, 300.

[58] *Id.* at 299, 300.

[59] *Id.* at 300.

[60] *Id.*

[61] *Id.* at 301.

[62] *Id.* at 309.

[63] *Id.* at 323.

[64] GEORGE GRANT, THE GEORGE GRANT READER 51 (William Christian & Sheila Grant eds., 1997).

[65] *Id.* at 61.

[66] *Id.*

[67] *Id.* at 52.

[68] In the 1930s in Canada, the Canadian Broadcasting Corporation, a public broadcasting system, was established to unify the country, displace American programming, and generally improve the cultural and moral condition of Canadians. ROBERT BOTHWELL, IAN DRUMMOND & JOHN ENGLISH, CANADA SINCE 1945: POWER, POLITICS, & PROVINCIALISM 93 (1989).

[69] Edward McWhinney, *The Supreme Court and the Bill of Rights—The Lessons of Comparative Jurisprudence*, 37 CAN. B. REV. 16-17 (1959).

[70] *Id.* at 17.

[71] *Id.* at 19 (citations omitted).
[72] *Id.*
[73] *Id.* at 20.
[74] *Id.* at 21.
[75] FRANK R. SCOTT, CIVIL LIBERTIES AND CANADIAN FEDERALISM 13 (1959).
[76] *Id.*
[77] *Id.* at 9.
[78] *Id.* at 11.
[79] *Id.* at 13.
[80] *Id.* at 12.
[81] *Id.* at 26.
[82] *Id.* at 30.
[83] HARRY KALVEN JR., A WORTHY TRADITION 119 (1988).
[84] Justices Stewart, Douglas, Frankfurter, Harlan, Vinson, and Warren were relativists. Justices Black and Goldberg were absolutists. Only one of the justices appointed after 1962 can be labeled as either, reflecting that the absolutist/relativist debate was no longer an issue among intellectuals. Justice Blackmun was an absolutist, arguing in *Parker v. Levy*, 417 U.S. 733, 765 (1974) that relativistic notions of right and wrong had reached a high level of prominence. "The law ought to be flexible enough to recognize the moral dimension of man and his instincts concerning that which is honorable, decent and right," he wrote.
[85] Dennis v. United States, 341 U.S. 494, 519 (1951).
[86] Sweezy v. New Hampshire, 354 U.S. 234, 266 (1957).
[87] *Dennis*, 341 U.S. at 556.
[88] Uphaus v. Wyman, 364 U.S. 388, 392 (1960).
[89] Braden v. United States, 365 U.S. 431, 445 (1961).
[90] Adler v. Bd. of Education, 342 U.S. 485, 497 (1952).
[91] Speiser v. Randall, 357 U.S. 513, 532 (1958).
[92] Am. Comm'n. Assoc. v. Douds, 339 U.S. 382, 394 (1950). The clear and present danger test was enunciated by Justice Holmes in *Schenck v. United States*, 249 U.S. 47 (1919).
[93] Dennis v. United States, 341 U.S. 494, 508 (1951).
[94] Carlson v. Landon, 342 U.S. 524, 555 (1952).
[95] *Dennis*, 341 U.S. at 580.

[96] 354 U.S. 298 (1957).

[97] Speiser v. Randall, 357 U.S. 513 (1958). Education and contrary arguments were the remedies for talk of revolution, and if those remedies were not sufficient, "the only meaning of free speech must be that the revolutionary ideas will be allowed to prevail," Black wrote in *Communist Party v. Subversive Activities Control Board*, 367 U.S. 1, 147-8 (1961), reiterating Justice Holmes' sentiment in *Abrams v. United States*, 250 U.S. 616 (1919).

[98] *Dennis*, 341 U.S. at 590.

[99] Speiser v. Randall, 357 U.S. 513, 536 (1958).

[100] Konigsberg v. State Bar of California, 366 U.S. 36, 78 (1961).

[101] Carlson v. Landon, 342 U.S. 524, 555-6 (1952).

[102] Communist Party v. Subversive Activities Control Bd., 367 U.S. 1, 168 (1961).

[103] *Dennis*, 341 U.S. at 584. Justice Clark called the American public education system the "genius of our democracy." Keyshian v. Bd. of Regents, 385 U.S. 589, 628 (1967).

[104] *Dennis*, 341 U.S. at 588.

[105] Am. Comm'n Assoc. v. Douds, 339 U.S. 382, 426 (1950).

[106] *Id.* at 427.

[107] *Dennis*, 341 U.S. at 564.

[108] *Id.* at 577.

[109] Harisiades v. Shaughnessy, 342 U.S. 580, 592 (1952).

[110] 337 U.S. 1 (1949).

[111] 412 U.S. 94 (1973).

[112] *Id.* at 167.

[113] *Id.* at 23.

[114] *See* WITNEY NORTH SEYMOUR, GENERAL INTRODUCTION, MR. JUSTICE JACKSON: FOUR LECTURES IN HIS HONOR 2 (Charles S. Desmond et al. eds. 1969).

[115] Charles S. Desmond, *The Role of the Country Lawyer*, in MR. JUSTICE JACKSON, *supra*, at 27.

[116] Paul A. Freund, *Jackson and Individual Rights*, in MR. JUSTICE JACKSON, *supra* note 113, at 47.

[117] Potter Stewart, *Jackson on Federal State Relationships*, in MR. JUSTICE JACKSON, *supra* note 113, at 62.

Endnote 259

[118] Am. Comm'n Assoc. v. Douds, 339 U.S. 382 (1950).
[119] Dennis v. United States, 341 U.S. 494 (1951).
[120] United States v. Rumely, 345 U.S. 41 (1953).
[121] Aptheker v. Secretary of State, 378 U.S. 500, 519 (1964).
[122] Wieman v. Updegraff, 344 U.S. 183, 193 (1952).
[123] Speiser v. Randall, 357 U.S. 513, 536 (1958).
[124] DeGregory v. Attorney General of New Hampshire, 383 U.S. 825, 829 (1966).
[125] Terminiello v. Chicago, 337 U.S. 1 (1949).
[126] Talley v. California, 362 U.S. 60 (1960).
[127] 331 U.S. 367 (1947).
[128] *Id.* at 383.
[129] *Id.* at 395.
[130] Pennekamp v. Florida, 328 U.S. 331, 357 (1946).
[131] 360 U.S. 525 (1959).
[132] Barr v. Mateo, 360 U.S. 564, 571 (1959).
[133] *Id.* at 577.
[134] W.F. Bowker, *Basic Rights and Freedoms: What are they?*, 37 CAN. B. REV. 65 (1959).
[135] Criminal Code, R.S.C., 1927, c. 36, s. 133(4).
[136] Criminal Code, R.S.C., 1936, c. 36, s. 133A.
[137] Boucher v. The King, [1950] 1 D.L.R. 657 (S.C.C.).
[138] Boucher v. The King, [1951] 2 D.L.R. 369, [1951] S.C.R. 265.
[139] *Boucher*, [1950] 1 D.L.R. at 678.
[140] *Id.* at 682.
[141] *Id.*
[142] *Id.* at 683.
[143] Boucher v. The King, [1951] 2 D.L.R. 369, 382, [1951] S.C.R. 265.
[144] Boucher v. The King, [1950] 1 D.L.R. 657, 682 (S.C.C.).
[145] *Boucher*, [1951] 2 D.L.R. at 407.
[146] *Id.* at 378.
[147] *Id.*
[148] Hartz argued that Americans did not come together because of a sense of community but because of a way of life. That being so, he concluded, anything threatening the American way of life was dangerous to the country

as a nation. Therefore, communism was seen as evil and un-American. HARTZ, *supra* note 20.

[149] [1953] 2 S.C.R. 95.
[150] *Id.* at 98.
[151] *Id.* at 99.
[152] Switzman v. Ebling, [1957] S.C.R. 282.
[153] *Id.* at 306.
[154] *Id.* at 305.
[155] *Id.*
[156] *Id.*
[157] *Id.* at 306.
[158] *Id.* at 328.
[159] [1952] 1 D.L.R. 657 (S.C.C.).
[160] (1960), 22 D.L.R. (2d) 277 (S.C.C.).
[161] *Id.*

CHAPTER 5

[1] EDWARD A. PURCELL JR., THE CRISIS OF DEMOCRATIC THEORY: SCIENTIFIC NATURALISM AND THE PROBLEM OF VALUE 267 (1973).

[2] GODFREY HODGSON, THE WORLD TURNED RIGHT SIDE UP: A HISTORY OF THE CONSERVATIVE ASCENDANCY IN AMERICA 118 (1996).

[3] DANIEL BELL, THE END OF IDEOLOGY (1960).

[4] ROBERT A. DAHL, PLURALIST DEMOCRACY IN THE UNITED STATES 18 (1967).

[5] *Id.* at 24.

[6] *Id.*

[7] *Id.* at 456.

[8] Frank S. Meyer, *Freedom, Tradition, Conservatism*, in THE MARCH OF FREEDOM: MODERN CLASSICS IN CONSERVATIVE THOUGHT 152 (Edwin J. Feulner Jr. ed. 1998).

[9] *Id.* at 155.

[10] *Id.* at 157, 158.

[11] C. WRIGHT MILLS, THE POWER ELITE (1956).

[12] The Port Huron Statement <http://lists.village.virginia.edu/sixties.HTML_docs/Resources/Primary/Manifestos/SDS_Port_Huron.html>.

[13] *Id.*

[14] THOMAS I. EMERSON, TOWARD A GENERAL THEORY OF THE FIRST AMENDMENT 8 (1966).

[15] J.A. CORRY & HENRY J. ABRAHAM, ELEMENTS OF DEMOCRATIC GOVERNMENT 3 (4th ed. 1964).

[16] *Id.* at 5.

[17] *Id.* at 8, 9.

[18] *Id.* at 10.

[19] *Id.* at 27-33.

[20] *Id.* at 234.

[21] *Id.* at 259.

[22] *Id.* at 261.

[23] *Id.* at 263. The same sentiment was expressed by Douglas Schmeiser in *Civil Liberties in Canada*. In discussing the treatment of Communists in the United States and Canada, he wrote, "The suppression of any organization in a democratic society is an indication of defeat, and perhaps, a convenient means of disguising that defeat." D.A. SCHMEISER, CIVIL LIBERTIES IN CANADA 215 (1964).

[24] GEORGE GRANT, THE GEORGE GRANT READER 89 (William Christian & Sheila Grant ed. 1997).

[25] *Id.*

[26] *Id.* at 94.

[27] *Id.* at 98.

[28] *Id.*

[29] *Id.* at 79. George Grant's *Lament for a Nation*, which was lamenting that it was impossible for Canada to retain independence as a nation in the face of the advance of the United States, produced an unprecedented outpouring of nationalism from a generation of young Canadians.

[30] DENIS MONIERE, IDEOLOGIES IN QUEBEC: THE HISTORICAL DEVELOPMENT (1981).

[31] *Id.* at 257.

[32] *Id.* at 256.

[33] *Id.* at 267.

[34] C.B. MACPHERSON, DEMOCRATIC THEORY: ESSAYS IN RETRIEVAL 3.

[35] *Id.* at 4.

[36] *Id.*

[37] *Id.* at 36.

[38] *Id.* at 37.

[39] *Id.* Macpherson was a Marxist and saw technology as providing the opportunity to finally achieve what Marx had sought—the end to the alienation of labor.

[40] *Id.* at 47.

[41] *Id.* at 79.

[42] *Id.*

[43] *Id.* at 51.

[44] *Id.*

[45] *Id.* at 54.

[46] For a definition of "preferred position," *see* DON R. PEMBER, MASS MEDIA LAW 572 (1996 ed.).

[47] Subversive speech, to use legal scholar Harry Kalven's term, is speech advocating overthrow of the government. HARRY KALVEN JR., A WORTHY TRADITION: FREEDOM OF SPEECH IN AMERICA 119 (Jamie Kalven ed. 1988).

[48] Reflexive speech, to use legal scholar Harry Kalven's term, is speech that causes the audience to take immediate steps to silence the speaker. *Id.*

[49] Like their predecessors in the 1950s, the conservative justices appointed in the last half of the period believed the state had the right to self-preservation, but they were more willing to make the state wait until the individual had crossed the line into action before taking steps to preserve itself than were the earlier judges. For example, Justice Powell in *Healy v. James* held that a university did not need to tolerate associational activities infringing campus rules but it should not assume that left-wing groups were going to interfere with campus life. Such a decision was possible because the threat of communism had subsided.

[50] 376 U.S. 254, 279-280 (1964).

[51] *Id.* at 270.

[52] Garrison v. Louisiana, 379 U.S. 64 (1964); Rosenblatt v. Baer, 383 U.S. 75 (1966); Mills v. Alabama, 384 U.S. 214 (1966); Ashton v. Kentucky, 384 U.S. 195 (1966); St. Amant v. Thompson, 390 U.S. 727

(1968); Monitor Patriot Co. v. Roy, 401 U.S. 265 (1971); Time Inc. v. Pape, 401 U.S. 279 (1971); Ocala Star-Banner Co. v. Damron, 401 U.S. 295 (1971); New York Times v. United States, 403 U.S. 713 (1971); CBS v. Democratic National Committee, 412 U.S. 94 (1973); Miami Herald v. Tornillo, 418 U.S. 241 (1974).

[53] 390 U.S. 727 (1968).

[54] *Id.* at 734.

[55] *Mills v. Alabama*, 384 U.S. at 218.

[56] *Id.* at 219; *Rosenblatt*, 383 U.S. at 95.

[57] *Mills v. Alabama*, 384 U.S. at 221.

[58] Garrison v. Louisiana, 379 U.S. 64, 75 (1964).

[59] 401 U.S. 295 (1971).

[60] 412 U.S. 94 (1973).

[61] Justice Burger argued the same thing in *Miami Herald v. Tornillo*, 418 U.S. 241 (1974), a case involving a right of reply statute and a newspaper. A right of reply intruded into the functions of editors, he argued. Compelling editors and publishers to publish that which reason tells them should not be published was what was at stake, for Burger.

[62] ALEXANDER MEIKLEJOHN, FREE SPEECH AND ITS RELATION TO SELF-GOVERNMENT 25 (1948).

[63] Under the Fairness Doctrine, broadcasters were required "(1) to devote a reasonable percentage of airtime to the discussion of public issues and (2) to present contrasting views in the case of controversial issues of public importance." The Federal Communications Commission declared the policy in 1949. It was repealed in 1987. KENT R. MIDDLETON, BILL F. CHAMBERLIN, AND MATTHEW D. BUNKER, THE LAW OF PUBLIC COMMUNICATION 551 (4th ed. 1997).

[64] CBS v. Democratic National Committee, 412 U.S. 94, 201 (1973).

[65] Am. Comm. Assoc. v. Douds, 339 U.S. 382, 421 (1950).

[66] Dennis v. United States 341 U.S. 494 (1951).

[67] In *Rosenblatt v. Baer*, 383 U.S. 75, Justice Douglas wrote that freedom of expression was applicable to speech at the lower levels of science and the humanities. Douglas cited Emerson in *New York Times v. United States*, 403 U.S. 713 (1971), and *CBS v. Democratic Nat'l. Comm.*, 412 U.S. 94 (1973).

[68] Rosenblatt v. Baer, 383 U.S. 75, 92 (1966).

[69] Cohen v. California, 403 U.S. 15 (1971).
[70] KALVEN, *supra* note 43, at 119.
[71] Vincent Blasi, *The Checking Value in First Amendment Theory*, 1977 AM. B. FOUND. RES. J. 523.
[72] *Id.* at 524.
[73] 372 U.S. 229 (1963).
[74] Cox v. Louisiana, 379 U.S. 536, 589 (1965).
[75] Rosenfeld v. New Jersey, 408 U.S. 901 (1972).
[76] Edwards v. South Carolina, 372 U.S. 229 (1963).
[77] Walker v. Birmingham, 388 U.S. 307 (1967).
[78] Cox v. Louisiana, 379 U.S. 536, 583-4 (1965). Justice Black held in *Adderley* that the state, no less than a private owner of property, had the power to preserve the property under its control for the purpose for which it was dedicated.

[79] Against Justice Black's conservative classical liberalism stood Justice Douglas' more relativist classical liberalism. In *Garner v. Louisiana*, for example, Douglas argued that although lunch counters in department stores were private property, they were infused with a public interest. It was necessary for Douglas to reach that conclusion to allow blacks to protest discriminatory laws by staging sit-ins on private property. Similarly, he held that a jail was a seat of government, especially when housing political prisoners, and therefore an obvious center for protest.

[80] Gregory v. Chicago, 394 U.S. 111, 125-6 (1969). Justice Black was not the only justice to lament the changing social order. Justice Blackmun, for example, thought it strange that someone could say to a police officer who was trying to restore access to a public building, "I'll kill you," and not be able to be prosecuted. Gooding v. Wilson, 405 U.S. 518 (1972). Justice Blackmun, in his conservatism, also saw the wearing of a jacket that said "Fuck the draft" on the back as conduct that would be punished, not as protected speech. Cohen v. California, 403 U.S. 15 (1971).

[81] 393 U.S. 503 (1969).
[82] *Id.* at 524.
[83] *Id.* at 525.
[84] Smith v. Goguen, 415 U.S. 566, 586 (1974).
[85] 418 U.S. 405 (1974).

[86] 394 U.S. 576 (1969).
[87] *Id.*
[88] Oil, Chemical and Atomic Workers Int'l v. Imperial Oil & A.G. (B.C.), [1963] S.C.R. 584.
[89] McKay v. The Queen, [1965] S.C.R. 798.
[90] *Oil, Chemical*, [1963] S.C.R. at 599.
[91] 431 U.S. 209 (1977).
[92] [1965] S.C.R. 798.
[93] *Id.* at 815-6.

CHAPTER 6

[1] C.B. MACPHERSON, POSSESSIVE INDIVIDUALISM (1964).
[2] The Charter is Part I of the Constitution Act, 1982, enacted as Sched. B to the Canada Act, 1982 (U.K.), c. 11. The Charter came into force on April 17, 1982.
[3] "Although Canada's historical traditions of government are very much part of British culture, modern constitutional developments suggest that the United States is beginning to have a dominant effect on Canada's constitutional self-image and structure." ALLAN C. HUTCHINSON, WAITING FOR CORAF: A CRITIQUE OF LAW & RIGHTS 15 (1995).
[4] Section 33 of the Charter provides that the legislatures of either the federal or the provincial governments can declare that an act shall operate notwithstanding a provision of the Charter. The Charter specifically protects language and educational rights, mobility rights, aboriginal rights, and denominational school rights.
[5] KENNETH M. DOLBEARE, AMERICAN POLITICAL THOUGHT 522, 524-525 (3d ed. 1996).
[6] RONALD DWORKIN, TAKING RIGHTS SERIOUSLY vii (1977).
[7] DOLBEARE, *supra* note 5, at 526.
[8] A.J. BEITZINGER, A HISTORY OF AMERICAN POLITICAL THOUGHT 316 (1972).
[9] MULFORD Q. SIBLEY, POLITICAL IDEAS AND IDEOLOGIES: A HISTORY OF POLITICAL THOUGHT 511 (1970).
[10] GEORGE F. WILL, STATECRAFT AS SOULCRAFT: WHAT GOVERNMENT DOES 17 (1983).

[11] *Id.* at 42.
[12] *Id.* at 43.
[13] *Id.* at 45.
[14] *Id.* at 29.
[15] *Id.* at 57.
[16] *Id.* at 60.
[17] *Id.* at 89.
[18] *Id.* at 19.
[19] *Id.* at 19, 55.
[20] FRIEDRICH HAYEK, LAW, LEGISLATION AND LIBERTY: THE POLITICAL ORDER OF A FREE PEOPLE (v. 3 1979).
[21] JOHN RAWLS, POLITICAL LIBERALISM xviii (1993).
[22] *Id.* at 15.
[23] JOHN RAWLS, A THEORY OF JUSTICE (1971).
[24] RAWLS, *supra* note 21, at 305.
[25] *Id.* at 6.
[26] *Id.* at 9.
[27] *Id.* at 18.
[28] *Id.* at 40-42.
[29] *Id.* at 19.
[30] *Id.* at 79.
[31] *Id.* at 134.
[32] *Id.* at 291.
[33] *Id.* at 294.
[34] A preferred position did not mean the basic liberties could not be regulated, however. Citing Alexander Meiklejohn, Rawls noted that rules of order, for example, were essential if freedom of speech was to serve its purpose. *Id.* at 295.
[35] JAMES T. KLOPPENBERG, THE VIRTUES OF LIBERALISM 8 (1998).
[36] *Id.* at 125.
[37] *Id.* at 103.
[38] *Id.* at 153.
[39] *Id.* at 154.
[40] *Id.* at 123.
[41] The shift in focus actually began after World War I but was greatly hastened after World War II through the influence of the mass media.

[42] PAUL M. SNIDERMAN, JOSEPH F. FLETCHER, PETER H. RUSSELL, AND PHILIP E. TETLOCK, THE CLASH OF RIGHTS: LIBERTY, EQUALITY, AND LEGITIMACY IN PLURALIST DEMOCRACY 2 (1996).

[43] *Supra* note 4.

[44] DAVID V.J. BELL, POWER, INFLUENCE, AND AUTHORITY 4 (1975).

[45] *Id.* at 10.

[46] *Id.* at 13.

[47] *Id.* at 21.

[48] *Id.* at 26.

[49] Bell used the following example. A "power" statement would be: If you marry that girl, I will cut you out of the will. An "influence" statement would be: If you marry that girl, you will be miserable the rest of your life. *Id.* at 25.

[50] *Id.* at 26.

[51] *Id.* at 18.

[52] *Id.* at 56.

[53] Substantive legitimacy, typified in Plato's *Republic* and also found in John Locke's work, was based on the quality of the ruler's acts and decisions. Therefore, any ruler who abused his authority by using it to serve personal ends as opposed to the public good was illegitimate and, at least in Locke's understanding, could be overthrown. Under substantive legitimacy, the public good was seen as fixed and determinable. *Id.* at 45.

[54] Procedural legitimacy was first outlined by Jean-Jacques Rousseau, according to Bell. Under procedural legitimacy, the "people" did not delegate power to representatives who were then sovereign within certain limits, as in substantive legitimacy, but rather agreed to legitimize only those actions arrived at through the general will. In England, procedural legitimacy took the form of parliamentary supremacy—Parliament could enact virtually any law and it would be constitutional. Although Bell does not state it, Canada too chose procedural legitimacy to the extent that it adopted the notion of parliamentary supremacy for the federal government. *Id.* at 46-47.

[55] *Id.* at 57.

[56] LESLIE ARMOUR, THE IDEA OF CANADA AND THE CRISIS OF COMMUNITY 15 (1981).

[57] *See e.g.*, HAYEK, *supra* note 20.

[58] ARMOUR, *supra* note 56, at x.
[59] *Id.* at xiii.
[60] *Id.* at 73.
[61] *Id.* at 117. According to Armour, English Canada was influenced by the idealism of Hegel, while French Canada was influenced by the philosophy of Thomas Aquinas.
[62] *Id.*
[63] *Id.* at 118.
[64] *Id.* at 109.
[65] *Id.* at 118.
[66] *Id.* at 121.
[67] *Id.* at 130.
[68] *Id.*
[69] *Id.* at 161.
[70] *Id.* at 131. Armour's conception of rights perhaps helps to explain the Supreme Court of Canada's continuing tendency to describe freedom of speech in terms of a citizen's right to facilitate the political process as opposed to the notion of individual self-fulfillment found in the American cases in the 1960s and 1970s.
[71] *Id.* at 127.
[72] *Id.* at 139.
[73] *Id.* at 129.
[74] *Id.* at 131.
[75] *Id.* at 136.
[76] CHARLES TAYLOR, RADICAL TORIES: THE CONSERVATIVE TRADITION IN CANADA 7 (1982).
[77] *Id.* at 57.
[78] *Id.*
[79] *Id.* at 109.
[80] *Id.* at 112.
[81] Another Canadian author, Gad Horowitz, described the Canadian conservatives as "red tories." "The red tory is a philosopher who combines elements of socialism and toryism so thoroughly in a single integrated Weltanschauung that it is impossible to say that he or she is a proponent of either one as against the other."Gad Horowitz, *Conservatism, Liberalism,*

and *Socialism in Canada: An Interpretation* in CANADA'S ORIGINS: LIBERAL, TORY OR REPUBLICAN? 32 (Janet Ajzenstat & Peter J. Smith eds. 1995).

[82] TAYLOR, *supra* note 76, at 115. Horowitz described this notion of social justice as the tory paternalistic concern for the condition of the people. Horowitz, *supra* note 81, at 30.

[83] TAYLOR, *supra* note 76, at 195.

[84] *Id.* at 213.

[85] JANET AJZENSTAT & PETER SMITH, CANADA'S ORIGINS: LIBERAL, TORY, OR REPUBLICAN 1 (1995).

[86] *Id.*

[87] *Id.* Ajzenstat and Smith used the term civic republicanism rather than classical republicanism. Classical republicanism will continue to be used for consistency.

[88] *Id.* at 2.
[89] *Id.* at 8.
[90] *Id.* at 111.
[91] *Id.* at 123.

[92] ALLAN C. HUTCHINSON, WAITING FOR CORAF: A CRITIQUE OF LAW & RIGHTS (1995).

[93] *Id.* at 12.
[94] *Id.* at 92.
[95] *Id.* at 25, 89.
[96] *Id.* at 89.
[97] *Id.* at 95.
[98] *Id.* at 12, 92.
[99] *Id.* at 185.
[100] *Id.* at 188.
[101] *Id.* at 210.
[102] *Id.* at 204.
[103] *Id.* at 213-214.
[104] *Id.* at 124, 132.
[105] *Id.* at 126.
[106] *Id.* at 209.
[107] *Id.* at 212.
[108] *Id.* at 216.
[109] *Id.*

[110] *Id.*

[111] *Id.* at 217.

[112] *Id.* at 220.

[113] Speech won in Elrod v Burns, 427 U.S. 347 (1976); Abood v. Detroit Bd. of Education, 431 U.S. 209 (1977); First Nat'l Bank of Boston v. Belloti, 435 U.S. 765 (1978); Landmark Communications, Inc. v. Virginia, 435 U.S. 829 (1978); Pruneyard Shopping Center v. Robins, 447 U.S. 74 (1980); Consolidated Edison Co. of N.Y. v. Public Service Comm'n of N.Y., 447 U.S. 530 (1980); and Carey v. Brown, 447 U.S. 455 (1980). There was a mixed decision in Buckley v. Valeo, 424 U.S. 1 (1976), and speech lost in Snepp v. United States, 444 U.S. 507 (1980).

[114] Speech lost in U.S. Postal Service v. Greenburgh, 453 U.S. 114 (1981); F.E.C. v. Nat'l Right to Work Comm., 459 U.S. 197 (1982); Connick v. Myers, 461 U.S. 138 (1983); City Council v. Taxpayers for Vincent, 466 U.S. 789 (1984); and Clark v. Community for Creative Non-Violence, 468 U.S. 288 (1984). Speech won in F.E.C. v. Nat'l Conservative Pol'l Action Comm., 470 U.S. 480 (1985).

[115] It is too early to determine the political philosophy of Justices Souter, Thomas, Breyer, and Ginsberg, at least in terms of political speech cases.

[116] HUTCHINSON, *supra* note 92, at 122.

[117] Texas v. Johnson, 491 U.S. 397 (1989); United States v. Eichman, 496 U.S. 310 (1990); Clark v. Community for Creative Non-Violence, 468 U.S. 288 (1984).

[118] Carey v. Brown, 447 U.S. 455 (1980); Boos v. Berry, 485 U.S. 312 (1988).

[119] Forsyth Cty v. Nationalist Movement, 505 U.S. 123 (1992).

[120] Clark, 468 U.S. 288 (1984).

[121] Street v. N.Y., 394 U.S. 576 (1969).

[122] 491 U.S. 397 (1989).

[123] The Court split along identical lines in *United States v. Eichman*, 496 U.S. 310 (1990).

[124] *Johnson*, 491 U.S. at 411.

[125] *Id.* at 419.

[126] *Id.* at 435.

Endnote 271

[127] Clark v. Community for Creative Non-Violence, 468 U.S. 288 (1984).
[128] Buckley v. Valeo, 424 U.S. 1 (1976).
[129] *Id.* at 287.
[130] *Id.* at 257.
[131] *Id.* at 264.
[132] *Id.* at 293.
[133] Buckley v. Am. Const'l Law Found., No. 97-930, slip op. at 6 (1999).
[134] Austin v. Michigan Chamber of Commerce, 494 U.S. 652 (1990).
[135] *Id.* at 695.
[136] *Id.* at 705.
[137] *Id.* at 706.
[138] First Nat'l Bank of Boston v. Bellotti, 435 U.S. 765 (1978).
[139] *Id.* at 802.
[140] In the 17 cases for which the two were on the bench together, they were on opposite sides in only four.
[141] F.E.C. v. Nat'l Conservative P.A.C., 470 U.S. 480 (1985).
[142] *Id.* at 498.
[143] *Id.* at 508.
[144] U.S. Postal Serv. v. Greenburgh Civic Ass'n, 453 U.S. 114 (1981).
[145] *Id.* at 152.
[146] 427 U.S. 347 (1976).
[147] *Id.* at 372.
[148] *Id.* at 382.
[149] *Id.* at 385.
[150] Connick v. Myers, 461 U.S. 138 (1983).
[151] *Id.* at 146.
[152] A.G. (Can.) & Dupond v. Montreal, [1978] 2 S.C.R. 770; Chernesky v. Armadale Publ'rs Ltd., [1979] 1 S.C.R. 1067; Fraser v. Pub. Serv. Staff Rel'ns Bd., [1985] 2 S.C.R. 455; O.P.S.E.U. v. Ont. (A.G.), [1987] 2 S.C.R. 2. In the cases of *Fraser* and *O.P.S.E.U.*, the Court did not apply the Charter because the Charter was either not in place when the case originally arose or was not argued before the lower courts.
[153] B.C.G.E.U. v. B.C. (A.G.), [1988] 2 S.C.R. 214; MacKay v. Manitoba, [1989] 2 S.C.R. 357; Que. (A.G.) v. Brunet, [1990] 1 S.C.R.

260; Comm. for the Commonwealth of Can. v. Can., [1991] 1 S.C.R. 139; Osborne v. Can. (Treas. Bd.), [1991] 2 S.C.R. 69; Lavigne v. O.P.S.E.U., [1991] 2 S.C.R. 211; Haig v. Can., [1993] 2 S.C.R. 995; Native Women's Ass'n of Can. v. Can., [1994] 3 S.C.R. 627; C.B.C. v. Can., [1995] 1 S.C.R. 157; Hill v. Church of Scientology, [1995] 2 S.C.R. 1130; Libman v. Que. (A.G.), [1997] 3 S.C.R. 569; R. v. Lucas (1998), 157 D.L.R. 4th 423 (S.C.C.); & Thomson Newspapers Co. v. Can. (A.G.) (1998), 159 D.L.R. 4th 385 (S.C.C.).

[154] *Dupond*, [1978] 2 S.C.R. 770.

[155] *Chernesky*, [1979] 1 S.C.R. 1067.

[156] *Fraser*, [1985] 2 S.C.R. 455; & O.P.S.E.U., [1987] 2 S.C.R. 2.

[157] It should be noted by way of explanation that in Canada, there is an extensive professional civil service staff. After an election, only the very top positions of a government agency are subject to change with a change in the party in power. The remainder of the agency is staffed by professional civil servants who provide continuity and stability. The notion, tied to the principle of responsible government, is that the institution of government will be maintained regardless of the party in power. Under the theory of responsible government, the prime minister and his or her party remain in power so long as they have the confidence of the people. The other parties represented in the House of Commons, the equivalent of the American House of Representatives, serve as a watchdog on the party in power. If those parties perceive that the people of Canada have lost faith in the party in power, they may at any time call for a vote of non-confidence. If the non-confidence vote succeeds, the party in power steps down and an immediate election is called. The theory is that under such a system the party in power will be accountable, or responsible, to the people in order to remain in power, hence the name "responsible government." Because of this theory of responsible government in which the party in power serves only so long as it has the confidence of the people, it is essential that a professional public servant staff remain in place, regardless of changes in party. These employees must remain neutral and impartial, loyal only to the institution of the government. The belief that the people's confidence in the institution of government will be undermined if they perceive public servants are not impartial is clearly seen in the pre-Charter cases.

[158] Fraser v. Pub. Serv. Staff Rel'ns Bd.,[1985] 2 S.C.R. 455.
[159] *Id.* at 467.
[160] *Id.* at 470.
[161] O.P.S.E.U. v. Ont. (A.G.), [1987] 2 S.C.R. 2.
[162] Despite Justice Dickson's comment about speech not being one single value, he did hold in *Chernesky v. Armadale Publ'rs Ltd.*, [1979] 1 S.C.R. 1067, that a free and general discussion was fundamental to democracy and that citizens as decision-makers could not be expected to exercise wise and informed judgments without exposure to a variety of ideas. Sounding very much like one of his American counterparts, he said that full disclosure protected against false doctrine.
[163] A.G. (Can.) & Dupond v. Montreal, [1978] 2 S.C.R. 770.
[164] *Id.* It was a time of civil unrest in the province of Quebec, and the authorities apparently attempted to prevent the outbreak of violence by banning public gatherings.
[165] *Id.* at 791.
[166] *Id.* at 797.
[167] *Id.* at 780.
[168] 30 & 31 Vict., c. 3 (1867) (U.K.).
[169] B.C.G.E.U. v. B.C. (A.G.), [1988] 2 S.C.R. 214.
[170] Section 2(b) of the Charter provides:
Everyone has the following fundamental freedoms:
> (b) freedom of thought, belief, opinion and expression, including freedom of the press and other media of communication.

[171] 314 U.S. 252 (1941).
[172] Comm. for the Commonwealth of Can. v. Can., [1991] 1 S.C.R. 139.
[173] Similarly, Justice LaForest argued that freedom of expression included the right to use government property dedicated to the use of the public, but that the public's use was subject to reasonable regulation to ensure the continued use for which the property was dedicated.
[174] Unlike the U.S. Supreme Court that must build limits into the substantive definition of constitutional rights themselves, section 1 of the Charter allows the Court to balance guaranteed rights against other societal interests without necessarily restricting the substantive scope of the Charter provisions. *See e.g.*, Christopher Manfredi, *The Canadian Supreme*

Court and American Judicial Review: United States Constitutional Jurisprudence and the Canadian Charter of Rights and Freedoms, 40 AM. J. COMP. L. 213 (1992).

[175] Comm. for the Commonwealth of Can. v. Can., [1991] 1 S.C.R. at 214.

[176] Id. at 232.

[177] [1991] 2 S.C.R. 211.

[178] 431 U.S. 209 (1977).

[179] Section 2(d) of the Charter provides:
2. Everyone has the following fundamental freedoms:
(d) freedom of association.

[180] [1997] 3 S.C.R. 569.

[181] [1995] 2 S.C.R. 1130.

[182] 376 U.S. 254 (1964).

[183] Hill v. Church of Scientology, [1995] 2 S.C.R. 1130.

[184] Criminal Code, R.S.C. 1985, c. C-46, §§ 298, 299, 300.

[185] (1998), 157 D.L.R. 4th 423 (S.C.C.).

[186] The Court did declare section 299(c) unconstitutional on the basis of overbreadth. Justices McLachlin and Major agreed with the constitutionality of the sections but disagreed that there was evidence to support the conviction of Mrs. Lucas. They argued she did not have the requisite intent.

CHAPTER 7

[1] Boucher v. The King, [1950] 1 D.L.R. 657 (S.C.C.).

[2] These characteristics are associated with a classical liberal political philosophy.

[3] These characteristics are most closely allied with classical conservatism. Canadian idealism sees individuals as basically good but seeking self-fulfillment through society.

Bibliography

PRIMARY SOURCES

American Political Thought

Arnold, Thurman W. *The Folklore of Capitalism.* New Haven: Yale University Press, 1937.
Bell, Daniel. *The End of Ideology.* Glencoe, IL: The Free Press, 1960.
Bickel, Alexander M. *The Morality of Consent.* New Haven: Yale University Press, 1975.
Bloom, Allan. *The Closing of the American Mind.* New York: Simon & Schuster, 1987.
Boorstin, Daniel J. *The Genius of American Politics.* Chicago: The University of Chicago Press, 1953.
Chafee, Zechariah Jr. *Freedom of Speech.* New York: Harcourt, Brace and Howe, 1920.
Croly, Herbert. *Progressive Democracy.* New York: The Macmillan Company, 1914.
―――. *The Promise of American Life.* New York: The Macmillan Company, 1911.
Dahl, Robert A. *Pluralist Democracy in the United States: Conflict and Consent.* Chicago: Rand McNally & Co., 1967.
―――. *A Preface to Democratic Theory.* Chicago: The University of Chicago Press, 1956.

Dewey, John. *Philosophy, Psychology and Social Practice.* Essays selected, edited and with a foreward by Joseph Ratner. New York: G.P. Putnam's Sons, 1963.

Dworkin, Ronald. *Taking Rights Seriously.* London: Gerald Duckworth & Co., 1977.

Emerson, Thomas I. *Toward a General Theory of the First Amendment.* New York: Random House, 1966.

Fromm, Erich. *Escape from Freedom.* New York: Rinehart & Company, Inc., 1941.

Hartz, Louis. *The Liberal Tradition in America: An Interpretation of American Political Thought Since the Revolution.* New York: Harcourt, Brace & World, Inc., 1955.

Hayek, F. A. *Law, Legislation, and Liberty: The Political Order of a Free People*, vol. 3. Chicago: The University of Chicago Press, 1979.

James, William. *Pragmatism.* Cambridge, Mass.: Harvard University Press, 1975.

Kirk, Russell. *The Conservative Mind: From Burke to Santayana.* Chicago: Henry Regnery Co., 1953.

Kloppenberg, James T. *The Virtues of Liberalism.* New York: Oxford University Press, 1998.

Lasswell, Harold D. *Propaganda Technique in the World War.* New York: Alfred A. Knopf, 1927.

Lippmann, Walter. *Public Opinion.* New York: Harcourt, Brace & Co., 1922.

MacKinnon, Catharine A. *Toward a Feminist Theory of the State.* Cambridge, Mass.: Harvard University Press, 1989.

Meiklejohn, Alexander. *Free Speech and its Relation to Self-Government.* Port Washington, NY: Kennikat Press, 1948.

Mills, C. Wright. *The Power Elite.* New York: Oxford University Press, 1956.

Niebuhr, Reinhold. *Moral Man and Immoral Society: A Study in Ethics and Politics.* New York: Charles Scribner's Sons, 1932.

Rawls, John. *Political Liberalism.* New York: Columbia University Press, 1993.

_____. *A Theory of Justice.* Cambridge, Mass.: The Belknap Press, 1971.

Skinner, B.F. *Walden Two*. Toronto: The Macmillan Company, 1948.
Smith, T.V. *The American Philosophy of Equality*. Chicago: The University of Chicago Press, 1927.
Spencer, Herbert. *First Principles*. 4th ed. 1880; reprint, New York: The De Witt Revolving Fund, Inc., 1958.
Sumner, William Graham. *What Social Classes Owe to Each Other*. London: Trubner & Co., 1885.
Viereck, Peter. *Conservatism Revisited: The Revolt Against Revolt, 1815-1949*. New York: Charles Scribner's Sons, 1949.
Will, George. *Statecraft as Soulcraft: What Government Does*. New York: Simon and Schuster, 1983.

Canadian Political Thought

Ajzenstat, Janet and Peter J. Smith, eds. *Canada's Origins: Liberal, Tory, or Republican?* Ottawa: Carleton University Press, 1995.
Armour, Leslie. *The Idea of Canada and the Crisis of Community*. Ottawa: Steel Rail Publishing, 1981.
Bell, David V. J. *Power, Influence, and Authority: An Essay in Political Linguistics*. New York: Oxford University Press, 1975.
Bennett, R.B. "Democracy on Trial." In *Canadian Problems as Seen by Twenty Outstanding Men of Canada*, 11-31. Toronto: Oxford University Press, n.d.
Cassidy, H.M. "An Unemployment Policy: Some Proposals." In *Canadian Problems as Seen by Twenty Outstanding Men of Canada*, 49-67. Toronto: Oxford University Press, n.d.
Corry, J.A. and Henry J. Abraham. *Elements of Democratic Government*. 4th ed. New York: Oxford University Press, 1964.
Executive Committee of Liberal-Conservative Summer School. *Canadian Problems as Seen by Twenty Outstanding Men of Canada*. Toronto: Oxford University Press, n.d.
Grant, George P. *The George Grant Reader*. Edited by William Christian and Shiela Grant. Toronto: University of Toronto Press, 1997.
Haultain, Arnold, "A Search for an Ideal." *Canadian Magazine* 22 (1904): 427-8.
Hutchinson, Allan C. *Waiting for Coraf: A Critique of Law and Rights*. Toronto: University of Toronto Press, 1995.

King, William Lyon Mackenzie. *Industry and Humanity: A Study in the Principles Underlying Industrial Reconstruction.* With an introduction by David Jay Bercuson. Toronto: University of Toronto Press, 1973.

Leacock, Stephen. *Social Criticism: The Unsolved Riddle of Social Justice and Other Essays.* Edited and with an introduction by Alan Bowker. Toronto: University of Toronto Press, 1996.

―――――. *Elements of Political Science.* Boston: Houghton Mifflin Company, 1921.

League for Social Reconstruction. *Social Planning for Canada.* Toronto: Thomas Nelson & Sons, 1935; reprint, Toronto: University of Toronto Press, 1975.

MacIver, R.M. *The Modern State.* Oxford: The Clarendon Press, 1926.

Macpherson, C.B. *Democratic Theory: Essays in Retrieval.* Oxford: Clarendon Press, 1973.

―――――. *The Political Theory of Possessive Individualism: Hobbes to Locke.* London: Oxford University Press, 1964.

McWhinney, Edward. "The Supreme Court and The Bill of Rights — The Lessons of Comparative Jurisprudence." *Canadian Bar Review* 37 (1959): 16–42.

Scott, F.R. *Civil Liberties and Canadian Federalism.* Toronto: University of Toronto Press, 1959.

Skelton, O.D. "Current Events." *Queen's Quarterly* 26 (1918): 128.

Taylor, Charles. *Radical Tories: The Conservative Tradition in Canada.* Toronto: House of Anansi Press Limited, 1982.

Watson, John. Comte, Mill, and Spencer: American Outlines of Philosophy. London: James MacLehose & Sons, 1895.

SECONDARY SOURCES

Adler, Mortimer J. *The Idea of Freedom: A Dialectical Examination of the Controversies about Freedom.* Vol. 2. Garden City, N.Y.: Doubleday & Co., 1961.

Alderson, Douglas A. "The Constitutionalization of Defamation: American and Canadian Approaches to the Constitutional Regulation of Speech." *Advocates Quarterly* 15 (1993): 385–424.

Beckton, Claire. "Freedom of Expression—Access to the Courts." *Canadian Bar Review* 61 (1983): 101–123.

Beer, Lawrence Ward. *Freedom of Expression in Japan: A Study in Comparative Law, Politics, and Society.* New York: Kodansha International Ltd., 1984.

Beitzinger, A.J. *A History of American Political Thought.* New York: Dodd, Mead and Company, 1972.

BeVier, Lillian R. "The First Amendment and Political Speech: An Inquiry into the Substance and Limits of Principle." *Stanford Law Review* 30 (1978): 299–358.

Blanchard, Margaret A. *Revolutionary Sparks: Freedom of Expression in Modern America.* New York: Oxford University Press, 1992.

Bothwell, Robert, Ian Drummond, and John English. *Canada Since 1945: Power, Politics and Provincialism.* rev. ed. Toronto: University of Toronto Press, 1989.

──────. *Canada: 1900–1945.* Toronto: University of Toronto Press, 1987.

Bork, Robert H. "Neutral Principles and Some First Amendment Problems." *Indiana Law Journal* 47 (1971): 1–35.

Bowker, W.F. "Basic Rights and Freedoms: What Are They?" *Canadian Bar Review* 37 (1959): 43–65.

Brett, Peter. "Reflections on the Canadian Bill of Rights." *Alberta Law Review* 7 (1969): 294–308.

Brooks, Stephen. *Canadian Democracy: An Introduction.* 2d ed. Toronto: Oxford University Press, 1996.

Dolbeare, Kenneth M. *American Political Thought.* 4th ed. Chatham, NJ: Chatham House Publishers, Inc., 1998.

──────. *American Political Thought.* 3rd ed. Chatham, NJ: Chatham House Publishers, Inc., 1996.

Dolbeare, Kenneth M. and Linda J. Medcalf. *American Ideologies Today: Shaping the New Politics of the 1990s.* 2nd ed. New York: McGraw-Hill, Inc., 1993.

Doody, Michael R. "Freedom of the Press, the Canadian Charter of Rights and Freedoms, and a New Category of Qualified Privilege. *Canadian Bar Review* 61 (1983): 124–150.

Eaton, William. "Canadian Judicial Review and the Federal Distribution of Power." *American Journal of Comparative Law* 7 (1958): 47–70.

Feulner, Edwin, Jr., ed. *The March of Freedom: Modern Classics in Conservative Thought.* Dallas: Spence Publishing Company, 1998.

Gibbins, Roger. "The Impact of the American Constitution on Contemporary Canadian Constitutional Politics." In *The Canadian and American Constitutions in Comparative Perspective*, ed. Marian C. McKenna, 131–145. Calgary: University of Calgary Press, 1993.

Ginsburg, Douglas. "Afterward to Ernst Freund and the First Amendment Tradition." *Chicago Law Review* 40 (1973): 243–247.

Glazebrook, G.P. de T. *A History of Canadian Political Thought.* Toronto: McClelland and Stewart Limited, 1966.

Gower, Karla K. "A Methodological Framework for Comparative Media Law." Paper presented to the Association for Education in Journalism and Mass Communication National Conference. August 1998.

──────. "The Homolka Press Ban: A Comparative Analysis of Canadian and American Approaches to the Fair Trial/Free Press Issue." *Southwestern Mass Communication Journal* 10 (1995): 47–60.

Graber, Mark. *Transforming Free Speech: The Ambiguous Legacy of Civil Libertarianism.* Berkeley: University of California Press, 1991.

Greenawalt, Kent. *Fighting Words: Individuals, Communities, and Liberties of Speech.* Princeton, NJ: Princeton University Press, 1995.

──────. "Free Speech in the United States and Canada." *Law and Contemporary Problems* 55 (1992): 5–33.

Gunther, Gerald. "Learned Hand and the Origins of the Modern First Amendment Doctrine: Some Fragments of History." *Stanford Law Review* 27 (1975): 719–773.

Hampsher-Monk, Iain. *A History of Modern Political Thought: Major Political Thinkers from Hobbes to Marx.* Oxford: Blackwell Publishers, 1992.

Hirschfeld, Charles. *Classics of Western Thought: The Modern World.* New York: Harcourt, Brace & World, Inc., 1964.

Hirst, David Wayne. German Propaganda in the United States, 1914–1917. Unpublished Dissertation Northwestern University, 1962.

Hodgson, Godfrey. *The World Turned Right Side Up: A History of the Conservative Ascendancy in America*. Boston: Houghton Mifflin Company, 1996.

Hofstadter, Richard. *Social Darwinism in American Thought*. Boston: The Beacon Press, 1955.

Holland, Kenneth M. "Federalism in a North American Context: The Contribution of the Supreme Courts of Canada, the United States and Mexico." In *The Canadian and American Constitutions in Comparative Perspective*, ed. Marian C. McKenna, 87–102. Calgary: University of Calgary Press, 1993.

Hughes, Thomas A. "The Actual Malice Rule: Why Canada Rejected the American Approach to Libel." *Communication Law and Policy* 3 (1998): 55–97.

Jacob, Herbert. *Law and Politics in the United States*. Boston: Little, Brown and Company, 1986.

Kalven, Harry, Jr. *A Worthy Tradition: Freedom of Speech in America*, ed. Jamie Kalven. New York: Harper & Row, Publishers, 1988.

———. "Professor Ernst Freund and *Debs v. United States*." *Chicago Law Review* 40 (1973): 235–239.

Katz, Ellis and G. Alan Tarr, eds. *Federalism and Rights*. Lanham, MD: Rowman and Littlefield Publishers, 1996.

Katz, Lewis R. "Reflections on Search and Seizure and Illegally Seized Evidence in Canada and the United States." *Canada–United States Law Journal* 3 (1980): 103–138.

Lahav, Pnina. "Holmes and Brandeis: Libertarian and Republican Justifications for Free Speech." *Journal of Law and Policy* 4 (1987): 451–482.

———. *Press law in Modern Democracies: A Comparative Study*. New York: Longman, 1985.

Leigh, Leonard H. "Civil Liberties and the Canadian Constitution." *Alberta Law Review* 1 (1958): 304–311.

L'Heureux-Dubé, The Honorable Madame Justice Claire. "Two Supreme Courts: A Study in Contrasts." In *The Canadian and American Constitutions in Comparative Perspective*, ed. Marian C. McKenna, 149–165. Calgary: University of Calgary Press, 1993.

Lipset, Seymour Martin. *Continental Divide: The Values and Institutions of the United States and Canada.* New York: Routledge, Chapman and Hall, Inc., 1990.

———. *Revolution and Counterrevolution: Change and Persistence in Social Structures.* Rev. ed. New Brunswick, NJ: Transaction Books, 1988.

———. "Revolution and Counterrevolution—Some Comments at a Conference Analyzing the Bicentennial of a Celebrated North American Divorce." In *Perspectives on Revolution and Evolution*, ed. Richard A. Preston, 22–45. Durham, NC: Duke University Press, 1979.

———. *The First New Nation: The United States in Historical and Comparative Perspective.* New York: Basic Books, Inc., 1963.

Manfredi, Christopher P. "The Canadian Supreme Court and American Judicial Review: United States Constitutional Jurisprudence and the Canadian Charter of Rights and Freedoms." *American Journal of Comparative Law* 40 (1992): 213–235.

———. "The Use of United States Decisions by the Supreme Court of Canada under the Charter of Rights and Freedoms." *Canadian Journal of Political Science* 23 (1990): 499–518.

———. "Adjudication, Policy-Making and the Supreme Court of Canada: Lessons from the Experience of the United States." *Canadian Journal of Political Science* 22 (1989): 313–335.

Massey, Calvin R. "The Locus of Sovereignty: Judicial Review, Legislative Supremacy, and Federalism in the Constitutional Traditions of Canada and the United States." *Duke Law Journal* 1990: 1229–1310.

McCormack, Thelma. "Censorship in Canada." *New York Law School Law Review* 38 (1993): 165–181.

McKenna, Marian, ed. *The Canadian and American Constitutions in Comparative Perspective.* Calgary: University of Calgary Press, 1993.

McKercher, William R. "The United States Bill of Rights: Implications for Canada." In *The U.S. Bill of Rights and the Canadian Charter of Rights and Freedoms*, ed. William McKercher, 7–26. Toronto: Ontario Economic Council, 1983.

Moniére, Denis. *Ideologies in Quebec: The Historical Development*. Translated by Richard Howard. Toronto: University of Toronto Press, 1981.

Morton, F. L. "The Politics of Rights: What Canadians Should Know About the American Bill of Rights." In *The Canadian and American Constitutions in Comparative Perspective*, ed. Marian C. McKenna, 107–130. Calgary: University of Calgary Press, 1993.

Murphy, Paul L. *The Shaping of the First Amendment: 1791 to the Present*. New York: Oxford University Press, 1992.

———. *World War I and the Origins of Civil Liberties in the United States*. New York: Norton Press, 1979.

Nunez, Rene. "Calibrating the Scales of Justice: Balancing Fundamental Freedoms in the United States and Canada." *Arizona Journal of International and Comparative Law* 14 (1997): 551–573.

Owram, Douglas. *The Government Generation: Canadian Intellectuals and the State, 1900–1945*. Toronto: University of Toronto Press, 1986.

Pember, Don R. *Mass Media Law*. Madison: Brown & Benchmark, 1996.

Preston, Richard A., ed. *Perspectives on Revolution and Evolution*. Durham, N.C.: Duke University Press, 1979.

Purcell, Edward A. Jr. *The Crisis of Democratic Theory: Scientific Naturalism and the Problem of Value*. Lexington: The University Press of Kentucky, 1973.

Rabban, David. "The Emergence of First Amendment Doctrine." *University of Chicago Law Review* 50 (1983): 1205–1355.

Ragan, Fred D. "Justice Oliver Wendell Holmes, Jr., Zechariah Chafee, Jr., and the Clear and Present Danger Test for Free Speech: The First Year, 1919." *Journal of American History* 58 (1971): 24–44.

Reid, Jennifer. "'A Society Made by History': The Mythic Source of Identity in Canada." *Canadian Review of American Studies* 27(1) (1997): 1–20.

Sandburg, Carl. *Abraham Lincoln, The War Years*. Vol. I. New York: Harcourt, Brace & Co., 1939.

Sanders, Michael L. and Philip M. Taylor. *British Propaganda During the First World War, 1914–18*. Hong Kong: The McMillan Press Ltd., 1982.

Schmeiser, Douglas A. "The Role of the Court in Shaping the Relationship of the Individual to the State, the Canadian Supreme Court." *Canada–U.S. Law Journal* 3 (1980): 67–80.

―――. *Civil Liberties in Canada.* London: Oxford University Press, 1964.

Sedler, Robert A. "The Constitutional Protection of Freedom of Religion, Expression, and Association in Canada and the United States: A Comparative Analysis." *Case Western Reserve Journal of International Law* 20 (1988): 577–621.

―――. "Constitutional Protection of Individual Rights in Canada: The Impact of the New Canadian Charter of Rights and Freedoms." *Notre Dame Law Review* 59 (1984): 1191–1242.

Shortt, S.E.D. *The Search for an Ideal: Six Canadian Intellectuals and Their Convictions in an Age of Transition, 1890–1930.* Toronto: University of Toronto Press, 1976.

Sibley, Mulford Q. *Political Ideas and Ideologies: A History of Political Thought.* New York: Harper & Row, 1970.

Simpson, Steven. "Cultural Crossroads: A Comparative Analysis of the Constitutional Protection for Freedom of Expression in Canada and the United States Following Passage of the Canadian Charter of Rights and Freedoms in 1982." Ph.D. diss., University of Washington, 1993.

Smith, Jennifer. "Canadian Confederation and the Influence of American Federalism." In *The Canadian and American Constitutions in Comparative Perspective*, ed. Marian C. McKenna, 65–85. Calgary: University of Calgary Press, 1993.

Stein, Amy R. "Libel Law and the Canadian Charter of Rights and Freedoms: Towards a Broader Protection for Media Defendants." *Fordham International Law Journal* 10 (1987): 750–762.

Stuart, Gordon T. *The Origins of Canadian Politics: A Comparative Approach.* Vancouver: University of British Columbia Press, 1986.

Vaughan, Stephen. *Holding Fast the Inner Lines: Democracy, Nationalism, and the Committee on Public Information.* Chapel Hill: University of North Carolina Press, 1980.

Verney, Douglas V. *Three Civilizations, Two Cultures, One State: Canada's Political Tradition.* Durham, N.C.: Duke University Press, 1986.

Vipond, Robert C. "1787 and 1867: The Federal Principle and Canadian Confederation Reconsidered." *Canadian Journal of Political Science* 22 (1989): 3–25.

Walden, Ruth. "A Government Action Approach to First Amendment Analysis." *Journalism Quarterly* 69 (1992): 65–88.

Westin, Alan F. "The United States Bill of Rights and the Canadian Charter: A Socio-Political Analysis." In *The U.S. Bill of Rights and the Canadian Charter of Rights and Freedoms*, ed. William McKercher, 27–50. Toronto: Ontario Economic Council, 1983.

Index

Abbott, Justice, 127, 155–156
Abraham, Henry, 138–139
Abrams v. United States, 52–53
Abood v. Detroit Board of Education, 155–156, 199–201
Absolutism, 101–104, 130, 214
　and the First Amendment, 98–99
　in the 1940s, 94
Actual malice, 21, 144, 204, 218
Ajzenstat, Janet, 174–175
Alderson, Douglas A., 7, 25
American Bill of Rights, 8, 11, 14–15, 102
American Communication Association v. Douds, 114
American Revolution, 7–8
Arkansas Education Television Commission v. Forbes, 188–189
Armour, Leslie, 170–172, 207
Arnold, Thurman, 73–75, 87

Attorney General and Dupond v. Montreal, 194–195
Austin v. Michigan Chamber of Commerce, 185–186
Authority,
　definition, 2
Authoritarianism, 25, 75
　and idealism, 61
　tendencies of state, 1

Bastariche, Justice, 203–204
Beckton, Claire, 16, 17
Beer, Lawrence, 24
Beetz, Justice, 194
Behavioralism, 93, 135, 139, 157–158, 210
Beitzinger, A. J., 48
Bell, Daniel, 96, 110, 134
Bell, David, 169–170, 173
Black, Hugo L., Justice, 83–84, 107–108, 109–112, 115, 117–119, 144–145, 150–152, 216

Blackmun, Harry A., Justice, 179
Blasi, Vincent, 149
Boorstin, Daniel, 110
 and relativism, 94–95
Bork, Robert H., 1
Boucher v. The King, 22,
 121–124, 217
Bowker, W. F., 22, 120–121
Brady, Alexander, 70
Brandeis, Louis, 54–55, 80–81,
 220
Brennan, William J., Justice,
 144, 145, 179, 182,
 183, 185, 189–190
Breyer, Stephen G., Justice, 179
Bridges v. California, 83, 196
British North America, 7–9
British North America Act,
 8–12, 14, 86, 101,
 103, 126, 168, 195
Brooks, Stephen, 59
Buchanan, James, M., 25
*Buckley v. American
 Constitutional Law
 Foundation*, 184–185
Buckley v. Valeo, 184
Burger, Warren E., Chief Justice,
 143, 145–146, 179,
 183, 184, 186

Canada,
 Confederation, 9
 evolution, 7
*Canada's Origins: Liberal, Tory,
 or Republican*, 174

Canadian Bill of Rights (1960),
 20, 101–102
Canadian Charter of Rights and
 Freedoms 162, 169,
 177, 211, 213,
 215–216, 219–220
 American influence on,
 14–15
 and Supreme Court, 17–19,
 195–206
 Section 1, 15–16, 197–198
 Section 2, 22, 195–197,
 199–202,
 Section 33, 15–17, 20
Canadian Criminal Code, 49,
 121, 205
Canadian Supreme Court. *See*
 Courts.
Cannon, Justice, 86
Cartwright, Justice, 128,
 155–156
Cassidy, H. M., 70
*CBS v. Democratic National
 Committee*, 113,
 145–147
Chafee, Zachariah, 44
Chilling effect argument,
 115–116, 120, 131,
 145, 184, 198,
 218–219, 221
Civil liberties
 factors shaping, 23–24
 in Canada, 103–104
Civil War, 8–9
Clark, Tom C., Justice, 116,
 118, 149–150

Index

Clark v. Community for Creative
    Nonviolence, 183
Clarke, John H., Justice, 79
Clear and Present Danger, 22,
    51–52, 54, 81, 108
Cohen v. California, 148
Cold War, 102, 106
Communism, 22, 77, 80, 88, 92,
    106, 120, 136, 214
    in the 1950s, 108–115,
    124–126, 128,
    130–131
Communitarianism, 3, 161, 168,
    175
Confederation, 8–9
Connick v. Myers, 190
Conservative Mind, The, 97
Conservatism,
    beginning of 20th century,
    46, 50, 55, 57
    classical, 96–97
    description of, 48, 96–97
    end of 19th century, 29, 33
    justices, 78–79, 88,
    105–106, 109, 111,
    113–114, 116–118,
    119, 121, 123–124,
    128, 129–130, 142,
    149–150, 152–154,
    156–157, 159, 179,
    181, 196, 213–215,
    218, 220, 221
    new, 92, 96–97, 99, 105,
    129, 134, 136
    political thinkers, 70, 93,
    134–135, 158, 163,
    166–167, 177,
    207–208, 210–211
    tories, 7, 169, 173–175
Conservatism Revisited: The
    Revolt Against Revolt,
    1815–1949, 97
Corporatism, 72–73
Corry, J. A., 138–139
Cory, Peter, Justice, 204–206
Courts,
    Supreme Court of Canada, 4,
    12–14, 15–16,
    213–221
    British North America
    Act, 85–86
    Charter of Rights and
    Freedoms, 195–206
    Communists, 124–127
    development, 13
    effect of Charter on,
    17–19
    election process,
    154–157, 202–204
    establishment, 10
    libel, 127–128,
    204–206, 192
    public employees,
    192–194
    reflexive speech,
    194–198
    subversive speech,
    121–124
    unions, 199–200
    WWI, 47, 49–50

United States Supreme
    Court, 13, 15–16, 18,
    21, 208, 213–221
  access to property,
    187–188
  broadcasting, 188–189
  communists, 80–83,
    109–112
  criminal contempt,
    83–85
  election finance,
    183–187
  flag-burning, 153,
    181–183
  freedom of press,
    116–117, 144–147
  libel, 117–119,
    144–145, 148
  pre-WWI cases, 48–49,
    51–52
  public employees,
    189–190
  reflexive speech,
    149–152
  subversive speech,
    112–116
  symbolic expression,
    152–153, 183
  WWI, 51–55, 79–80
Cox v. Louisiana, 150
Craig v. Harney, 116–117
Crisis of Community, The, 171
Croly, Herbert, 38–39, 43

Dahl, Robert, 135–136, 141
  and pluralism, 96

Darwinism, social, 28, 31, 51,
    92
Democracy, 1–3, 11
Dennis v. United States,
    109–110, 114–115,
    147
Depression, Great, 59–60, 70,
    73–74, 75, 87–88, 92
Desrosiers, Fr., 72
Dewey, John, 36–37, 43, 53,
    55, 67
Dickson, David, Justice, 196
Douglas, William O., Justice,
    108, 109–113, 115,
    119, 145–147, 150
Douglas v. Tucker, 127–128
Duff, Lyman P., Chief Justice, 86
Dworkin, Ronald, 163

Eaton, William, 10
Edwards v. South Carolina,
    149–150
*Elements of Democratic
    Government*, 138
Elements of Political Science, 41
Elrod v. Burns, 189–190
Emerson, Thomas I., 1,
    137–138, 147–148
Empiricism, 36–37
Enlightenment, 1, 25, 56
Espionage Act 1917, 44, 47,
    51–52

*Farmers Education and
    Cooperative Union of*

Index

of America v. WDAY, 117–118
Fauteux, Justice, 155
FEC v. National Conservative Political Action Committee, 187
Federalism, 6
  U.S. vs. Canada, 8–11
First National Bank of Boston v. Bellotti, 186–187
Folklore of Capitalism, 73
Fortas, Abe, Justice, 144, 153
Frankfurter, Felix, Justice, 78, 84–85, 107, 114–115, 117–120, 147, 196
Fraser v. Public Service Staff Relations Board, 192–193
Freedom of expression, 1–3, 6, 17. See also Courts
  attitude of state toward, 1
  hallmark of democracy, 1
  restrictions on, 2
  social contract, 49
  theories of, 23–26
  U.S. vs. Canada, 21–23
Freedom of press, 2, 48–49. See also Courts
French-Canadians. See also Quebec
  attitudes of, 7–8
  Quiet Revolution, 139–140, 158
Frohwerk v. United States, 51
Fromm, Erich, 87–88
  on freedom of expression, 75

Genius of American Politics, The, 94
Gibbons, Roger, 19–20
Ginsberg, Ruth Bader, Justice, 179
Gitlow v. New York, 79–80, 81
Globe and Mail v. Boland, 128
Goldberg, Arthur J., Justice, 144
Gonthier, Justice, 199, 203
Graber, Mark, 37, 55
Grant, George P., 100–101, 134, 139, 213
Great Britain, 9, 12, 69, 91, 101, 104, 136, 168–169
Greenawalt, Kent, 22

Harlan, John M., Justice, 50
Harlan, John M. II, Justice, 118, 148
Hartz, Louis, 99, 108, 110
  and liberalism, 95–96
  on individualism, 95
Haultain, Arnold, 27
Hayek, Friedrich, 165–166, 177
Hegelian, 24, 36, 39, 171
  Hegel, 31, 36
Herndon v. Lowry, 80
Hill v. Church of Scientology, 204–205
Hobbes, Thomas, 166
Holland, Kenneth, 10–11, 18–19

Holmes, Oliver Wendell, Justice, 51–53, 54–55, 80–82, 220
Hughes, Charles E., Chief Justice, 82, 85, 87
Hutchinson, Allan, 175–177, 180

Idealism, 28, 32–34,
  at end of 19th century, 32–34
  justices, 47, 50, 55–56, 78–79, 86, 105–106, 120, 122–123, 130, 157, 191–192, 197, 199, 201, 204–206, 213–217, 220
  political thinkers, 41–42, 60–64, 68–69, 72, 77, 129, 135, 158, 211–212
Individual rights,
  effect of Charter on, 19
  protection of, 11–14
Individualism, 3, 8, 33, 195
  Possessive, 161, 163, 167, 177, 213
  Socialized, 61, 69, 79, 86, 88, 89, 93, 106, 129–130, 156, 211, 214, 216–217, 220–221

Jackson, Robert H., Justice, 82–83, 109, 111–114, 115–116, 117, 123
James, William, 36, 52–53, 67

Judson, Justice, 156

Kalven, Harry, Jr., 106, 148
Katz, Ellis, 6
Katz, Lewis, 12
Kellock, Justice, 122
Kennedy, Anthony M., Justice, 179, 183, 186, 189
King, William Lyon Mackenzie, 39
King v. Hoaglin, 50
Kirk, Russell, 97
Kloppenberg, James, 168, 175, 177

LaForest, Justice, 199–200
Lahav, Pnina, 2, 209
  on freedom of the press, 24–26
Laissez-faire, doctrine of, 30–31, 34, 35–36, 40, 56, 65, 72, 77, 97, 104, 140, 184, 191
  criticism of, 37–38
  in Canada, 28, 39–40
  in U.S., 28
Lament for a Nation, 139
Lamer, Justice, 197, 203
Laskin, Bora, Justice, 194–195
Lavigne v. OPSEU, 199–201
Leacock, Stephen, 173
  on socialism, 44–45
  theory of state, 41–43
League for Social Reconstruction, 71–72
Leigh, Leonard, 12

Index

L'Heureux-Dubé, Claire, 197–198, 202, 203
Libel, 21, 217, 218. *See also* Courts.
Liberal, 2, 25, 57, 60, 76
Liberal Tradition in America, The, 95
Liberalism, 1, 25, 162–163, 169
definition, 6
Liberty, 12–13, 24–25, 34–35, 58, 62–63, 77, 89, 113–114, 116, 123, 127, 131, 209, 221–222
definition, 2
Libman v. Quebec, 202–204
Lippmann, Walter, 64–66, 87
Lipset, Seymour M., 6, 7–8, 9, 12–13
Locke, John, 166
Locke, Justice, 123

Macdonald, John A., Sir, 9
MacIver, R. M., 61–64, 69, 76–77,
MacPherson, C. B., 134, 140–142, 161, 213
Macphail, Andrew, 31
Maitland, Justice, 155–157
Manfredi, Christopher P., 14, 15–16, 16–17, 18, 20
Marshall, Thurgood, Justice, 179, 183, 184–185, 188
Massey, Calvin, 9, 10–11, 12, 16

McCarthy, Joseph, Senator, 94
McCarthyism, 95–96, 98, 106, 120, 143
McIntyre, Justice, 196
McKay v. The Queen, 156–157
McKercher, William R., 14–15, 16, 17–18
McLachlin, Beverly, Justice, 198–199, 200
McWhinney, Edward, 102–103, 104
Meiklejohn, Alexander, 98–99, 110, 137, 144, 146
Meyer, Frank, S., 136
Mills, C. Wright, 99–100, 136
Milwaukee Publishing Co. v. Burleson, 79
Modern State, The, 61
Moniére, Denis, 140
Morton, F. L., 19, 20
Murphy, Justice Frank, 116–117

Native Women's Association of Canada v. Canada, 201–202
Nativism, 60, 64
Natural rights, 12, 37, 47, 50–51, 213
Neibuhr, Reinhold, 66–67, 76, 87
Neoconservatives, 136
New Left, 134–135, 157
New York Times v. Sullivan, 21, 144, 204
Nolan, Justice, 126

Ocala Star-Banner v. Damron, 145
O'Connor, Sandra Day, Justice, 179
Owram, Douglas, 32

Parliament, 13, 22, 127
Parliamentary democracy, 101–102, 103, 127, 129
Parliamentary supremacy, doctrine of, 9, 12, 16, 162, 169
Patterson v. Colorado, 48, 50–51
Pierce v. United States, 53–54, 55
Pitney, Mahlon, Justice, 53–54
Pluralism, 96–97, 99–100, 104–105, 129, 135–136, 142, 156, 158, 162, 166, 179, 210
  description, 91–92
Political speech, definition, 3-4
Powell, Lewis F., Justice, 143, 152–153, 179, 190, 201
Pragmatism, 34–35, 36–37, 45–46, 52, 56–57, 61, 67, 68, 71, 74, 75–76, 78, 81–85, 88–89, 91, 97, 105, 108–109, 114–115, 119, 129–130, 134, 137, 142–143, 146, 149, 153–154, 158, 191–192, 196–198, 208, 210, 213–216, 220, 221
Preface to Democratic Theory, 96
Preston, Richard A., 7
Price, William, 71
Privy Council, 4, 10
Progressive Democracy, 38
Progressive Era, 34–35, 56–57, 59, 68, 74, 209–210, 214
Propaganda, 64–65, 139
Public law, 24–25
Public Opinion, 65
Purcell, Edward, 133

Quebec, 72–73, 103, 121, 124, 126, 133, 134–135, 139–140, 158
Quebec Act, 8

Radical Tories, 173
Rand, Justice, 22, 122–123, 125–127, 217
Rawls, John, 166–168
Realism, 60
Red Scare, 60, 95
Reflexive speech, 143–144, 148–149, 151, 157, 180, 181, 183, 191, 216. *See also* Courts
Rehnquist, William H., Chief Justice, 143, 153, 179,

Index

182–183, 184–185, 187–188
Reid, Jennifer, 8
Relativism, 96–99, 104–105, 106–109, 111, 119, 129–130, 134, 139, 141, 157–158, 210, 214
  description, 91–92, 94
Republicanism, classical, 48, 55, 65, 78, 79–82, 87–89, 142, 143, 146, 163–164, 168, 174–175
  justices, 181–191, 192, 206–207, 208, 214, 215, 220–221
R. v. Bainbridge, 50
R. v. Lucas, 205–206
R. v. Trainor, 52
Rinfret, Chief Justice, 126
Ritchie, Justice, 155
Roberts, Owen J., Justice, 82, 85
Rosenblatt v. Baer, 148
Rousseau, Jean-Jacques, 166, 174
Routledge, Riley B., Justice, 83
RWDSU, Local 580 v. Dolphin Delivery Ltd., 15

St. Amant v. Thompson, 144
Sanford, Edward T., Justice, 79–80
Scalia, Antonin, Justice, 179, 186–187
Schaefer v. United States, 54–55
Schenck v. United States, 51–53
Schmeiser, Douglas, A., 13
Scientific naturalism, 92, 102
Scott, Frank R., 103–104
Sedition, 22, 49–50, 52, 55–56, 121–123, 126
Sedition Act 1918, 47
Sedler, Robert A., 15, 18, 24
Simpson, Steven, 16
Skelton, O. D., 41
Skinner, B. F., 97
  and behavioralism, 93
Slippery slope argument, 115–116, 120, 131, 219, 221
Smith, Jennifer, 8–9
Smith, Peter, 174–175
Smith, T. V., 66–68
Smith v. Rhuland, 125
Social Darwinism, *see* Individualism.
Social engineering, 93, 129, 210
Social Planning for Canada, 71
Socialism, 43, 45, 69, 136, 142, 180
Sopinka, John, Justice, 199
Souter, David H., Justice, 179
Sovereignty, 7, 165
Spence v. Washington, 153
Spencer, Herbert, 29–30, 32, 46–47, 49, 51–52, 55, 57
Stapleford, F. N., 61
Statecraft as Soulcraft, 164

Stephens, John P., Justice, 179, 188–189
Stewart, Potter, Justice, 146, 148, 150, 179
Street v. New York, 153
Stuart, Judge, 52
Students for a Democratic Society, 134, 136–138, 148
Subversive speech, 116, 153–154, 180, 215. *See also* Courts
definition, 106
Sumner, William Graham, 29–31, 47, 48–49

Tarr, Alan, 6
Taschereau, Justice, 123, 155
Taylor, Charles, 172–174, 207
Terminiello v. Chicago, 112–114
Texas v. Johnson, 181–183
Thomas, Clarence, Justice, 179, 185
Thomas v. Collins, 82
Tinker v. Des Moines, 152
Toledo Newspapers Co. v. U.S., 48–49
Tory. *See* Conservatism
Totalitarianism, 92, 94, 98, 114
Turner v. Williams, 49

Ultramontanism, 72–73
United States,
founding principles, 6
revolution, 8

United States Constitution, 8–9, 18, 49, 52–53, 65, 82–83, 98, 107–109, 110, 112, 151, 183
Bill of Rights, 11, 14–16
First Amendment, 44, 47–48, 51, 82–83, 84, 98–99, 107–108, 109–112, 115, 130, 144–150, 153–154, 158, 180, 182–183, 175–187, 188–190, 212
United States Supreme Court. *See* Courts
U.S. Postal Service v. Greenburgh Civic Assoc., 188
Utilitarianism, 71, 141

Van Devanter, Willis, Justice, 80
Viereck, Peter, 97–98
Vinson, Fred, Chief Justice, 108, 114–115

Waiting for Coraf: A Critique of Law and Rights, 175
Walden Two, 93
Warren, Chief Justice Earl, 150
Watson, John, 32–33
Westin, Alan, 12, 23–24
What is Conservatism?, 136
What Social Classes Owe Each Other, 30
White, Byron R., Justice, 144, 145, 153, 179,

Index

    182–184, 186–187, 190
Whittaker, Charles E., Justice, 118
Whitton, Charlotte, 72
Will, George, 164–165, 177
Wilson, Bertha, Justice, 199
Wilson, Woodrow, 43
Winnipeg General Strike, 61
World War I, 22, 35, 56, 58–59, 68–69, 87–88, 95, 171, 210–211
    Effect on progressivism, 40–43
    Effect on idealism, 40–41
    Aftermath, 60–62, 64
World War II, 91, 93, 95, 101, 119, 129, 136, 168–169, 210–211

Yates v. United States, 11